Undergraduate Topics in Computer Science

Undergraduate Topics in Computer Science' (UTiCS) delivers high-quality instructional content for undergraduates studying in all areas of computing and information science. From core foundational and theoretical material to final-year topics and applications, UTiCS books take a fresh, concise, and modern approach and are ideal for self-study or for a one- or two-semester course. The texts are all authored by established experts in their fields, reviewed by an international advisory board, and contain numerous examples and problems. Many include fully worked solutions.

For other volumes:
http://www.springer.com/series/7592

John Vince

Mathematics for Computer Graphics

3rd Edition

 Springer

Prof. John Vince, MTech, PhD, DSc, CEng, FBCS
www.johnvince.co.uk

Series editor
Ian Mackie

Undergraduate Topics in Computer Science ISSN 1863-7310
ISBN: 978-1-84996-022-9   e-ISBN: 978-1-84996-023-6
DOI: 10.1007/978-1-84996-023-6
Springer London Dordrecht Heidelberg New York

British Library Cataloguing in Publication Data
A catalogue record for this book is available from the British Library

Library of Congress Control Number: 2009942716

Cover design: SPi Publisher Services

Printed on acid-free paper

Springer is part of Springer Science+Business Media (www.springer.com)

*This book is dedicated to my grandchildren:
Megan, Mia and Lucie.*

Preface

Mathematics is a beautiful subject. Its symbols, notation and abstract structures permit us to define, manipulate and resolve extremely complex problems. However, the symbols by themselves are meaningless – they are nothing more than a calligraphic representation of a mental idea. If one does not understand such symbols, then the encoded idea remains a secret.

Having spent most of my life using mathematics, I am still conscious of the fact that I do not understand much of the notation used by mathematicians. And even when I feel that I understand a type of notation, I still ask myself "Do I really understand its meaning?" For instance, I originally studied to be an electrical engineer and was very familiar with $i = \sqrt{-1}$, especially when used to represent out-of-phase voltages and currents. I can manipulate complex numbers with some confidence, but I must admit that I do not understand the physical meaning of i^i. This hole in my knowledge makes me feel uncomfortable, but I suppose it is reassuring to learn that some of our greatest mathematicians have had problems understanding some of their own inventions.

Some people working in computer graphics have had a rigorous grounding in mathematics and can exploit its power to solve their problems. However, in my experience, the majority of people have had to pick up their mathematical skills on an *ad hoc* basis depending on the problem at hand. They probably had no intention of being mathematicians, nevertheless they still had to study mathematics and apply it intelligently, which is where this book comes in.

To begin with, this book is not for mathematicians. They would probably raise their hands in horror about the level of mathematical rigour I have employed, or probably not employed! This book is for people working in computer graphics who know that they have to use mathematics in their day-to-day work, and don't want to get too embroiled in axioms, truths and Platonic realities.

This book originally appeared as part of Springer's excellent *"Essential"* series, and was revised to include chapters on analytical geometry, barycentric coordinates and worked examples. This edition includes a new chapter on geometric algebra, which I have written about in my books *Geometric Algebra for Computer Graphics* and *Geometric Algebra: An Algebraic System for Computer Games and Animation*.

Although I prepared the first book using Microsoft WORD, for this last edition I have used LaTeX2_ε which has greatly improved the layout. This, however, has required me to type in every equation again, which was not only tedious, but an opportunity to correct a handful of typos that always seem to find there way into books. I have also redrawn all the illustrations to bring a consistent graphical appearance to the book. LaTeX2_ε is an amazing software system – extremely fast and robust. The entire book only takes 4 s to typeset, which permitted me to edit the final draft and recompile every time I changed a single punctuation mark!

Whilst writing this book I have borne in mind what it was like for me when I was studying different areas of mathematics for the first time. In spite of reading and rereading an explanation several times it could take days before "the penny dropped" and a concept became apparent. Hopefully, the reader will find the following explanations useful in developing their understanding of these specific areas of mathematics, and enjoy the sound of various pennies dropping!

Once again, I am indebted to Beverley Ford, General Manager, Springer UK, and Helen Desmond, Assistant Editor for Computer Science, for persuading me to give up holidays and hobbies in order to complete this book! I would also like to thank Springer's technical support team for their help with LaTeX2_ε.

Ringwood,   John Vince
January 2010

Contents

Chapter 1
Mathematics

1.1 Introduction

When I was taught mathematics at junior school in the late 1950s, there were no computers or calculators. Calculations, whether they were addition, subtraction, multiplication, division or square roots, had to be worked out in one's head or with pencil and paper. We learnt our 'times tables' by reciting them over and over again until we could give the product of any pair of numbers up to 12 in a fraction of a second – numbers higher than 12 were computed long hand.

I was fortunate in having a teacher who appreciated the importance of mathematics, and without knowing it at the time, I began a journey into a subject area that would eventually bring my knowledge of mathematics to life in computer graphics.

Today, students have access to calculators that are virtually miniature computers. They are programmable and can even display graphs on small LCD screens. Unfortunately, the policy pursued by some schools has ensured that generations of children are unable to compute simple arithmetic operations without the aid of a calculator. I believe that such children have been disadvantaged, as they are unable to visualize the various patterns that exist in numbers such as odd numbers (1, 3, 5, 7, ...), even numbers (2, 4, 6, 8, ...), prime numbers (2, 3, 5, 7, 11, ...), squares (1, 4, 9, 16, 25, ...) and Fibonacci numbers (0, 1, 1, 2, 3, 5, 8, ...). They will not know that it is possible to multiply a two-digit number, such as 17, by 11, simply by adding 1 to 7 and placing the result in the middle to make 187.

Although I do appreciate the benefits of calculators, I believe that they are introduced into the curriculum far too early. Children should be given the opportunity to develop a sense of number and the possibility of developing a love for mathematics, before they discover the tempting features of a digital calculator.

'I am no good at mathematics' is a common response from most people when asked about their mathematical abilities. Some suggest that their brain is unable to cope with numbers, some claim that it's boring, whilst others put it down to inadequate teaching. Personally, I am not very good at mathematics, but I delight in reading books about mathematicians and the history of mathematics, and applying

J. Vince, *Mathematics for Computer Graphics*, Undergraduate Topics
in Computer Science, DOI 10.1007/978-1-84996-023-6_1,

mathematics to solve problems in computer graphics. I am easily baffled by pages of abstract mathematical symbols, but readily understand the application of mathematics in a practical context.

It was only when I started programming computers to produce drawings and pictures, that I really appreciated the usefulness of mathematics. Multiplication became synonymous with scaling; division created perspective; sines and cosines rotated objects; tangents produced shearing, and geometry and trigonometry provided the analytical tools to solve all sorts of other problems. Such a toolkit is readily understood and remembered.

1.2 Is Mathematics Difficult?

'Is mathematics difficult?' I suppose that there is no real answer to this question, because it all depends upon what we mean by 'mathematics' and 'difficult'. But if the question is rephrased slightly: 'Is the mathematics of computer graphics difficult?' then the answer is a definite no. What's more, I believe that the subject of computer graphics can instill in someone a love for mathematics. Perhaps 'love' is too strong a word, but I am convinced that it is possible to 'make friends' with mathematics.

For me, mathematics should be treated like a foreign language: You only require to learn an appropriate vocabulary to survive while visiting another country. If you attempt to memorize an extended vocabulary, and do not put it to practice, it is highly likely that you will forget it. Mathematics is the same. I know that if I attempted to memorize some obscure branch of mathematics, such as vector calculus, I would forget it within days if I did not put it to some practical use.

Fortunately, the mathematics needed for computer graphics is reasonably simple and covers only a few branches such as algebra, trigonometry, vectors, geometry, transforms, interpolation, curves and patches. Although these topics do have an advanced side to them, in most applications we only need to explore their intermediate levels.

1.3 Who Should Read This Book?

I have written this book as a reference for anyone intending to study computer graphics, computer animation, computer games or virtual reality, especially for people who want to understand the technical aspects. Although it is possible to study these topics without requiring the support of mathematics, increasingly, there are situations and projects that require animators, programmers and technical directors to resort to mathematics to resolve unforeseen technical problems. This may be in the form of a script or an extra piece of program code.

1.4 Aims and Objectives of This Book

One of the aims of this book is to bring together a range of useful mathematical topics that are relevant to computer graphics. And the real objective is to provide programmers and animators with an understanding of mathematics so that they can solve all sorts of problems with confidence.

I have attempted to do this by exploring a range of mathematical topics without intimidating the reader with mathematical symbols and abstract ideas. Hopefully, I will be able to explain each topic in a simple and practical manner, with a variety of practical examples.

This is far from an exhaustive study of the mathematics associated with computer graphics. Each chapter introduces the reader to a new topic, and should leave the reader confident and capable of studying more advanced books.

1.5 Assumptions Made in This Book

I suppose that I do expect that readers will have some understanding of arithmetic and the general knowledge of the principles of mathematics, such as the ideas of algebra. But, apart from that, each subject will be introduced as though it were the first time it had been discovered.

In the chapter on curves and surfaces I have used a little calculus. Readers who have not studied this subject should not be concerned about missing some vital piece of information. I only included it to keep the explanation complete.

1.6 How to Use This Book

I would advise starting at the beginning and proceeding chapter by chapter. Where a subject seems familiar, just jump ahead until a challenge is discovered. Once you have read the book, keep it handy so that you can refer to it when the occasion arises.

Although I have tried to maintain a sequence to the mathematical ideas, so that one idea leads to another, in some cases this has proved impossible. For example, determinants are referred to in the chapter on vectors, but they are described in detail in the next chapter on transforms. Similarly, the later chapter on analytic geometry contains some basic ideas of geometry, but its position was dictated by its use of vectors. Consequently, on some occasions, the reader will have to move between chapters to read about related topics.

Chapter 2
Numbers

2.1 Introduction

All sorts of number system have been proposed by previous civilizations, but our current system is a positional number system using a base ten. The number 1234 means the sum of one thousand, plus two hundreds, plus three tens, plus four ones, which can be expressed as

$$1234 = 1 \times 1000 + 2 \times 100 + 3 \times 10 + 4 \times 1.$$

It should be obvious that the base ten is nothing special, it just so happens that human beings have evolved with ten digits, which we use for counting. This suggests that any number can be used as a base: 2, 3, 4, 5, 6, 7, etc. In fact, the decimal number system is not very convenient for computer technology, where electronic circuits switch on and off trillions of times a second using binary numbers – numbers to a base 2 – with great ease. In this text there is no real need to explore such numbers. This is left to programmers who have to master number systems such as binary (base 2), octal (base 8) and hexidecimal (base 16).

The only features of numbers we have to revise in this chapter are the sets of numbers that exist, what they are used for, and any problems that arise when they are stored in a computer. In some cases, the sets of number are represented by a single letter such as $\mathbf{R}$ for real and $\mathbf{Z}$ for integers. It is also common practice to declare a symbol λ (lambda) as being a member of a particular set using $\lambda \in \mathbf{R}$ which implies that lambda (λ) is a member of $(\in)$ the set of real numbers $(\mathbf{R})$ and is thus a real quantity.

Let us begin with the natural numbers.

J. Vince, *Mathematics for Computer Graphics*, Undergraduate Topics
in Computer Science, DOI 10.1007/978-1-84996-023-6_2,
© Springer-Verlag London Limited 2010

2.2 Natural Numbers

The *natural numbers* [1, 2, 3, 4, ...] are used for counting, ordering and labelling and represented by the set **N**. When zero is added to the set, **N*** is used. Note that negative numbers are not included. We often use natural numbers to subscript a quantity to distinguish one element from another, e.g., x_1, x_2, x_3, x_4....

2.3 Prime Numbers

A natural number that can be divided only by 1 and itself, without leaving a remainder, is called a *prime number*. Examples are [2, 3, 5, 7, 11, 13, 17]. There are 25 primes less than 100, 168 primes less than 1,000 and 455,052,512 primes less than 10,000,000,000. The *fundamental theory of arithmetic* states 'Any positive integer (other than 1) can be written as the product of prime numbers in one and only one way.' For example:

$$25 = 5 \times 5$$
$$26 = 2 \times 13$$
$$27 = 3 \times 3 \times 3$$
$$28 = 2 \times 2 \times 7$$
$$29 = 29$$
$$30 = 2 \times 3 \times 5$$
$$92365 = 5 \times 7 \times 7 \times 13 \times 29.$$

In 1742 Christian Goldbach conjectured that every even integer greater than 2 could be written as the sum of two primes:

$$4 = 2 + 2$$
$$14 = 11 + 3$$
$$18 = 11 + 7, \text{ etc.}$$

No one has ever found an exception to this conjecture, and no one has ever confirmed it.

Although prime numbers are enigmatic and have taxed the brains of the greatest mathematicians, unfortunately they play no part in computer graphics!

2.4 Integers

Integers include the natural numbers and their negative counterparts: [..−3, −2, −1, 0, 1, 2, 3, 4, ..] and are represented by the set **Z** and **Z*** without zero.

2.5 Rational Numbers

Rational or *fractional* numbers are numbers that can be represented as a fraction and are represented by the set **Q**. For example, $2, \sqrt{16}, 0.25$ are rational numbers because

$$2 = \frac{4}{2}$$
$$\sqrt{16} = 4 = \frac{8}{2}$$
$$0.25 = \frac{1}{4}.$$

Some rational numbers can be stored accurately inside a computer, but many others can only be stored approximately. For example, $4/3 = 1.333\,333$ produces an infinite sequence of threes and has to be truncated when stored as a binary number.

2.6 Irrational Numbers

Irrational numbers cannot be represented as fractions. Examples are

$$\sqrt{2} = 1.414213562...$$
$$\pi = 3.141592653...$$
$$e = 2.718281828...$$

Such numbers never terminate and are always subject to a small error when stored within a computer.

2.7 Real Numbers

Rational and irrational numbers together comprise the set of *real numbers* which are represented by the letter **R**. **R*** is used to represent the set of real numbers without zero. Typical examples are $1.5, 0.004, 12.999$ and 23.0.

2.8 The Number Line

It is convenient to organize numbers in the form of an axis to give them a spatial significance. Figure 2.1 shows such a *number line* which forms an axis as used in graphs and coordinate systems. The number line also helps us understand complex numbers which are the 'king' of all numbers.

Fig. 2.1 The number line.

2.9 Complex Numbers

Leonhard Euler (1707–1783) (whose name rhymes with *boiler*) played a significant role in putting *complex numbers* on the map. His ideas on rotations are also used in computer graphics to locate objects and virtual cameras in space, as we shall see later on.

Complex numbers resolve some awkward problems that arise when attempting to solve certain types of equations and are represented by the set **C**. For example, $x^2 - 4 = 0$ has solutions $x = \pm 2$. But $x^2 + 4 = 0$ has no solutions using real numbers. However, the number line provides a graphical interpretation for a new type of number: the complex number. The name is rather misleading: it is not complex, it is rather simple.

Consider the scenario depicted in Fig. 2.2. Any number on the number line is related to the same number with the opposite sign via an anticlockwise rotation of 180°. For example, if 2 is rotated 180° about zero, it becomes -2, and if -3 is rotated 180° about zero it becomes 3.

We can now write $-2 = (-1) \times 2$, or $3 = -1 \times -3$, where -1 is effectively a rotation through 180°. But a rotation of 180° can be interpreted as two consecutive rotations of 90°, and the question now arises: What does a rotation of 90° signify? Well, let's assume that we don't know what the answer is going to be – even though some of you do – we can at least give a name to the operation, and what better name to use than i.

So the letter i represents an anticlockwise rotation of 90°. Therefore 2i is equivalent to lifting 2 out of the number line, rotating it 90° and leaving it hanging in limbo. But if we take this '*imaginary*' number and subject it to a further 90° rotation, i.e., 2ii, it becomes -2. Therefore, we can write $2ii = -2$, which means that $ii = -1$. But if this is so, $i = \sqrt{-1}$! Therefore, i is not really a number, but an operator – an operator that effectively rotates a number anticlockwise through 90°.

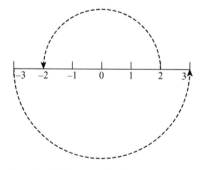

Fig. 2.2 Rotating numbers through 180° reverses their sign.

So now we have two types of number: ordinary numbers and complex numbers. Ordinary numbers are the everyday numbers we use for counting and so on, whereas complex numbers have a mixture of real and imaginary components, and help resolve a wide range of mathematical problems. For example, a complex number z is represented as

$$z = a + bi$$

where a and b are real quantities, but b is multiplied by i, which makes it imaginary.

Complex numbers obey all the normal laws of algebra. For example, if we multiply $(a + bi)$ by $(c + di)$ we obtain:

$$(a + bi)(c + di) = ac + adi + bci + bdi^2.$$

Collecting up like terms and substituting -1 for i^2 we get

$$(a + bi)(c + di) = ac + (ad + bc)i - bd$$

and simplifies to

$$(a + bi)(c + di) = ac - bd + (ad + bc)i$$

which is another complex number.

Something interesting happens when we multiply a complex number by its *conjugate*, which is the same complex number but with the sign of the imaginary part reversed:

$$(a + bi)(a - bi) = a^2 - abi + bai - b^2i^2.$$

Collecting up like terms and simplifying we obtain

$$(a + bi)(a - bi) = a^2 + b^2$$

which is a real number because the imaginary part has been cancelled out by the action of the conjugate.

Figure 2.3 shows how complex numbers can be represented graphically: the horizontal number line represents the *real component*, and the vertical number line represents the *imaginary component*.

For example, the complex number $P(1 + 2i)$ in Fig. 2.3 is rotated $90°$ to Q by multiplying it by i. Let's do this, and remember that $i^2 = -1$:

$$i(1 + 2i) = i + 2i^2$$
$$= i - 2$$
$$= -2 + i.$$

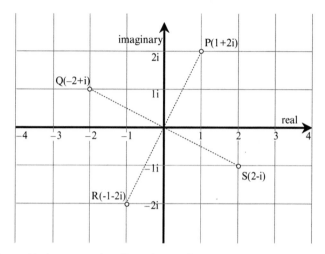

Fig. 2.3 The graphical representation of complex numbers.

The point $Q(-2+i)$ is rotated another $90°$ to R by multiplying it by i:

$$i(-2+i) = -2i+i^2$$
$$= -2i-1$$
$$= -1-2i.$$

The point $R(-1-2i)$ is rotated another $90°$ to S by multiplying it by i:

$$i(-1-2i) = -i-2i^2$$
$$= -i+2$$
$$= 2-i.$$

Finally, the point $S(2-i)$ is rotated $90°$ back to P by multiplying it by i:

$$i(2-i) = 2i-i^2$$
$$= 2i+1$$
$$= 1+2i.$$

Historically, complex numbers have not played a big part in computer graphics, but imaginary quantities are very important in quaternions and geometric algebra, which are covered in later chapters. Complex numbers are intimately related to Cartesian coordinates, in that the ordered pair $(x,y) \equiv (x+yi)$, and that they led to the discovery of vectors and quaternions.

Before concluding this chapter, I cannot fail to include the famous equation discovered by Euler:

$$e^{i\pi} + 1 = 0$$

which integrates $0, 1, e, \pi$ and i in a simple and beautiful arrangement, and is on a par with Einstein's $e = mc^2$.

2.10 Summary

Apart from the natural numbers, integers, rational, irrational, prime, real and
complex numbers, there are also Fermat, Mersenne, amicable, chromic, cubic,
Fibonacci, pentagonal, perfect, random, square and tetrahedral numbers, which
although equally interesting, don't concern us in this text.

Now that we know something about the important number sets, let's revise some
ideas behind algebra.

Chapter 3
Algebra

3.1 Introduction

This chapter reviews the basic elements of algebra to prepare the reader for the algebraic manipulations used in later chapters. And although algebra can be a very abstract mathematical tool, we only need to explore those practical features relevant to its application to computer graphics.

3.2 Notation

The word '*algebra*' comes from the Arabic *al-jabr w'al-muqabal* meaning 'restoration and reduction'. Today's algebraic notation has evolved over thousands of years where different civilizations developed ways of annotating mathematical and logical problems. In retrospect, it does seem strange that centuries passed before the 'equals' sign (=) was invented and concepts such as 'zero' (CE 876) were introduced, especially as they now seem so important. But we are not at the end of this evolution, because new forms of annotation and manipulation will continue to emerge as new mathematical ideas are invented.

One fundamental concept of algebra is the idea of giving a name to an unknown quantity. For example, m is often used to represent the slope of a 2D line, and c is the line's y-coordinate where it intersects the y-axis. René Descartes (1596–1650) formalized the idea of using letters from the beginning of the alphabet (a, b, c, etc.) to represent arbitrary quantities, and letters at the end of the alphabet ($p, q, r, s, t, \ldots, x, y, z$) to represent quantities such as pressure (p), temperature (t), and coordinates (x, y, z).

With the aid of the basic arithmetic operators $+, -, \times, \div$ we can develop expressions that describe the behaviour of a physical process or a specific computation. For example, the expression $ax + by - d$ equals zero for a straight line. The variables x and y are the coordinates of any point on the line and the values of a, b, d

J. Vince, *Mathematics for Computer Graphics*, Undergraduate Topics in Computer Science, DOI 10.1007/978-1-84996-023-6_3,

determine the position and orientation of the line. There is an implied multiplication between ax and by which would be expressed as $a*x$ and $b*y$ using a programming language.

The '$=$' sign permits the line equation to be expressed as a self-evident statement:

$$0 = ax + by - d.$$

Such a statement implies that the expressions on the left- and right-hand sides of the $=$ sign are 'equal' or 'balanced'. So whatever is done to one side must also be done to the other in order to maintain equality or balance. For example, if we add d to both sides, the straight-line equation becomes

$$d = ax + by.$$

Similarly, we could double or treble both expressions, divide them by 4, or add 6, without disturbing the underlying relationship.

Algebraic expressions also contain a wide variety of other notation, such as:

$$\sqrt{x} = \text{square root of } x$$
$$\sqrt[n]{x} = n\text{th root of } x$$
$$x^n = x \text{ to the power } n$$
$$\sin x = \text{sine of } x$$
$$\cos x = \text{cosine of } x$$
$$\tan x = \text{tangent of } x$$
$$\log x = \text{logarithm of } x$$
$$\ln x = \text{natural logarithm of } x.$$

Parentheses are used to isolate part of an expression in order to select a sub-expression that is manipulated in a particular way. For example, the parentheses in $c(a + b) + d$ ensure that the variables a and b are added together before being multiplied by c and finally added to d.

3.3 Algebraic Laws

On the whole, mathematics is well behaved. This is because it is subject to a system of laws or axioms that describe how mathematical statements are to be manipulated. Negative numbers and zero always seem to cause problems and we just have to remember that the product of two negative numbers results in a positive number and that

$$x/0 \quad \text{equals infinity}$$
$$0/x \quad \text{equals 0, and}$$
$$0/0 \quad \text{is undefined.}$$

There are three basic axioms that are fundamental to manipulating algebraic expressions: associative, commutative and distributive. In the following descriptions, the term binary operation represents the arithmetic operations $+, -$ or $\times$, which are always associated with a pair of numbers or variables.

3.3.1 Associative Law

The *associative law* in algebra states that when three or more elements are linked together through a binary operation, the result is independent of how each pair of elements is grouped. The associative law of addition is

$$a + (b + c) = (a + b) + c$$
$$\text{e.g. } 1 + (2 + 3) = (1 + 2) + 3.$$

This seems so obvious that it is almost unnecessary to state such an axiom. But it must be included as it reminds us that grouping is immaterial when adding a string of numbers.

The associative law of multiplication also seems unnecessary, but reminds us that grouping is also immaterial when multiplying a string of numbers:

$$a \times (b \times c) = (a \times b) \times c$$
$$\text{e.g. } 1 \times (2 \times 3) = (1 \times 2) \times 3.$$

However, note that subtraction is not associative:

$$a - (b - c) \neq (a - b) - c$$
$$\text{e.g. } 1 - (2 - 3) \neq (1 - 2) - 3.$$

which may seem surprising, but at the same time confirms the need for clear axioms.

3.3.2 Commutative Law

The *commutative law* in algebra states that when two elements are linked through some binary operation, the result is independent of the order of the elements. The commutative law of addition is

$$a + b = b + a$$
$$\text{e.g. } 1 + 2 = 2 + 1.$$

The commutative law of multiplication is

$$a \times b = b \times a$$
$$\text{e.g. } 1 \times 2 = 2 \times 1.$$

Again, these may seem so obvious that they are unnecessary. But the algebra of numbers must be clear on such products. Note that subtraction is not commutative

$$a - b \neq b - a$$
$$\text{e.g. } 1 - 2 \neq 2 - 1.$$

3.3.3 Distributive Law

The *distributive law* in algebra describes an operation which when performed on a combination of elements is the same as performing the operation on the individual elements. The distributive law does not work in all cases of arithmetic. For example, multiplication over addition holds:

$$a(b + c) = ab + ac$$
$$\text{e.g. } 2(3 + 4) = 6 + 8.$$

whereas addition over multiplication does not:

$$a + (b \times c) \neq (a + b) \times (a + c)$$
$$\text{e.g. } 3 + (4 \times 5) \neq (3 + 4) \times (3 + 5).$$

Although most of these laws seem to be natural for numbers, they do not necessarily apply to all mathematical constructs. For instance, the vector product, which multiplies two vectors together, is not commutative.

3.4 Solving the Roots of a Quadratic Equation

To put the above laws and notation into practice, let us take a simple example to illustrate the logical steps in solving a problem. The task involves solving the roots of a quadratic equation, i.e., those values of x that make the equation equal zero. And as the starting equation involves an x^2 term, at some stage we will have to take a square root. Therefore, the strategy is to create a situation that makes it easy to take a square root.

We begin with the quadratic equation where $a \neq 0$:

$$ax^2 + bx + c = 0.$$

Step 1: Subtract c from both sides:

$$ax^2 + bx = -c.$$

Step 2: Divide both sides by a:

$$x^2 + \frac{b}{a}x = -\frac{c}{a}.$$

Step 3: Add $b^2/4a^2$ to both sides to create a perfect square on the left side:

$$x^2 + \frac{b}{a}x + \frac{b^2}{4a^2} = \frac{b^2}{4a^2} - \frac{c}{a}.$$

Step 4: Factorize the left side

$$\left(x + \frac{b}{2a}\right)^2 = \frac{b^2}{4a^2} - \frac{c}{a}.$$

Step 5: Make $4a^2$ the common denominator for the right side:

$$\left(x + \frac{b}{2a}\right)^2 = \frac{b^2 - 4ac}{4a^2}.$$

Step 6: Take the square root of both sides:

$$x + \frac{b}{2a} = \frac{\pm\sqrt{b^2 - 4ac}}{2a}.$$

Step 7: Subtract $b/2a$ from both sides:

$$x = \frac{\pm\sqrt{b^2 - 4ac}}{2a} - \frac{b}{2a}.$$

Step 8: Rearrange the right side:

$$x = \frac{-b \pm \sqrt{b^2 - 4ac}}{2a}$$

which provides the roots for any quadratic equation.

3.5 Indices

A notation for repeated multiplication is with the use of *indices*. For instance, in the above example with a quadratic equation x^2 is used to represent $x \times x$. This notation leads to a variety of situations where laws are required to explain how the result is to be computed.

3.5.1 Laws of Indices

The laws of indices are expressed as follows:

$$a^m \times a^n = a^{m+n}$$
$$a^m \div a^n = a^{m-n}$$
$$(a^m)^n = a^{mn}$$

which are easily verified using some simple examples.

3.5.2 Examples

$$2^3 \times 2^2 = 8 \times 4 = 32 = 2^5$$
$$2^4 \div 2^2 = 16 \div 4 = 4 = 2^2$$
$$(2^2)^3 = 64 = 2^6.$$

From the above laws, it is evident that

$$a^0 = 1$$
$$a^{-p} = \frac{1}{a^p}$$
$$a^{\frac{1}{q}} = \sqrt[q]{a}$$
$$a^{\frac{p}{q}} = \sqrt[q]{a^p}.$$

3.6 Logarithms

Two people are associated with the invention of logarithms: John Napier (1550–1617) and Joost Bürgi (1552–1632). Both men were frustrated by the time they spent multiplying numbers together, and both realized that multiplication could be replaced by addition using logarithms. Logarithms exploit the addition and subtraction of indices shown above, and are always associated with a base. For example, if $a^x = n$, then $\log_a n = x$, where a is the base. When no base is indicated, it is assumed to be 10. A concrete example brings the idea to life:

$$\text{if } 10^2 = 100 \text{ then } \log 100 = 2$$

which can be interpreted as "10 has to be raised to the power (index) 2 to equal 100". The log operation finds the power of the base for a given number. Thus a multiplication can be translated into an addition using logs:

$$36 \times 24 = 864$$
$$\log 36 + \log 24 = \log 864$$
$$1.55630250077 + 1.38021124171 = 2.93651374248.$$

In general, the two bases used in calculators and computer software are 10 and 2.718281846... The latter is e, a *transcendental* number. (A transcendental number is not a root of any algebraic equation. Joseph Liouville proved the existence of such numbers in 1844. π, the ratio of the circumference of a circle to its diameter, is another example). To distinguish one type of logarithm from the other, logarithms to the base 10 are written as log, and logarithms to the base e are written ln. From the above notation, it is evident that

$$\log(ab) = \log a + \log b$$
$$\log\left(\frac{a}{b}\right) = \log a - \log b$$
$$\log(a^n) = n\log a.$$

3.7 Further Notation

Mathematicians use all sorts of symbols to substitute for natural language expressions. Here are some examples:

$<$ less than

$>$ greater than

$\leq$ less than or equal to

$\geq$ greater than or equal to

$\simeq$ approximately equal to

$\equiv$ equivalent to

$\neq$ not equal to.

For example, $0 \leq t \leq 1$ is interpreted as: t is greater than or equal to 0, and is less than or equal to 1. Basically, this means t varies between 0 and 1.

3.8 Summary

The above description of algebra should be sufficient for the reader to understand the remaining chapters. However, one should remember that this is only the beginning of a very complex subject.

Chapter 4
Trigonometry

4.1 Introduction

When we split the word 'trigonometry' into its constituent parts, '*tri*' '*gon*' '*metry*', we see that it is to do with the measurement of three-sided polygons, i.e., triangles. It is a very ancient subject, and one the reader requires to understand for the analysis and solution of problems in computer graphics.

Trigonometric functions arise in vectors, transforms, geometry, quaternions and interpolation, and in this chapter we survey some of the basic features with which the reader should be familiar.

The measurement of angles is at the heart of trigonometry, and today two units of angular measurement have survived into modern usage: *degrees* and *radians*. The degree (or sexagesimal) unit of measure derives from defining one complete rotation as 360°. Each degree divides into 60 min, and each minute divides into 60 s. The number 60 has survived from Mesopotamian days and is rather incongruous when used alongside today's decimal system – which is why the radian has secured a strong foothold in modern mathematics.

The radian of angular measure does not depend upon any arbitrary constant. It is the angle created by a circular arc whose length is equal to the circle's radius. And because the perimeter of a circle is $2\pi r$, 2π radians correspond to one complete rotation. As 360° correspond to 2π radians, 1 radian corresponds to $180°/\pi$, which is approximately 57.3°.

The reader should try to memorize the following relationships between radians and degrees:

$$\frac{\pi}{2} \equiv 90° \qquad \pi \equiv 180°$$

$$\frac{3\pi}{2} \equiv 270° \qquad 2\pi \equiv 360°.$$

J. Vince, *Mathematics for Computer Graphics*, Undergraduate Topics in Computer Science, DOI 10.1007/978-1-84996-023-6_4,
© Springer-Verlag London Limited 2010

4.2 The Trigonometric Ratios

Ancient civilizations knew that triangles, whatever their size, possessed some inherent properties, especially the ratios of sides and their associated angles. This meant that if such ratios were known in advance, problems involving triangles with unknown lengths and angles could be computed using these ratios.

To give you some idea why we employ the current notation, consider the history of the word sine. The Hindu word *ardha-jya* meaning 'half-chord' was abbreviated to *jya* ('chord'), which was translated by the Arabs into *jiba*, and corrupted to *jb*. Other translators converted this to *jaib*, meaning 'cove', 'bulge' or 'bay', which in Latin is *sinus*.

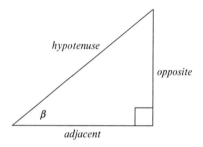

Fig. 4.1 Labeling a right-angle triangle for the trigonometric ratios.

Today, the trigonometric ratios are known by the abbreviations sin, cos, tan, csc, sec and cot. Figure 4.1 shows a right-angled triangle where the trigonometric ratios are given by:

$$\sin\beta = \frac{opposite}{hypotenuse} \qquad \cos\beta = \frac{adjacent}{hypotenuse} \qquad \tan\beta = \frac{opposite}{adjacent}$$

$$\csc\beta = \frac{1}{\sin\beta} \qquad \sec\beta = \frac{1}{\cos\beta} \qquad \cot\beta = \frac{1}{\tan\beta}.$$

The sin and cos functions have limits ± 1, whereas tan has limits $\pm\infty$. The signs of the functions in the four quadrants are

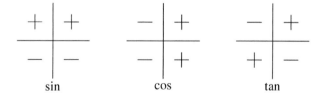

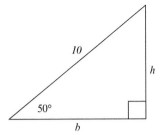

Fig. 4.2 h and b are unknown.

4.3 Example

Figure 4.2 shows a triangle where the hypotenuse and one angle are known. The other sides are calculated as follows:

$$\frac{h}{10} = \sin 50°$$
$$h = 10 \sin 50° = 10 \times 0.76601 = 7.66$$
$$\frac{b}{10} = \cos 50°$$
$$b = 10 \cos 50° = 10 \times 0.64279 = 6.4279.$$

4.4 Inverse Trigonometric Ratios

As every angle has its associated ratio, functions are required to convert one into the other. The sin, cos and tan functions convert angles into ratios, and the inverse functions $\sin^{-1}$, $\cos^{-1}$ and $\tan^{-1}$ convert ratios into angles. For example, $\sin 45° \approx 0.707$, therefore $\sin^{-1} 0.707 \approx 45°$. Although sine and cosine functions are *cyclic* functions (i.e., they repeat indefinitely) the inverse functions return angles over a specific period.

4.5 Trigonometric Relationships

There is an intimate relationship between the sin and cos definitions, and are formally related by
$$\cos \beta = \sin(\beta + 90°).$$

Also, the theorem of Pythagoras can be used to derive other formulae such as

$$\frac{\sin\beta}{\cos\beta} = \tan\beta$$
$$\sin^2\beta + \cos^2\beta = 1$$
$$1 + \tan^2\beta = \sec^2\beta$$
$$1 + \cot^2\beta = \csc^2\beta.$$

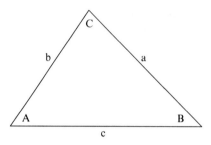

Fig. 4.3 An arbitrary triangle.

4.6 The Sine Rule

The sine rule relates angles and side lengths for a triangle. Figure 4.3 shows a triangle labeled such that side a is opposite angle A, side b is opposite angle B, etc.

The sine rule states

$$\frac{a}{\sin A} = \frac{b}{\sin B} = \frac{c}{\sin C}.$$

4.7 The Cosine Rule

The cosine rule expresses the $\sin^2\beta + \cos^2\beta = 1$ relationship for the arbitrary triangle shown in Fig. 4.3. In fact, there are three versions:

$$a^2 = b^2 + c^2 - 2bc\cos A$$
$$b^2 = c^2 + a^2 - 2ca\cos B$$
$$c^2 = a^2 + b^2 - 2ab\cos C.$$

Three further relationships also hold

$$a = b\cos C + c\cos B$$
$$b = c\cos A + a\cos C$$
$$c = a\cos B + b\cos A.$$

4.8 Compound Angles

Two sets of compound trigonometric relationships show how to add and subtract two different angles and multiples of the same angle. The following are some of the most common relationships:

$$\sin(A \pm B) = \sin A \cos B \pm \cos A \sin B$$
$$\cos(A \pm B) = \cos A \cos B \mp \sin A \sin B$$
$$\tan(A \pm B) = \frac{\tan A \pm \tan B}{1 \mp \tan A \tan B}$$
$$\sin 2\beta = 2\sin \beta \cos \beta$$
$$\cos 2\beta = \cos^2 \beta - \sin^2 \beta$$
$$\cos 2\beta = 2\cos^2 \beta - 1$$
$$\cos 2\beta = 1 - 2\sin^2 \beta$$
$$\sin 3\beta = 3\sin \beta - 4\sin^3 \beta$$
$$\cos 3\beta = 4\cos^3 \beta - 3\cos \beta$$
$$\cos^2 \beta = \frac{1}{2}(1 + \cos 2\beta)$$
$$\sin^2 \beta = \frac{1}{2}(1 - \cos 2\beta).$$

4.9 Perimeter Relationships

Finally, with reference to Fig. 4.3, we come to the relationships that integrate angles with the perimeter of a triangle:

$$s = \frac{1}{2}(a + b + c)$$
$$\sin\left(\frac{A}{2}\right) = \sqrt{\frac{(s-b)(s-c)}{bc}}$$

$$\sin\left(\frac{B}{2}\right) = \sqrt{\frac{(s-c)(s-a)}{ca}}$$

$$\sin\left(\frac{C}{2}\right) = \sqrt{\frac{(s-a)(s-b)}{ab}}$$

$$\cos\left(\frac{A}{2}\right) = \sqrt{\frac{s(s-a)}{bc}}$$

$$\cos\left(\frac{B}{2}\right) = \sqrt{\frac{s(s-b)}{ca}}$$

$$\cos\left(\frac{C}{2}\right) = \sqrt{\frac{s(s-c)}{ab}}$$

$$\sin A = \frac{2}{bc}\sqrt{s(s-a)(s-b)(s-c)}$$

$$\sin B = \frac{2}{ca}\sqrt{s(s-a)(s-b)(s-c)}$$

$$\sin C = \frac{2}{ab}\sqrt{s(s-a)(s-b)(s-c)}.$$

4.10 Summary

No derivation has been given for the formulae in this chapter, and the reader who is really interested will find plenty of books that show their origins. Hopefully, the formulae will be a useful reference when studying the rest of the book, and perhaps will be of some use when solving problems in the future. I should draw the reader's attention to two maths books that I have found a source of information and inspiration: *Handbook of Mathematics and Computational Science* by John Harris and Horst Stocker (1998), and *Mathematics from the Birth of Numbers* by Jan Gullberg (1997).

Chapter 5
Cartesian Coordinates

5.1 Introduction

René Descartes (1596–1650) is often credited with the invention of the xy-plane, but Pierre de Fermat (1601–1665) was probably the first inventor. In 1636 Fermat was working on a treatise titled *Ad locus planos et solidos isagoge*, which outlined what we now call *analytic geometry*. Unfortunately, Fermat never published his treatise, although he shared his ideas with other mathematicians such as Blaise Pascal (1623–1662). At the same time Descartes devised his own system of analytic geometry and in 1637 published his results in the prestigious journal *Géométrie*. In the eyes of the scientific world, the publication date of a technical paper determines when a new idea or invention is released into the public domain. Consequently, ever since this publication Descartes has been associated with the xy-plane, which is why it is called the *Cartesian plane*. If Fermat had been more efficient in publishing his research results, the xy-plane could have been called the Fermatian plane (*A History of Mathematics* by Boyer and Merzbach, 1989)!

5.2 The Cartesian xy-Plane

The Cartesian xy-plane provides a mechanism for visualizing pairs of related variables into a graphical format. The variables are normally x and y, as used to describe a function such as $y = 0.5x + 1$. Every value of x has a corresponding value of y, which can be located on intersecting axes as shown in Fig. 5.1. The set of points forms a familiar straight line associated with equations of the form $y = mx + c$. By convention, the axis for the independent variable x is horizontal, and the dependent variable y is vertical. The axes intersect at $90°$ at a point called the *origin*. As previously mentioned, Descartes suggested that the letters x and y should be used to represent variables, and letters at the opposite end of the alphabet should substitute numbers. Which is why equations such as $y = ax^2 + bx + c$ are written the way they are.

J. Vince, *Mathematics for Computer Graphics*, Undergraduate Topics in Computer Science, DOI 10.1007/978-1-84996-023-6_5,
© Springer-Verlag London Limited 2010

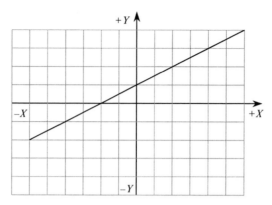

Fig. 5.1 The equation $y = 0.5x + 1$ using the xy Cartesian plane.

Measurements to the right and left of the origin are positive and negative respectively, and measurements above and below the origin share a similar sign convention. Together, the axes are said to create a *left-handed* set of axes, because it is possible, using one's left hand, to align the thumb with the x-axis and the first finger with the y-axis. We will say more about left and right-handed axes in Chapter 6.

The Cartesian plane is such a simple idea that it is strange that it took so long to be discovered. But even though it was invented almost 400 years ago, it is central to computer graphics. However, although it is true that René Descartes showed how an orthogonal coordinate system could be used for graphs and coordinate geometry, coordinates had been used by ancient Egyptians, almost 2,000 years earlier!

Any point P on the Cartesian plane is identified by an ordered pair of numbers (x, y) where x and y are called the *Cartesian coordinates* of P. Mathematical functions and geometric shapes can then be represented as lists of coordinates inside a computer program.

5.2.1 Function Graphs

A wide variety of functions, such as $y = mx + c$ (linear), $y = ax^2 + bx + c$ (quadratic), $y = ax^3 + bx^2 + cx + d$ (cubic), $y = a\sin x$ (trigonometric), etc., create familiar graphs that readily identify the function's origins. Linear functions are straight lines, quadratics are parabolas, cubics have an 's' shape, and trigonometric functions often have a wave-like trace. Such graphs are used in computer animation to control the movement of objects, lights and the virtual camera. But instead of depicting the relationship between x and y, the graphs show the relationship between an activity such as movement, rotation, size, brightness, colour, etc., with time. Figure 5.2 shows an example where the horizontal axis marks the progress of time in animation frames, and the vertical axis records the corresponding brightness of a virtual light source. Such a function forms part of the animator's user interface, and communicates in a

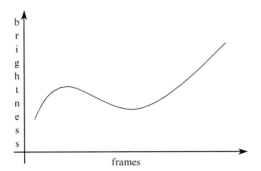

Fig. 5.2 A function curve relating brightness to frame number.

very intuitive manner the brightness of the light source for every frame of animation. The animator can then make changes to the function with the aid of interactive software tools.

5.2.2 Geometric Shapes

Computer graphics requires that 2D shapes and 3D objects have a numerical description of some sort. Shapes include polygons, circles, arbitrary curves, mathematical functions, fractals, etc., and objects can be faceted, smooth, bumpy, furry, gaseous, etc. For the moment though, we will only consider 2D shapes.

5.2.3 Polygonal Shapes

A polygon is constructed from a sequence of *vertices* (points) as shown in Fig. 5.3. A straight line is assumed to link each pair of neighbouring vertices; intermediate points on the line are not explicitly stored. There is no convention for starting a chain of vertices, but software will often dictate whether polygons have a clockwise or anticlockwise vertex sequence. If the vertices in Fig. 5.3 had been created in an anticlockwise sequence, they could be represented in a tabular form as shown, where the starting vertex is (1, 1), but this is arbitrary. We can now subject this list of vertex coordinates to a variety of arithmetic and mathematical operations. For example, if we double the values of *x* and *y* and redraw the vertices, we discover that the shape's geometric integrity is preserved, but its size is doubled with respect to the origin. Similarly, if we divide the values of *x* and *y* by 2, the shape is still preserved, but its size is halved with respect to the origin. On the other hand, if we add 1 to every *x*-coordinate and 2 to every *y*-coordinate and redraw the vertices, the shape's size remains the same but it is displaced 1 unit horizontally and 2 units vertically. This arithmetic manipulation of vertices is the basis of shape and object transforms and is described in Chapter 7.

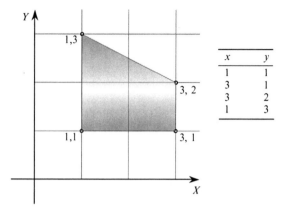

Fig. 5.3 A simple polygon created with four vertices shown in the table.

5.2.4 Areas of Shapes

The area of a polygonal shape is readily calculated from its chain of coordinates. For example, given the following list of coordinates:

x	y
x_0	y_0
x_1	y_1
x_2	y_2
x_3	y_3

the area is computed by

$$area = \frac{1}{2}[(x_0y_1 - x_1y_0) + (x_1y_2 - x_2y_1) + (x_2y_3 - x_3y_2) + (x_3y_0 - x_0y_3)].$$

If you check to see what is happening, you will notice that the calculation sums the results of multiplying an x by the next y, minus the next x by the previous y. When the last vertex is selected it is paired with the first vertex to complete the process. The result is then halved to reveal the area. As a simple test, let's apply this formula to the shape described in Fig. 5.3

$$area = \frac{1}{2}[(1 \times 1 - 3 \times 1) + (3 \times 2 - 3 \times 1) + (3 \times 3 - 1 \times 2) + (1 \times 1 - 1 \times 3)]$$

$$area = \frac{1}{2}[-2 + 3 + 7 - 2] = 3.$$

which by inspection, is the true area. The beauty of this technique is that it works with any number of vertices and any arbitrary shape. In Chapter 6 we will discover how it works.

Another feature of the technique is that if the set of coordinates is clockwise, the area is negative. Which means that the calculation computes vertex orientation as well as area. To illustrate this feature, the original vertices are reversed to a clockwise sequence as follows:

$$area = \frac{1}{2}[(1 \times 3 - 1 \times 1) + (1 \times 2 - 3 \times 3) + (3 \times 1 - 3 \times 2) + (3 \times 1 - 1 \times 1)]$$

$$area = \frac{1}{2}[2 - 7 - 3 + 2] = -3.$$

The minus sign indicates that the vertices are in a clockwise sequence.

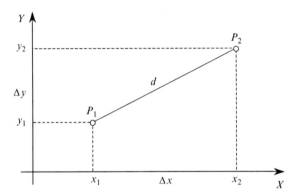

Fig. 5.4 Calculating the distance between two points.

5.2.5 Theorem of Pythagoras in 2D

We can calculate the distance between two points by applying the theorem of Pythagoras. Figure 5.4 shows two arbitrary points $P_1(x_1, y_1)$ and $P_2(x_2, y_2)$. The distance $\Delta x = x_2 - x_1$ and $\Delta y = y_2 - y_1$. Therefore, the distance d between P_1 and P_2 is given by

$$d = \sqrt{(\Delta x)^2 + (\Delta y)^2}.$$

5.3 3D Coordinates

In the 2D Cartesian plane a point is located by its x- and y-coordinates. But when we move to 3D there are two choices for positioning the third z-axis. Figure 5.5 shows the two possibilities, which are described as *left-* and *right-handed* axial systems. The left-handed system allows us to align our left hand with the axes such that the thumb aligns with the x-axis, the first finger aligns with the y-axis and the middle finger aligns with the z-axis. The right-handed system allows the same system of alignment, but using our right hand. The choice between these axial systems is arbitrary, but one should be aware of the system employed by commercial computer graphics packages. The main problem arises when projecting 3D points onto a 2D plane, which, in general, has a left-handed axial system. This will become obvious when we look at perspective projections. In this text we will keep to a right-handed system as shown in Fig. 5.6, which also shows a point P with its coordinates. It also worth noting that handedness has no meaning in spaces with four dimensions or more.

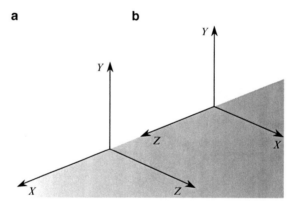

Fig. 5.5 (**a**) A left-handed system. (**b**) A right-handed system.

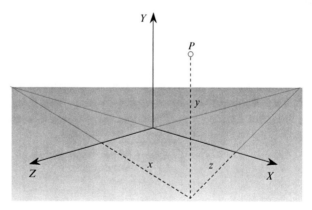

Fig. 5.6 A right-handed axial system showing the coordinates of a point P.

5.3.1 Theorem of Pythagoras in 3D

The theorem of Pythagoras in 3D is a natural extension of the 2D rule. In fact, it even works in higher dimensions. Given two arbitrary points $P_1(x_1, y_1, z_1)$ and $P_2(x_2, y_2, z_2)$, we need to compute $\Delta x = x_2 - x_1$, $\Delta y = y_2 - y_1$ and $\Delta z = z_2 - z_1$, from which the distance d between P_1 and P_2 is given by

$$d = \sqrt{(\Delta x)^2 + (\Delta y)^2 + (\Delta z)^2}.$$

5.3.2 3D Polygons

The simplest 3D polygon is a triangle, which is always *planar*, i.e., the three vertices lie on a common plane. Planarity is very important in computer graphics because rendering algorithms assume that polygons are planar. For instance, it is quite easy to define a quadrilateral in 3D where the vertices are not located on one plane. When such a polygon is rendered and animated, spurious highlights can result, simply because the geometric techniques (which assume the polygon is planar) give rise to errors.

5.3.3 Euler's Rule

In 1619, Descartes discovered quite a nice relationship between vertices, edges and the faces of a 3D polygonal object:

$$faces + vertices = edges + 2.$$

As a simple test, consider a cube: it has 12 edges, 6 faces and 8 vertices, which satisfies this equation. This rule can be applied to a geometric database to discover whether it contains any spurious features. Unfortunately for Descartes, for some unknown reason, the rule is named after Euler!

5.4 Summary

The Cartesian plane and its associated coordinates are the basis for all mathematics used for computer graphics. By changing the values of the coordinates, we effectively change the shape of objects and their position in space. Furthermore, by creating a virtual lighting environment and associating colour and reflective properties with surfaces they can be rendered with realistic textures, shadows and surface finishes. Basically, this is what computer graphics is about: simulating the real world numerically!

We will see in following chapters how 2D shapes are manipulated using simple functions, and how the plane can be extended into a three-dimensional Cartesian space that becomes the domain for creating objects, curves, surfaces, and a virtual environment where they can be animated and visualized.

Chapter 6
Vectors

6.1 Introduction

Vectors are a relatively new arrival to the world of mathematics, dating only from the nineteenth century. They provide us with some elegant and powerful techniques for computing angles between lines and the orientation of surfaces. They also provide a coherent framework for computing the behaviour of dynamic objects in computer animation and illumination models in rendering.

We often employ a single number to represent quantities that we use in our daily lives such as height, age, shoe size, waist and chest measurement. The magnitude of this number depends on our age and whether we use metric or imperial units. Such quantities are called *scalars*. In computer graphics scalar quantities include colour, height, width, depth, brightness, number of frames, etc.

On the other hand, there are some things that require more than one number to represent them: wind, force, weight, velocity and sound are just a few examples. These cannot be represented accurately by a single number. For example, any sailor knows that wind has a magnitude and a direction. The force we use to lift an object also has a value *and* a direction. Similarly, the velocity of a moving object is measured in terms of its speed (e.g., miles per hour) and a direction such as north-west. Sound, too, has intensity and a direction. These quantities are called *vectors*. In computer graphics, vectors generally require two or three numbers, and these are the only type we consider in this chapter.

Mathematicians such as Caspar Wessel (1745–1818), Jean Argand (1768 – 1822) and John Warren (1796–1852) were simultaneously exploring complex numbers and their graphical representation. And in 1843, Sir William Rowan Hamilton (1788–1856) made his breakthrough with *quaternions*. In 1853, Hamilton published his book *Lectures on Quaternions* in which he described terms such as *vector*, *transvector* and *provector*. Hamilton's work was not widely accepted until in 1881, when the American mathematician Josiah Gibbs (1839–1903), published his treatise *Vector Analysis*, describing modern *vector analysis*.

J. Vince, *Mathematics for Computer Graphics*, Undergraduate Topics
in Computer Science, DOI 10.1007/978-1-84996-023-6_6,
© Springer-Verlag London Limited 2010

Gibbs was not a fan of the imaginary quantities associated with Hamilton's quaternions, but saw the potential of creating a vectorial system from the imaginary i, j and k into the unit basis vectors **i, j** and **k**, which is what we use today.

Some mathematicians were not happy with the direction vector analysis had taken. Hermann Gunther Grassmann (1809–1877) for example, believed that his own *geometric calculus* was far superior to Hamilton's quaternions and the vector techniques of Gibbs, but he died without managing to convince any of his fellow mathematicians. Fortunately, William Kingdon Clifford (1845–1879) recognized the brilliance of Grassmann's ideas and formalized what today has become known as *geometric algebra.*

With the success of Gibbs' vector analysis, quaternions faded into obscurity, only to be rediscovered in the 1970s when they were employed by the flight simulation community to control the dynamic behavior of a simulator's motion platform. A decade later they found their way into computer graphics where they are used for rotations about arbitrary axes. A decade later Clifford's geometric algebra was discovered by the computer graphics community, and today it is beginning to extend traditional vector techniques.

Now this does not mean that vector analysis is dead – far from it. Vast quantities of computer graphics software depends upon the vector mathematics developed over a century ago, and will continue to employ it for many years to come. Therefore, this current chapter is very important for the reader. Nevertheless, geometric algebra is destined to emerge as a powerful mathematical framework that could eventually replace vector analysis some day, which is why Chapter 12 is also very important.

6.2 2D Vectors

In computer graphics we employ 2D and 3D vectors. In this chapter we first consider vector notation within a 2D context and then extend the ideas into 3D.

6.2.1 Vector Notation

A scalar such as x is just a name for a single numeric quantity. However, because a vector contains two or more numbers, its symbolic name is printed using a **bold** font to distinguish it from a scalar variable. Examples being **n, i** and **q**. When a scalar variable is assigned a value we employ the standard algebraic notation

$$x = 3.$$

However, when a vector is assigned its numeric values, the following notation is used

$$\mathbf{n} = \begin{bmatrix} 3 \\ 4 \end{bmatrix}$$

which is called a *column* vector. The numbers 3 and 4 are called the *components* of **n**, and their position within the brackets is important. A *row* vector transposes the components horizontally $\mathbf{n} = \begin{bmatrix} 3 & 4 \end{bmatrix}^T$ as it is sometimes convenient for presentation purposes, and the superscript ^{T} reminds us of the column to row transposition.

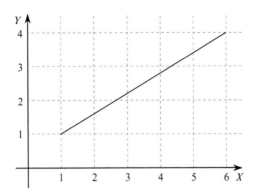

Fig. 6.1 A vector represented by a line segment. However, although the vector has magnitude, it does not have direction.

6.2.2 Graphical Representation of Vectors

Because vectors have to encode direction as well as magnitude, an arrow could be used to indicate direction and a number to represent magnitude. Such a scheme is often used in weather maps. And although this is a useful graphical interpretation of such data, it is not practical for algebraic manipulation.

Cartesian coordinates provide an excellent mechanism for representing vectors and allows them to be incorporated within the classical framework of mathematics. Figure 6.1 shows a short line segment which could be used to represent a vector. The length of the line represents the vector's magnitude, and the line's orientation defines its direction. But as you can see from the figure, the line does not have a direction. Even if we attach an arrowhead to the line, which is standard practice for annotating vectors in books and scientific papers, the arrowhead has no mathematical reality.

The line's direction is determined by first identifying the vector's tail and then measuring its components along the *x*- and *y*-axes. For example, in Fig. 6.2 the vector **r** has its tail defined by $(x_1, y_1) = (1, 2)$ and its head by $(x_2, y_2) = (3, 4)$.

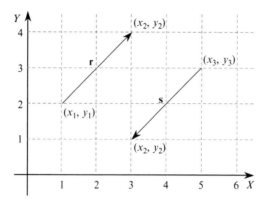

Fig. 6.2 Two vectors **r** and **s** have the same magnitude but opposite directions.

Vector **s**, on the other hand, has its tail defined by $(x_3, y_3) = (5, 3)$ and its head by $(x_4, y_4) = (3, 1)$ The x- and y-components for **r** are computed as follows

$$x_r = (x_2 - x_1) \qquad\qquad y_r = (y_2 - y_1)$$
$$x_r = 3 - 1 \qquad\qquad y_r = 4 - 2$$
$$x_r = 2 \qquad\qquad y_r = 2$$

and the components for **s** are computed as follows

$$x_s = (x_4 - x_3) \qquad\qquad y_s = (y_4 - y_3)$$
$$x_s = 3 - 5 \qquad\qquad y_s = 1 - 3$$
$$x_s = -2 \qquad\qquad y_s = -2.$$

It is the negative value of x_s and y_s that encode the vector's direction. In general, given that the coordinates of a vector's head and tail are (x_h, y_h) and (x_t, y_t) respectively, its components Δx and Δy are given by

$$\Delta x = (x_h - x_t) \qquad\qquad \Delta y = (y_h - y_t).$$

One can readily see from this notation that a vector does not have a unique position in space. It does not matter where we place a vector, so long as we preserve its length and orientation its components will not alter.

6.2.3 Magnitude of a Vector

The *magnitude* of a vector **r** is written $|\mathbf{r}|$ and is computed by applying the theorem of Pythagoras to its components:

$$|\mathbf{r}| = \sqrt{(\Delta x)^2 + (\Delta y)^2}.$$

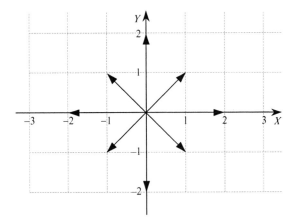

Fig. 6.3 Eight vectors whose coordinates are shown in Table 6.1.

To illustrate these ideas, consider a vector defined by $(x_h, y_h) = (4, 5)$ and $(x_t, y_t) = (1, 1)$. The x- and y-components are 3 and 4 respectively. Therefore its magnitude is equal to $\sqrt{3^2 + 4^2} = 5$. Figure 6.3 shows eight vectors, and their geometric properties are listed in Table 6.1.

Table 6.1 Values associated with the eight vectors in Fig. 6.3

x_h	y_h	x_t	y_t	Δx	Δy	$|\text{vector}|$
2	0	0	0	2	0	2
0	2	0	0	0	2	2
−2	0	0	0	−2	0	2
0	−2	0	0	0	−2	2
1	1	0	0	1	1	$\sqrt{2}$
−1	1	0	0	−1	1	$\sqrt{2}$
−1	−1	0	0	−1	−1	$\sqrt{2}$
1	−1	0	0	1	−1	$\sqrt{2}$

6.3 3D Vectors

The above vector examples are in 2D, but it is extremely simple to extend this notation to embrace an extra dimension. Figure 6.4 shows a 3D vector **r** with its head, tail, components and magnitude annotated. The vector, its components and magnitude are given by

$$\mathbf{r} = \begin{bmatrix} \Delta x & \Delta y & \Delta z \end{bmatrix}^T$$

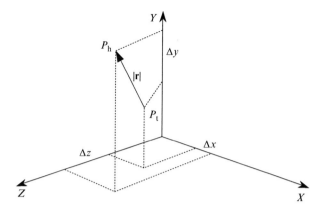

Fig. 6.4 The vector **r** has components Δx, Δy, Δz, which are the differences between the head and tail coordinates.

$$\Delta x = (x_h - x_t)$$
$$\Delta y = (y_h - y_t)$$
$$\Delta z = (z_y - z_t)$$
$$|\mathbf{r}| = \sqrt{(\Delta x)^2 + (\Delta y)^2 + (\Delta z)^2}.$$

As 3D vectors play a very important role in computer animation, all future examples will be three-dimensional.

6.3.1 Vector Manipulation

As vectors are different to scalars, a set of rules has been developed to control how the two mathematical entities interact with one another. For instance, we need to consider vector addition, subtraction and multiplication, and how a vector is modified by a scalar. Let's begin with multiplying a vector by a scalar.

6.3.2 Multiplying a Vector by a Scalar

Given a vector **n**, 2**n** means that the vectors components are doubled. For example, if

$$\mathbf{n} = \begin{bmatrix} 3 \\ 4 \\ 5 \end{bmatrix} \quad \text{then} \quad 2\mathbf{n} = \begin{bmatrix} 6 \\ 8 \\ 10 \end{bmatrix}$$

which seems logical. Similarly, if we divide **n** by 2, its components are halved. Note that the vector's direction remains unchanged – only its magnitude changes.

In general, if

$$\mathbf{n} = \begin{bmatrix} n_1 \\ n_2 \\ n_3 \end{bmatrix} \quad \text{then} \quad \lambda\mathbf{n} = \begin{bmatrix} \lambda n_1 \\ \lambda n_2 \\ \lambda n_3 \end{bmatrix} \text{ where } \quad [\lambda \in \mathbb{R}].$$

There is no way we can resolve the expression 2+ **n**, for it is not obvious which component of **n** is to be increased by 2. If all the components of **n** have to be increased by 2, then we simply add another vector whose components equal 2. However, if we can add a scalar to an imaginary (e.g., $2 + 3i$), why can't we add a scalar to a vector (e.g., $2 + \mathbf{n}$)? Well, the answer to this question is two-fold. First, if we change the meaning of 'add' to mean 'associated with', then there is nothing to stop us from 'associating' a scalar with a vector as we do with complex numbers. Second, the axioms controlling our algebra must be clear on this matter. Unfortunately, the axioms of traditional vector analysis do not support the 'association' of scalars with vectors in this way. However, geometric algebra does! Furthermore, geometric algebra even permits division by a vector, which does sound strange. Consequently, whilst reading the rest of this chapter keep an open mind about what is allowed and what is not allowed. At the end of the day, virtually anything is possible, so long as we have a well-behaved axiomatic system.

6.3.3 Vector Addition and Subtraction

Given vectors **r** and **s**, $\mathbf{r} \pm \mathbf{s}$ is defined as

$$\mathbf{r} = \begin{bmatrix} x_r \\ y_r \\ z_r \end{bmatrix} \quad \mathbf{s} = \begin{bmatrix} x_s \\ y_s \\ z_s \end{bmatrix} \quad \text{then} \quad \mathbf{r} \pm \mathbf{s} = \begin{bmatrix} x_r \pm x_s \\ y_r \pm y_s \\ z_r \pm z_s \end{bmatrix}.$$

Vector addition is commutative:

$$\mathbf{a} + \mathbf{b} = \mathbf{b} + \mathbf{a}$$

$$\text{e.g.} \quad \begin{bmatrix} 1 \\ 2 \\ 3 \end{bmatrix} + \begin{bmatrix} 4 \\ 5 \\ 6 \end{bmatrix} = \begin{bmatrix} 4 \\ 5 \\ 6 \end{bmatrix} + \begin{bmatrix} 1 \\ 2 \\ 3 \end{bmatrix}.$$

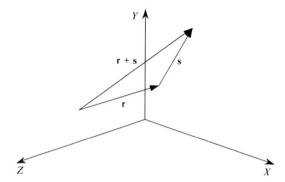

Fig. 6.5 Vector addition $\mathbf{r} + \mathbf{s}$.

However, like scalar subtraction, vector subtraction is not commutative

$$\mathbf{a} - \mathbf{b} \neq \mathbf{b} - \mathbf{a}$$

$$\text{e.g.} \quad \begin{bmatrix} 4 \\ 5 \\ 6 \end{bmatrix} - \begin{bmatrix} 1 \\ 2 \\ 3 \end{bmatrix} \neq \begin{bmatrix} 1 \\ 2 \\ 3 \end{bmatrix} - \begin{bmatrix} 4 \\ 5 \\ 6 \end{bmatrix}.$$

Let's illustrate vector addition and subtraction with two examples. Figure 6.5 shows the graphical interpretation of adding two vectors $\mathbf{r}$ and $\mathbf{s}$. Note that the tail of vector $\mathbf{s}$ is attached to the head of vector $\mathbf{r}$. The resultant vector $\mathbf{t} = \mathbf{r} + \mathbf{s}$ is defined by adding the corresponding components of $\mathbf{r}$ and $\mathbf{s}$ together. Figure 6.6 shows a graphical interpretation for $\mathbf{r} - \mathbf{s}$. This time the components of vector $\mathbf{s}$ are reversed to produce an equal and opposite vector. Then it is attached to $\mathbf{r}$ and added as described above.

6.3.4 Position Vectors

Given any point $P(x, y, z)$, a *position vector* $\mathbf{p}$ can be created by assuming that P is the vector's head and the origin is its tail. Because the tail coordinates are $(0, 0, 0)$ the vector's components are x, y, z. Consequently, the vector's magnitude $|\mathbf{p}|$ equals $\sqrt{x^2 + y^2 + z^2}$. For example, the point $P(4, 5, 6)$ creates a position vector $\mathbf{p}$ relative to the origin:

$$\mathbf{p} = \begin{bmatrix} 4 \\ 5 \\ 6 \end{bmatrix} \quad \text{and} \quad |\mathbf{p}| = \sqrt{4^2 + 5^2 + 6^2} \approx 20.88.$$

We will see how position vectors are used in Chapter 8 when we examine analytic geometry.

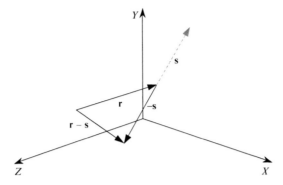

Fig. 6.6 Vector subtraction $\mathbf{r} - \mathbf{s}$.

6.3.5 Unit Vectors

By definition, a *unit vector* has a magnitude of 1. A simple example is $\mathbf{i}$ where

$$\mathbf{i} = \begin{bmatrix} 1 \\ 0 \\ 0 \end{bmatrix} \quad \text{and} \quad |\mathbf{i}| = 1.$$

Unit vectors are extremely useful when we come to vector multiplication. As we shall discover later, the multiplication of vectors involves taking their magnitude, and if this is unity, the multiplication is greatly simplified. Furthermore, in computer graphics applications vectors are used to specify the orientation of surfaces, the direction of light sources and the virtual camera. Again, if these vectors have a unit length, the computation time associated with vector operations can be minimized.

Converting a vector into a unit form is called *normalizing* and is achieved by dividing a vector's components by its magnitude. To formalize this process, consider a vector $\mathbf{r}$ whose components are x, y, z. The magnitude $|\mathbf{r}| = \sqrt{x^2 + y^2 + z^2}$ and the unit form of $\mathbf{r}$ is given by

$$\hat{\mathbf{r}} = \frac{1}{|\mathbf{r}|} \begin{bmatrix} x \\ y \\ z \end{bmatrix}.$$

This process can be confirmed by showing that the magnitude of $\hat{\mathbf{r}}$ is 1:

$$|\hat{\mathbf{r}}| = \sqrt{\left(\frac{x}{|\hat{\mathbf{r}}|}\right)^2 + \left(\frac{y}{|\hat{\mathbf{r}}|}\right)^2 + \left(\frac{z}{|\hat{\mathbf{r}}|}\right)^2}$$

$$= \frac{1}{|\hat{\mathbf{r}}|} \sqrt{x^2 + y^2 + z^2}$$

$$|\hat{\mathbf{r}}| = 1.$$

To put this into context, consider the conversion of **r** into a unit form:

$$\mathbf{r} = \begin{bmatrix} 1 \\ 2 \\ 3 \end{bmatrix}$$

$$|\mathbf{r}| = \sqrt{1^2 + 2^2 + 3^2} = \sqrt{14}$$

$$\hat{\mathbf{r}} = \frac{1}{\sqrt{14}} \begin{bmatrix} 1 \\ 2 \\ 3 \end{bmatrix} \approx \begin{bmatrix} 0.267 \\ 0.535 \\ 0.802 \end{bmatrix}.$$

6.3.6 Cartesian Vectors

Now that we have investigated the scalar multiplication of vectors, vector addition and unit vectors, we can combine all three to permit the algebraic manipulation of vectors. To begin with, we will define three Cartesian unit vectors **i, j, k** that are aligned with the x-, y- and z-axes respectively:

$$\mathbf{i} = \begin{bmatrix} 1 \\ 0 \\ 0 \end{bmatrix}, \quad \mathbf{j} = \begin{bmatrix} 0 \\ 1 \\ 0 \end{bmatrix}, \quad \mathbf{k} = \begin{bmatrix} 0 \\ 0 \\ 1 \end{bmatrix}.$$

Therefore, any vector aligned with the x-, y- or z-axes can be defined by a scalar multiple of the unit vectors **i, j** and **k** respectively. For example, a vector 10 units long aligned with the x-axis is simply 10**i**. And a vector 20 units long aligned with the z-axis is 20**k**. By employing the rules of vector addition and subtraction, we can compose a vector **r** by summing three *Cartesian unit vectors* as follows:

$$\mathbf{r} = a\mathbf{i} + b\mathbf{j} + c\mathbf{k}.$$

This is equivalent to writing **r** as

$$\mathbf{r} = \begin{bmatrix} a \\ b \\ c \end{bmatrix}$$

which means that the magnitude of **r** is readily computed as

$$|\mathbf{r}| = \sqrt{a^2 + b^2 + c^2}.$$

Any pair of Cartesian vectors such as $\mathbf{r}$ and $\mathbf{s}$ can be combined as follows

$$\mathbf{r} = a\mathbf{i} + b\mathbf{j} + c\mathbf{k}$$
$$\mathbf{s} = d\mathbf{i} + e\mathbf{j} + f\mathbf{k}$$
$$\mathbf{r} \pm \mathbf{s} = (a \pm d)\mathbf{i} + (b \pm e)\mathbf{j} + (c \pm f)\mathbf{k}.$$

For example, given

$$\mathbf{r} = 2\mathbf{i} + 3\mathbf{j} + 4\mathbf{k}$$
$$\mathbf{s} = 5\mathbf{i} + 6\mathbf{j} + 7\mathbf{k}$$

then

$$\mathbf{r} + \mathbf{s} = 7\mathbf{i} + 9\mathbf{j} + 11\mathbf{k}$$

and

$$|\mathbf{r} + \mathbf{s}| = \sqrt{7^2 + 9^2 + 11^2} \approx 15.84.$$

6.3.7 Vector Multiplication

Although vector addition and subtraction are useful in resolving various problems, vector multiplication provides some powerful ways of computing angles and surface orientations.

The multiplication of two scalars is very familiar: for example, 6×7 or $7 \times 6 = 42$. We often visualize this operation, as a rectangular area where 6 and 7 are the dimensions of a rectangle's sides, and 42 is the area. However, when we consider the multiplication of vectors we are basically multiplying two 3D lines together, which is not an easy operation to visualize.

The mathematicians who defined the structure of vector analysis provided two ways to multiply vectors together: one gives rise to a scalar result and the other a vector result. We will start with the *scalar product*.

6.3.8 Scalar Product

We could multiply two vectors $\mathbf{r}$ and $\mathbf{s}$ by using the product of their magnitudes: $|\mathbf{r}|\,|\mathbf{s}|$. Although this is a valid operation it does not get us anywhere because it ignores the orientation of the vectors, which is one of their important features. The concept, however, is readily developed into a useful operation by including the angle between the vectors.

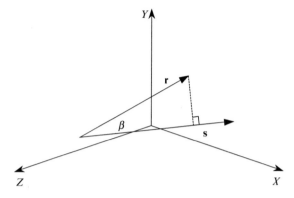

Fig. 6.7 The projection of **r** on **s** creates the basis for the scalar product.

Figure 6.7 shows two vectors **r** and **s** that have been drawn, for convenience, such that their tails touch. Taking **s** as the reference vector, which is an arbitrary choice, we compute the projection of **r** on **s**, which takes into account their relative orientation. The length of **r** on **s** is $|\mathbf{r}|\cos\beta$. We can now multiply the magnitude of **s** by the projected length of **r**: $|\mathbf{s}||\mathbf{r}|\cos\beta$ This scalar product is written

$$\mathbf{r}\cdot\mathbf{s} = |\mathbf{r}||\mathbf{s}|\cos\beta. \tag{6.1}$$

The dot symbol '·' is used to represent scalar multiplication, to distinguish it from the vector product, which, we will discover, employs a '×' symbol. Because of this symbol, the scalar product is often referred to as the *dot product*.

So far we have only defined what we mean by the dot product. We now need to discover how to compute it. Fortunately, everything is in place to perform this task. To begin with, we define two Cartesian vectors **r** and **s**, and proceed to multiply them together using the dot product definition:

$$\mathbf{r} = a\mathbf{i} + b\mathbf{j} + c\mathbf{k}$$
$$\mathbf{s} = d\mathbf{i} + e\mathbf{j} + f\mathbf{k}$$

therefore,

$$\begin{aligned}
\mathbf{r}\cdot\mathbf{s} &= (a\mathbf{i} + b\mathbf{j} + c\mathbf{k}) \cdot (d\mathbf{i} + e\mathbf{j} + f\mathbf{k}) \\
&= a\mathbf{i} \cdot (d\mathbf{i} + e\mathbf{j} + f\mathbf{k}) \\
&\quad + b\mathbf{j} \cdot (d\mathbf{i} + e\mathbf{j} + f\mathbf{k}) \\
&\quad + c\mathbf{k} \cdot (d\mathbf{i} + e\mathbf{j} + f\mathbf{k}) \\
\mathbf{r}\cdot\mathbf{s} &= ad\mathbf{i} \cdot \mathbf{i} + ae\mathbf{i} \cdot \mathbf{j} + af\mathbf{i} \cdot \mathbf{k} \\
&\quad + bd\mathbf{j} \cdot \mathbf{i} + be\mathbf{j} \cdot \mathbf{j} + bf\mathbf{j} \cdot \mathbf{k} \\
&\quad + cd\mathbf{k} \cdot \mathbf{i} + ce\mathbf{k} \cdot \mathbf{j} + cf\mathbf{k} \cdot \mathbf{k}.
\end{aligned}$$

Before we proceed any further, we can see that we have created various dot product terms such as $\mathbf{i}\cdot\mathbf{i}$, $\mathbf{i}\cdot\mathbf{j}$, $\mathbf{i}\cdot\mathbf{k}$ etc. These terms can be divided into two groups: those that reference the same unit vector, and those that reference different unit vectors.

Using the definition of the dot product (6.1), terms such as $\mathbf{i}\cdot\mathbf{i}$, $\mathbf{j}\cdot\mathbf{j}$ and $\mathbf{k}\cdot\mathbf{k}=1$, because the angle between $\mathbf{i}$ and $\mathbf{i}$, $\mathbf{j}$ and $\mathbf{j}$, or $\mathbf{k}$ and $\mathbf{k}$, is $0°$; and $\cos 0° = 1$. But because the other vector combinations are separated by $90°$, and $\cos 90° = 0$, all remaining terms collapse to zero. Bearing in mind that the magnitude of a unit vector is 1, we can write

$$|\mathbf{r}||\mathbf{s}|\cos\beta = ad + be + cf.$$

This result confirms that the dot product is indeed a scalar quantity. Now let's see how it works in practice.

6.3.9 Example of the Scalar Product

To find the angle between two vectors $\mathbf{r}$ and $\mathbf{s}$

$$\mathbf{r} = \begin{bmatrix} 2 \\ 3 \\ 4 \end{bmatrix} \quad \text{and} \quad \mathbf{s} = \begin{bmatrix} 5 \\ 6 \\ 10 \end{bmatrix}$$

$$|\mathbf{r}| = \sqrt{2^2 + 0^2 + 4^2} \approx 4.472$$
$$|\mathbf{s}| = \sqrt{5^2 + 6^2 + 10^2} \approx 12.689.$$

Therefore,

$$|\mathbf{r}||\mathbf{s}|\cos\beta = 2 \times 5 + 0 \times 6 + 4 \times 10 = 50$$
$$12.689 \times 4.472 \times \cos\beta = 50$$
$$\cos\beta = \frac{50}{12.689 \times 4.472} \approx 0.8811$$
$$\beta = \cos^{-1} 0.8811 \approx 28.22°.$$

The angle between the two vectors is approximately $28.22°$.

It is worth pointing out at this stage that the angle returned by the dot product ranges between $0°$ and $180°$. This is because, as the angle between two vectors increases beyond $180°$ the returned angle β is always the smallest angle associated with the geometry.

6.3.10 The Dot Product in Lighting Calculations

Lambert's law states that the intensity of illumination on a diffuse surface is proportional to the cosine of the angle between the surface normal vector and the light source direction. This arrangement is shown in Fig. 6.8. The light source is located at (20, 20, 40) and the illuminated point is (0, 10, 0).

In this situation we are interested in calculating $\cos\beta$, which when multiplied by the light source intensity gives the incident light intensity on the surface. To begin with, we are given the normal vector $\hat{\mathbf{n}}$ to the surface. In this case $\hat{\mathbf{n}}$ is a unit vector, and its magnitude $|\hat{\mathbf{n}}| = 1$:

$$\hat{\mathbf{n}} = \begin{bmatrix} 0 \\ 1 \\ 0 \end{bmatrix}.$$

The direction of the light source from the surface is defined by the vector $\mathbf{s}$:

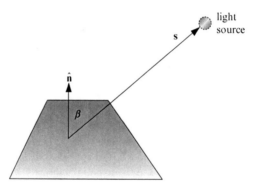

Fig. 6.8 Lambert's law states that the intensity of illumination on a diffuse surface is proportional to the cosine of the angle between the surface normal vector and the light source direction.

$$\mathbf{s} = \begin{bmatrix} 20 - 0 \\ 20 - 10 \\ 40 - 0 \end{bmatrix} = \begin{bmatrix} 20 \\ 10 \\ 40 \end{bmatrix}$$

$$|\mathbf{s}| = \sqrt{20^2 + 10^2 + 40^2} \approx 45.826$$

$$|\hat{\mathbf{n}}||\mathbf{s}|\cos\beta = 0 \times 20 + 1 \times 10 + 0 \times 40 = 10$$

$$1 \times 45.826 \times \cos\beta = 10$$

$$\cos\beta = \frac{10}{45.826} \approx 0.218.$$

Therefore the light intensity at the point $(0,10,0)$ is 0.218 of the original light intensity at $(20,20,40)$, but does not take into account the attenuation due to the inverse-square law of light propagation.

6.3.11 The Scalar Product in Back-Face Detection

A standard way of identifying back-facing polygons relative to the virtual camera is to compute the angle between the polygon's surface normal and the line of sight between the camera and the polygon. If this angle is less than $90°$ the polygon is visible; if it is equal to or greater than $90°$ the polygon is invisible. This geometry is shown in Fig. 6.9. Although it is obvious from Fig. 6.9 that the right-hand polygon is invisible to the camera, let's prove algebraically that this is so. Let the camera be located at $(0,0,0)$ and the polygon's vertex is $(10,10,40)$. The normal vector is $[5 \quad 5 \ -2]^T$.

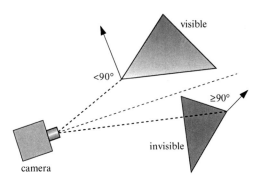

Fig. 6.9 The angle between the surface normal and the camera's line of sight determines the polygon's visibility.

$$\mathbf{n} = \begin{bmatrix} 0 \\ 1 \\ 0 \end{bmatrix}$$

$$|\mathbf{n}| = \sqrt{5^2 + 5^2 + (-2)^2} \approx 7.348.$$

The camera vector $\mathbf{c}$ is

$$\mathbf{c} = \begin{bmatrix} 0-10 \\ 0-10 \\ 0-40 \end{bmatrix} = \begin{bmatrix} -10 \\ -10 \\ -40 \end{bmatrix}$$

$$|\mathbf{c}| = \sqrt{(-10)^2 + (-10)^2 + (-40)^2} \approx 42.426$$

therefore,

$$|\mathbf{n}||\mathbf{c}|\cos\beta = 5 \times (-10) + 5 \times (-10) + (-2) \times (-40)$$
$$7.348 \times 42.426 \times \cos\beta = -20$$
$$\cos\beta = \frac{-20}{7348 \times 42.426} \approx -0.0634$$
$$\beta = \cos^{-1}(-0.0634) \approx 93.635°$$

which shows that the polygon is invisible.

6.3.12 The Vector Product

As mentioned above, there are two ways to multiply vectors. The first is the scalar product, and the second is the *vector product*, which is also called the *cross product* due to the '×' symbol used in its notation. It is based on the assumption that two vectors $\mathbf{r}$ and $\mathbf{s}$ can be multiplied together to produce a third vector $\mathbf{t}$:

$$\mathbf{r} \times \mathbf{s} = \mathbf{t}$$

where

$$|\mathbf{t}| = |\mathbf{r}||\mathbf{s}|\sin\beta \qquad (6.2)$$

and β is the angle between $\mathbf{r}$ and $\mathbf{s}$.

We will discover that the vector $\mathbf{t}$ is normal (90°) to the plane containing the vectors $\mathbf{r}$ and $\mathbf{s}$. Which makes it an ideal way of computing the surface normal to a polygon. Once again, let's define two vectors and proceed to multiply them together using the × operator:

$$\mathbf{r} = a\mathbf{i} + b\mathbf{j} + c\mathbf{k}$$
$$\mathbf{s} = d\mathbf{i} + e\mathbf{j} + f\mathbf{k}$$

therefore,

$$\mathbf{r} \times \mathbf{s} = (a\mathbf{i} + b\mathbf{j} + c\mathbf{k}) \times (d\mathbf{i} + e\mathbf{j} + f\mathbf{k})$$
$$= a\mathbf{i} \times (d\mathbf{i} + e\mathbf{j} + f\mathbf{k})$$
$$+ b\mathbf{j} \times (d\mathbf{i} + e\mathbf{j} + f\mathbf{k})$$
$$+ c\mathbf{k} \times (d\mathbf{i} + e\mathbf{j} + f\mathbf{k})$$
$$\mathbf{r} \times \mathbf{s} = ad\mathbf{i} \times \mathbf{i} + ae\mathbf{i} \times \mathbf{j} + af\mathbf{i} \times \mathbf{k}$$
$$+ bd\mathbf{j} \times \mathbf{i} + be\mathbf{j} \times \mathbf{j} + bf\mathbf{j} \times \mathbf{k}$$
$$+ cd\mathbf{k} \times \mathbf{i} + ce\mathbf{k} \times \mathbf{j} + cf\mathbf{k} \times \mathbf{k}.$$

As we found with the dot product, there are two groups of vector terms: those that reference the same unit vector, and those that reference different unit vectors.

Using the definition for the cross product (6.2), operations such as $\mathbf{i} \times \mathbf{i}$, $\mathbf{j} \times \mathbf{j}$ and $\mathbf{k} \times \mathbf{k}$ result in a vector whose magnitude is 0. This is because the angle between the vectors is $0°$, and $\sin 0° = 0$. Consequently these terms disappear and we are left with

$$\mathbf{r} \times \mathbf{s} = ae\mathbf{i} \times \mathbf{j} + af\mathbf{i} \times \mathbf{k} + bd\mathbf{j} \times \mathbf{i} + bf\mathbf{j} \times \mathbf{k} + cd\mathbf{k} \times \mathbf{i} + ce\mathbf{k} \times \mathbf{j}. \tag{6.3}$$

The mathematician Sir William Rowan Hamilton struggled for many years when working on quaternions to resolve the meaning of a similar result. At the time, he was not using vectors, as they had yet to be defined, but the imaginary terms i, j and k. Hamilton's problem was to resolve the products ij, jk, ki and their opposites ji, kj and ik. What did the products mean? He reasoned that $ij = k$, $jk = i$ and $ki = j$, but could not resolve their opposites. One day in 1843, when he was out walking, thinking about this problem, he thought the impossible: $ij = k$, but $ji = -k$, $jk = i$, but $kj = -i$, and $ki = j$, but $ik = -j$. To his surprise, this worked, but it contradicted the commutative multiplication law of scalars where $6 \times 7 = 7 \times 6$. We now accept that the commutative multiplication law is there to be broken!

Although Hamilton had discovered 3D complex numbers, to which he gave the name *quaternion*, they were not popular with everyone. And as mentioned earlier, Josiah Gibbs saw that converting the imaginary i, j and k terms into the unit vectors $\mathbf{i}$, $\mathbf{j}$ and $\mathbf{k}$ created a stable algebra for manipulating vectors, and for over a century we have been using Gibbs' vector notation.

The question we must ask is "Was Gibbs right?" to which the answer is probably "no!" The reason for this is that although the scalar product works in space of any number of dimensions, the vector (cross) product does not. It obviously does not work in 2D as there is no direction for the resultant vector. It obviously works in 3D, but in 4D and above there is no automatic spatial direction for the resultant vector. So, the vector product is possibly a special condition of some other structure. Hermann Grassmann knew this but did not have the mathematical reputation to convince his fellow mathematicians.

In Chapter 12 on geometric algebra we return to this problem and discover that the terms $\mathbf{i} \times \mathbf{j}$, $\mathbf{j} \times \mathbf{k}$, $\mathbf{k} \times \mathbf{i}$ and their opposites are entities in there own right. We also discover that geometric algebra incorporates the 3D vector product and a much better version of quaternions.

For the moment though, let's continue with Hamilton's rules and reduce the cross product terms of (6.3) to

$$\mathbf{r} \times \mathbf{s} = ae\mathbf{k} - af\mathbf{j} - bd\mathbf{k} + bf\mathbf{i} + cd\mathbf{j} - ce\mathbf{i}. \tag{6.4}$$

Equation (6.4) can be tidied up to bring like terms together:

$$\mathbf{r} \times \mathbf{s} = (bf - ce)\mathbf{i} + (cd - af)\mathbf{j} + (ae - bd)\mathbf{k}. \tag{6.5}$$

Now let's repeat the original vector equations to see how equation (6.5) is computed:

$$\mathbf{r} = a\mathbf{i} + b\mathbf{j} + c\mathbf{k}$$
$$\mathbf{s} = d\mathbf{i} + e\mathbf{j} + f\mathbf{k}$$

$$\mathbf{r} \times \mathbf{s} = (bf - ce)\mathbf{i} + (cd - af)\mathbf{j} + (ae - bd)\mathbf{k}. \qquad (6.6)$$

To compute the **i** scalar term we consider the scalars associated with the other two unit vectors, i.e., b, c, e, and f, and cross-multiply and subtract them to form $(bf - ce)$.

To compute the **j** scalar term we consider the scalars associated with the other two unit vectors, i.e., a, c, d, and f, and cross-multiply and subtract them to form $(cd - af)$.

To compute the **k** scalar term we consider the scalars associated with the other two unit vectors, i.e., a, b, d, and e, and cross-multiply and subtract them to form $(ae - bd)$.

The middle operation seems out of step with the other two, but in fact it preserves a cyclic symmetry often found in mathematics. Nevertheless, some authors reverse the sign of the **j** scalar term and cross-multiply and subtract the terms to produce $-(af - cd)$ which maintains a visual pattern for remembering the cross-multiplication. Equation (6.6) now becomes

$$\mathbf{r} \times \mathbf{s} = (bf - ce)\mathbf{i} - (af - cd)\mathbf{j} + (ae - bd)\mathbf{k}. \qquad (6.7)$$

However, we now have to remember to introduce a negative sign for the **j** scalar term!

Although we have not yet covered *determinants*, their notation allows us to write (6.7) as

$$\mathbf{r} \times \mathbf{s} = \begin{vmatrix} b & c \\ e & f \end{vmatrix} \mathbf{i} - \begin{vmatrix} a & c \\ d & f \end{vmatrix} \mathbf{j} + \begin{vmatrix} a & b \\ d & e \end{vmatrix} \mathbf{k}. \qquad (6.8)$$

A 2×2 determinant is the difference between the product of the diagonal terms.

Therefore, to derive the cross product of two vectors we first write the vectors in the correct sequence. Remembering that $\mathbf{r} \times \mathbf{s}$ does not equal $\mathbf{s} \times \mathbf{r}$. Second, we compute the three scalar terms and form the resultant vector, which is perpendicular to the plane containing the original vectors.

Let's illustrate the vector product with some examples. First we will confirm that the vector product works with the unit vectors **i**, **j** and **k**.

We start with

$$\mathbf{r} = 1\mathbf{i} + 0\mathbf{j} + 0\mathbf{k}$$
$$\mathbf{s} = 0\mathbf{i} + 1\mathbf{j} + 0\mathbf{k}$$

and then compute (6.7)

$$\mathbf{r} \times \mathbf{s} = (0 \times 0 - 0 \times 1)\mathbf{i} - (1 \times 0 - 0 \times 0)\mathbf{j} + (1 \times 1 - 0 \times 0)\mathbf{k}.$$

The **i** scalar and **j** scalar terms are both zero, but the **k** scalar term is 1, which makes $\mathbf{i} \times \mathbf{j} = \mathbf{k}$.

Now let's show what happens when we reverse the vectors. This time we start with

$$\mathbf{r} = 0\mathbf{i} + 1\mathbf{j} + 0\mathbf{k}$$
$$\mathbf{s} = 1\mathbf{i} + 0\mathbf{j} + 0\mathbf{k}$$

and then compute (6.7)

$$\mathbf{r} \times \mathbf{s} = (1 \times 0 - 0 \times 0)\mathbf{i} - (0 \times 0 - 0 \times 1)\mathbf{j} + (0 \times 0 - 1 \times 1)\mathbf{k}.$$

The **i** scalar and **j** scalar terms are both zero, but the **k** scalar term is -1, which makes $\mathbf{j} \times \mathbf{i} = -\mathbf{k}$. So we see that the vector product is *antisymmetric*, i.e., there is a sign reversal when the vectors are reversed. Similarly, it can be shown that

$$\mathbf{j} \times \mathbf{k} = \mathbf{i}$$
$$\mathbf{k} \times \mathbf{i} = \mathbf{j}$$
$$\mathbf{k} \times \mathbf{j} = -\mathbf{i}$$
$$\mathbf{i} \times \mathbf{k} = -\mathbf{j}.$$

Let's now consider two vectors **r** and **s** and compute the normal vector **t**. The vectors are chosen so that we can anticipate approximately the answer. For the sake of clarity, the vector equations include the scalar multipliers 0 and 1. Normally, these would be omitted. Figure 6.10 shows the vectors **r** and **s** and the normal vector **t**, and Table 6.2 contains the coordinates of the vertices forming the two vectors

$$\mathbf{r} = \begin{bmatrix} x_3 - x_2 \\ y_3 - y_2 \\ z_3 - z_2 \end{bmatrix} \quad \text{and} \quad \mathbf{s} = \begin{bmatrix} x_1 - x_2 \\ y_1 - y_2 \\ z_1 - z_2 \end{bmatrix}$$

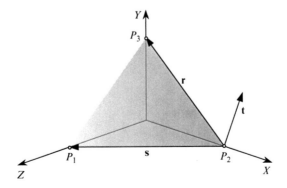

Fig. 6.10 The vector **t** is normal to the vectors **r** and **s**.

Table 6.2 Coordinates of the vertices used in Fig. 6.10

Vertex	x	y	z
P_1	0	0	1
P_2	1	0	0
P_3	0	1	0

$$P_1 = (0,0,1)$$
$$P_2 = (1,0,0)$$
$$P_3 = (0,1,0)$$
$$\mathbf{r} = -1\mathbf{i} + 1\mathbf{j} + 0\mathbf{k}$$
$$\mathbf{s} = -1\mathbf{i} + 0\mathbf{j} + 1\mathbf{k}$$

$$\mathbf{r} \times \mathbf{s} = [1 \times 1 - 0 \times 0]\mathbf{i}$$
$$- [-1 \times 1 - (-1) \times 0]\mathbf{j}$$
$$+ [-1 \times 0 - (-1) \times 1]\mathbf{k}$$
$$\mathbf{t} = \mathbf{i} + \mathbf{j} + \mathbf{k}.$$

This confirms what we expected from Fig. 6.10. Let us now reverse the vectors to illustrate the importance of vector sequence.

$$\mathbf{s} = -1\mathbf{i} + 0\mathbf{j} + 1\mathbf{k}$$
$$\mathbf{r} = -1\mathbf{i} + 1\mathbf{j} + 0\mathbf{k}$$

$$\mathbf{s} \times \mathbf{r} = [0 \times 0 - 1 \times 1]\mathbf{i}$$
$$- [-1 \times 0 - (-1) \times 1]\mathbf{j}$$
$$+ [-1 \times 1 - (-1) \times 0]\mathbf{k}$$
$$\mathbf{t} = -\mathbf{i} - \mathbf{j} - \mathbf{k}$$

which is in the opposite direction to $\mathbf{r} \times \mathbf{s}$ and confirms that the vector product is non-commutative.

6.3.13 The Right-Hand Rule

The *right-hand rule* is an *aide mémoire* for working out the orientation of the cross product vector. Given the operation $\mathbf{r} \times \mathbf{s}$, if the right-hand thumb is aligned with $\mathbf{r}$, the first finger with $\mathbf{s}$, and the middle finger points in the direction of $\mathbf{t}$. However, we must remember that this only holds in 3D. In 4D and above it makes no sense.

6.4 Deriving a Unit Normal Vector for a Triangle

Figure 6.11 shows a triangle with vertices defined in an anticlockwise sequence from its visible side. This is the side from which we want the surface normal to

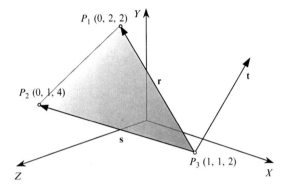

Fig. 6.11 The normal vector **t** is derived from the cross product **r** × **s**.

point. Using the following information we will compute the surface normal using the cross product and then convert it to a unit normal vector.

Create vector **r** between P_1 and P_3, and vector **s** between P_2 and P_3:

$$\mathbf{r} = -1\mathbf{i} + 1\mathbf{j} + 0\mathbf{k}$$
$$\mathbf{s} = -1\mathbf{i} + 0\mathbf{j} + 2\mathbf{k}$$
$$\mathbf{r} \times \mathbf{s} = (1 \times 2 - 0 \times 0)\mathbf{i}$$
$$- (-1 \times 2 - 0 \times -1)\mathbf{j}$$
$$+ (-1 \times 0 - 1 \times -1)\mathbf{k}$$
$$\mathbf{t} = 2\mathbf{i} + 2\mathbf{j} + \mathbf{k}$$
$$|\mathbf{t}| = \sqrt{2^2 + 2^2 + 1^2} = 3$$
$$\hat{\mathbf{t}}_u = \frac{2}{3}\mathbf{i} + \frac{2}{3}\mathbf{j} + \frac{1}{3}\mathbf{k}.$$

The unit vector $\hat{\mathbf{t}}_u$ can now be used in illumination calculations, and as it has unit length, dot product calculations are simplified.

6.5 Areas

Before we leave the cross product let's investigate the physical meaning of $|\mathbf{r}|\,|\mathbf{s}|\sin\beta$. Figure 6.12 shows two 2D vectors **r** and **s**. The height $h = |\mathbf{s}|\sin\beta$, therefore the area of the parallelogram is

$$area = |\mathbf{r}|\,h = |\mathbf{r}||\mathbf{s}|\sin\beta.$$

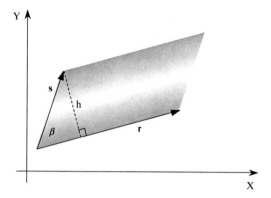

Fig. 6.12 The area of the parallelogram formed by two vectors **r** and **s** equals $|\mathbf{r}||\mathbf{s}|\sin\beta$.

But this is the magnitude of the cross product vector **t**. Thus when we calculate $\mathbf{r}\times\mathbf{s}$, the length of the normal vector **t** equals the area of the parallelogram formed by **r** and **s**. Which means that the triangle formed by halving the parallelogram is half the area.

$$area\ of\ parallelogram = |\mathbf{t}|$$
$$area\ of\ triangle = \frac{1}{2}|\mathbf{t}|.$$

This means that it is a relatively easy exercise to calculate the surface area of an object constructed from triangles or parallelograms. In the case of a triangulated surface, we simply sum the magnitudes of the normals and halve the result.

6.5.1 Calculating 2D Areas

Figure 6.13 shows three vertices of a triangle $P_0(x_0, y_0)$, $P_1(x_1, y_1)$ and $P_2(x_2, y_2)$ formed in an anti-clockwise sequence. We can imagine that the triangle exists on the $z = 0$ plane, therefore the z-coordinates are zero. The vectors **r** and **s** are computed as follows:

$$\mathbf{r} = \begin{bmatrix} x_1 - x_0 \\ y_1 - y_0 \\ 0 \end{bmatrix} \quad and \quad \mathbf{s} = \begin{bmatrix} x_2 - x_0 \\ y_2 - y_0 \\ 0 \end{bmatrix}$$

$$\mathbf{r} = (x_1 - x_0)\mathbf{i} + (y_1 - y_0)\mathbf{j}$$
$$\mathbf{s} = (x_2 - x_0)\mathbf{i} + (y_2 - y_0)\mathbf{j}$$
$$|\mathbf{r} \times \mathbf{s}| = (x_1 - x_0)(y_2 - y_0) - (x_2 - x_0)(y_1 - y_0)$$
$$= x_1(y_2 - y_0) - x_0(y_2 - y_0) - x_2(y_1 - y_0) + x_0(y_1 - y_0)$$

$$= x_1 y_2 - x_1 y_0 - x_0 y_2 + x_0 y_0 - x_2 y_1 + x_2 y_0 + x_0 y_1 - x_0 y_0$$
$$= x_1 y_2 - x_1 y_0 - x_0 y_2 - x_2 y_1 + x_2 y_0 + x_0 y_1$$
$$= (x_0 y_1 - x_1 y_0) + (x_1 y_2 - x_2 y_1) + (x_2 y_0 - x_0 y_2).$$

But the area of the triangle formed by the three vertices is $\frac{1}{2}|\mathbf{r} \times \mathbf{s}|$. Therefore

$$area = \frac{1}{2}[(x_0 y_1 - x_1 y_0) + (x_1 y_2 - x_2 y_1) + (x_2 y_0 - x_0 y_2)]$$

which is the formula disclosed in Chapter 2!

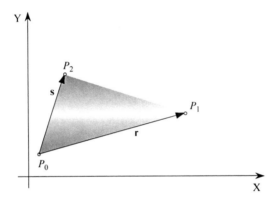

Fig. 6.13 The area of the triangle formed by the vectors $\mathbf{r}$ and $\mathbf{s}$ is half the magnitude of their cross product.

6.6 Summary

Vectors are extremely useful and relatively easy to use. They are vital to rendering algorithms and shaders, and most of the time we only need to use the scalar and cross products. However, I have tried to prepare you for an alternative algebra for vectors: geometric algebra. As we shall see in Chapter 12, geometric algebra shows that mathematics took the wrong direction when it embraced Gibbs' vector analysis. Hermann Grassmann had been right all along. If the mathematicians of the day had adopted Grassmann's ideas, today we would be familiar with vectors, bivectors, trivectors, quaternions, etc. But we are where we are, and we must prepare ourselves for some new ideas.

Even if you already knew something about vectors, I hope that this chapter has introduced some new ideas and illustrated the role vectors play in computer graphics.

Chapter 7
Transforms

7.1 Introduction

Transforms are used to scale, translate, rotate, reflect and shear shapes and objects. For example, if we start with a 2D point $P(x,y)$, it can be transformed into $P'(x',y')$ by manipulating the original coordinates x and y using

$$x' = ax + by + e$$
$$y' = cx + dy + f.$$

Similarly, a 3D point $P(x,y,z)$ can be transformed into $P'(x',y',z')$ using

$$x' = ax + by + cz + k$$
$$y' = dx + ey + fz + l$$
$$z' = gx + hy + jz + m.$$

By choosing different values for $a,b,c,....$ we can translate, shear, scale, reflect or rotate a shape.

Although algebra is the basic notation for transforms, it is also possible to express them as *matrices*, which provide certain advantages for viewing the transform and for interfacing to various types of computer graphics hardware. We begin with an algebraic approach and then introduce matrix notation.

7.2 2D Transforms

7.2.1 Translation

Cartesian coordinates provide a one-to-one relationship between number and shape, such that when we change a shape's coordinates, we change its geometry. For example, if $P(x,y)$ is a vertex on a shape, when we apply the operation $x' = x + 3$ we

J. Vince, *Mathematics for Computer Graphics*, Undergraduate Topics in Computer Science, DOI 10.1007/978-1-84996-023-6_7,

create a new point $P'(x',y)$ three units to the right. Similarly, the operation $y' = y+1$ creates a new point $P'(x,y')$ displaced one unit vertically. By applying both of these transforms to every vertex to the original shape, the shape is displaced as shown in Fig. 7.1.

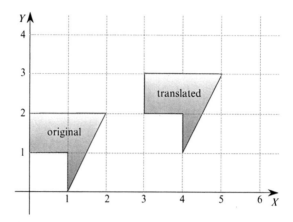

Fig. 7.1 The translated shape results by adding 3 to every x-coordinate, and 1 to every y-coordinate to the original shape.

7.2.2 Scaling

Shape scaling is achieved by multiplying coordinates as follows:

$$x' = 2x$$
$$y' = 1.5y.$$

This transform results in a horizontal scaling of 2 and a vertical scaling of 1.5 as illustrated in Fig. 7.2. Note that a point located at the origin does not change its place, so scaling is relative to the origin.

7.2.3 Reflection

To make a reflection of a shape relative to the y-axis, we simply reverse the sign of the x-coordinates, leaving the y-coordinates unchanged:

$$x' = -x$$
$$y' = y$$

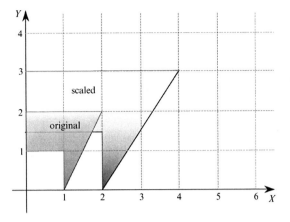

Fig. 7.2 The scaled shape results by multiplying the *x*-coordinates by 2 and the *y*-coordinates by 1.5.

and to reflect a shape relative to the *x*-axis we reverse the *y*-coordinates:

$$x' = x$$
$$y' = -y.$$

Examples of reflections are shown in Fig. 7.3.

Before proceeding, we pause to introduce matrix notation so that we can develop further transforms using algebra and matrices simultaneously.

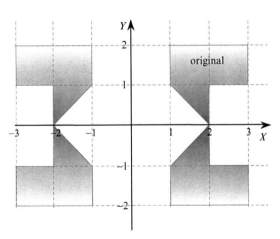

Fig. 7.3 The top right-hand shape gives rise to three reflections simply by reversing the signs of its coordinates.

7.3 Matrices

Matrix notation was researched by the British mathematician Arthur Cayley around 1858. Caley formalized matrix algebra, along with the American mathematicians Benjamin and Charles Pierce. Also, by the start of the nineteenth century Carl Gauss (1777–1855) had shown that transforms were not commutative, i.e., $T_1 \times T_2 \neq T_2 \times T_1$ (where T_1 and T_2 are transforms) and Caley's matrix notation would clarify such observations. For example, consider the transform T_1:

$$T_1 = \begin{cases} x' = ax + by \\ y' = cx + dy \end{cases} \tag{7.1}$$

and another transform T_2 that transforms T_1:

$$T_2 \times T_1 = \begin{cases} x'' = Ax' + By' \\ y'' = Cx' + Dy'. \end{cases}$$

If we substitute the full definition of T_1 we get

$$T_2 \times T_1 = \begin{cases} x'' = A(ax + by) + B(cx + dy) \\ y'' = C(ax + by) + D(cx + dy) \end{cases}$$

which simplifies to

$$T_2 \times T_1 = \begin{cases} x'' = (Aa + Bc)x + (Ab + Bd)y \\ y'' = (Ca + Dc)x + (Cb + Dd)y. \end{cases}$$

Caley proposed separating the constants from the variables, which permits us to write (7.1) as:

$$T_1 = \begin{bmatrix} x' \\ y' \end{bmatrix} = \begin{bmatrix} a & b \\ c & d \end{bmatrix} \begin{bmatrix} x \\ y \end{bmatrix}$$

where the 2×2 matrix of constants in the middle describe the transform. The algebraic form is recreated by taking the top variable x', introducing the = sign, and multiplying the top row of constants $[a \quad b]$ individually by the last column vector containing x and y. We then examine the second variable y', introduce the = sign, and multiply the bottom row of constants $[c \quad d]$ individually by the last column vector containing x and y to create

$$x' = ax + by$$
$$y' = cx + dy.$$

Using Caley's notation, the product $\mathbf{T}_2 \times \mathbf{T}_1$ is

$$\begin{bmatrix} x'' \\ y'' \end{bmatrix} = \begin{bmatrix} A & B \\ C & D \end{bmatrix} \begin{bmatrix} x' \\ y' \end{bmatrix}.$$

But the notation also intimates that

$$\begin{bmatrix} x'' \\ y'' \end{bmatrix} = \begin{bmatrix} A & B \\ C & D \end{bmatrix} \begin{bmatrix} a & b \\ c & d \end{bmatrix} \begin{bmatrix} x' \\ y' \end{bmatrix}$$

and when we multiply the two inner matrices together they must produce

$$x'' = (Aa + Bc)x + (Ab + Bd)y$$
$$y'' = (Ca + Dc)x + (Cb + Dd)y$$

or in matrix form

$$\begin{bmatrix} x'' \\ y'' \end{bmatrix} = \begin{bmatrix} Aa + Bc & Ab + Bd \\ Ca + Dc & Cb + Dd \end{bmatrix} \begin{bmatrix} x \\ y \end{bmatrix}$$

otherwise the two system of notation will be inconsistent. This implies that

$$\begin{bmatrix} Aa + Bc & Ab + Bd \\ Ca + Dc & Cb + Dd \end{bmatrix} = \begin{bmatrix} A & B \\ C & D \end{bmatrix} \begin{bmatrix} a & b \\ c & d \end{bmatrix}$$

which demonstrates how matrices must be multiplied. Here are the rules for matrix multiplication:

$$\begin{bmatrix} Aa + Bc & \dots \\ \dots & \dots \end{bmatrix} = \begin{bmatrix} A & B \\ \dots & \dots \end{bmatrix} \begin{bmatrix} a & \dots \\ c & \dots \end{bmatrix}.$$

1: The top left-hand corner element $Aa + Bc$ is the product of the top row of the first matrix by the left column of the second matrix.

$$\begin{bmatrix} \dots & Ab + Bd \\ \dots & \dots \end{bmatrix} = \begin{bmatrix} A & B \\ \dots & \dots \end{bmatrix} \begin{bmatrix} \dots & b \\ \dots & d \end{bmatrix}.$$

2: The top right-hand element $Ab + Bd$ is the product of the top row of the first matrix by the right column of the second matrix.

$$\begin{bmatrix} \dots & \dots \\ Ca + Dc & \dots \end{bmatrix} = \begin{bmatrix} \dots & \dots \\ C & D \end{bmatrix} \begin{bmatrix} a & \dots \\ c & \dots \end{bmatrix}.$$

3: The bottom left-hand element $Ca + Dc$ is the product of the bottom row of the first matrix by the left column of the second matrix.

$$\begin{bmatrix} \cdots & \cdots \\ \cdots & Cb+Dd \end{bmatrix} = \begin{bmatrix} \cdots & \cdots \\ C & D \end{bmatrix} \begin{bmatrix} \cdots & b \\ \cdots & d \end{bmatrix}.$$

4: The bottom right-hand element $Cb + Dd$ is the product of the bottom row of the first matrix by the right column of the second matrix.

It is now a trivial exercise to confirm Gauss's observation that $\mathbf{T}_1 \times \mathbf{T}_2 \neq \mathbf{T}_2 \times \mathbf{T}_1$. For if we reverse the transforms $\mathbf{T}_2 \times \mathbf{T}_1$ to $\mathbf{T}_1 \times \mathbf{T}_2$ we get

$$\begin{bmatrix} aA+bC & aB+bD \\ cA+dC & cB+dD \end{bmatrix} = \begin{bmatrix} a & b \\ c & d \end{bmatrix} \begin{bmatrix} A & B \\ C & D \end{bmatrix}$$

which shows conclusively that the product of two transforms is not commutative.

One immediate problem with this notation is that there is no apparent mechanism to add or subtract a constant such as e or f:

$$x' = ax + by + e$$
$$y' = cx + dy + f.$$

Mathematicians resolved this in the nineteenth century by the use of *homogeneous coordinates*. But before we look at this idea, it must be pointed out that currently there are two systems of matrix notation in use.

7.3.1 Systems of Notation

Over time, two systems of matrix notation have evolved: one where the matrix multiplies a column vector, as described above, and another where a *row vector* multiplies the matrix:

$$\begin{bmatrix} x' & y' \end{bmatrix} = \begin{bmatrix} x & y \end{bmatrix} \begin{bmatrix} a & c \\ b & d \end{bmatrix} = \begin{bmatrix} ax+by & cx+dy \end{bmatrix}.$$

Note how the elements of the matrix are transposed to accommodate the algebraic correctness of the transform. There is no preferred system of notation, and you will find technical books and papers supporting both. For example, *Computer Graphics: Principles and Practice* (Foley et al. 1990) employs the column vector notation, whereas *Graphics Gems* (Glassner et al. 1990) employs the row vector notation. The important thing to remember is that the rows and columns of the matrix are transposed when moving between the two systems.

7.3.2 The Determinant of a Matrix

Given a 2×2 matrix:

$$\begin{bmatrix} a & b \\ c & d \end{bmatrix}$$

its determinant is the scalar quantity $ad - cb$ and represented by

$$\begin{vmatrix} a & b \\ c & d \end{vmatrix}.$$

For example, the determinant of

$$\begin{bmatrix} 3 & 2 \\ 1 & 2 \end{bmatrix}$$

is

$$\begin{vmatrix} 3 & 2 \\ 1 & 2 \end{vmatrix} = 3 \times 2 - 2 \times 1 = 4.$$

Later, we will discover that the determinant of a 2×2 matrix determines the change in area that occurs when a polygon is transformed by the matrix. For example, if the determinant is 1, there is no change in area, but if the determinant is 2, the polygon's area is doubled.

7.4 Homogeneous Coordinates

Homogeneous coordinates surfaced in the early nineteenth century where they were independently proposed by Möbius (who also invented a one-sided curled band, the Möbius strip), Feuerbach, Bobillier, and Plücker. Möbius named them *barycentric coordinates*, and they have also been called *areal coordinates* because of their area-calculating properties.

Basically, homogeneous coordinates define a point in a plane using three coordinates instead of two. Initially, Plücker located a homogeneous point relative to the sides of a triangle, but later revised his notation to the one employed in contemporary mathematics and computer graphics. This states that for a point (x, y) there exists a homogeneous point (xt, yt, t) where t is an arbitrary number. For example, the point $(3, 4)$ has homogeneous coordinates $(6, 8, 2)$, because $3 = 6/2$ and $4 = 8/2$. But the homogeneous point $(6, 8, 2)$ is not unique to $(3, 4)$; $(12, 16, 4)$, $(15, 20, 5)$ and $(300, 400, 100)$ are all possible homogeneous coordinates for $(3, 4)$.

The reason why this coordinate system is called 'homogeneous' is because it is possible to transform functions such as $f(x, y)$ into the form $f(x/t, y/t)$ without disturbing the degree of the curve. To the non-mathematician this may not seem anything to get excited about, but in the field of projective geometry it is a very powerful concept.

For our purposes we can imagine that a collection of homogeneous points of the form (xt, yt, t) exist on an xy-plane where t is the z-coordinate as illustrated in

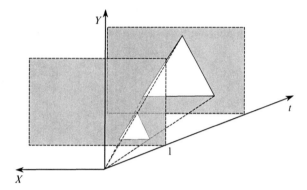

Fig. 7.4 2D homogeneous coordinates can be visualized as a plane in 3D space generally where $t = 1$, for convenience.

Fig. 7.4. The figure shows a triangle on the $t = 1$ plane, and a similar triangle, much larger, on a more distant plane. Thus instead of working in two dimensions, we can work on an arbitrary xy-plane in three dimensions. The t- or z-coordinate of the plane is immaterial because the x- and y-coordinates are eventually scaled by t. However, to keep things simple it seems a good idea to choose $t = 1$. This means that the point (x, y) has homogeneous coordinates $(x, y, 1)$ making scaling superfluous.

If we substitute 3D homogeneous coordinates for traditional 2D Cartesian coordinates we must attach 1 to every (x, y) pair. When a point $(x, y, 1)$ is transformed, it emerges as $(x', y', 1)$, and we discard the 1. This may seem a futile exercise, but it resolves the problem of creating a translation transform. Consider the following transform on the homogeneous point $(x, y, 1)$:

$$
\begin{bmatrix} x' \\ y' \\ 1 \end{bmatrix} = \begin{bmatrix} a & b & e \\ c & d & f \\ 0 & 0 & 1 \end{bmatrix} \begin{bmatrix} x \\ y \\ 1 \end{bmatrix}.
$$

This expands to

$$
x' = ax + by + e
$$
$$
y' = cx + dy + f
$$
$$
1 = 1
$$

which solves the above problem of adding a constant.

Let's now go on to see how homogeneous coordinates are used in practice.

7.4.1 2D Translation

The algebraic and matrix notation for 2D translation is

$$x' = x + t_x$$
$$y' = y + t_y$$

or using matrices

$$\begin{bmatrix} x' \\ y' \\ 1 \end{bmatrix} = \begin{bmatrix} 1 & 0 & t_x \\ 0 & 1 & t_y \\ 0 & 0 & 1 \end{bmatrix} \begin{bmatrix} x \\ y \\ 1 \end{bmatrix}.$$

7.4.2 2D Scaling

The algebraic and matrix notation for 2D scaling is

$$x' = s_x x$$
$$y' = s_y y$$

or using matrices

$$\begin{bmatrix} x' \\ y' \\ 1 \end{bmatrix} = \begin{bmatrix} s_x & 0 & 0 \\ 0 & s_y & 0 \\ 0 & 0 & 1 \end{bmatrix} \begin{bmatrix} x \\ y \\ 1 \end{bmatrix}.$$

The scaling action is relative to the origin, i.e., the point $(0,0)$ remains unchanged. All other points move away from the origin when $s_x > 1$, or move towards the origin when $s_x < 1$. To scale relative to another point (p_x, p_y) we first subtract (p_x, p_y) from (x, y) respectively. This effectively makes the reference point (p_x, p_y) the new origin. Second, we perform the scaling operation relative to the new origin, and third, add (p_x, p_y) back to the new (x, y) respectively to compensate for the original subtraction. Algebraically this is

$$x' = s_x(x - p_x) + p_x$$
$$y' = s_y(y - p_y) + p_y$$

which simplifies to

$$x' = s_x x + p_x(1 - s_x)$$
$$y' = s_y y + p_y(1 - s_y)$$

or as a homogeneous matrix

$$
\begin{bmatrix} x' \\ y' \\ 1 \end{bmatrix} = \begin{bmatrix} s_x & 0 & p_x(1-s_x) \\ 0 & s_y & p_y(1-s_y) \\ 0 & 0 & 1 \end{bmatrix} \begin{bmatrix} x \\ y \\ 1 \end{bmatrix}. \tag{7.2}
$$

For example, to scale a shape by 2 relative to the point $(1,1)$ the matrix is

$$
\begin{bmatrix} x' \\ y' \\ 1 \end{bmatrix} = \begin{bmatrix} 2 & 0 & -1 \\ 0 & 2 & -1 \\ 0 & 0 & 1 \end{bmatrix} \begin{bmatrix} x \\ y \\ 1 \end{bmatrix}.
$$

7.4.3 2D Reflections

The matrix notation for reflecting about the y-axis is

$$
\begin{bmatrix} x' \\ y' \\ 1 \end{bmatrix} = \begin{bmatrix} -1 & 0 & 0 \\ 0 & 1 & 0 \\ 0 & 0 & 1 \end{bmatrix} \begin{bmatrix} x \\ y \\ 1 \end{bmatrix}
$$

or about the x-axis

$$
\begin{bmatrix} x' \\ y' \\ 1 \end{bmatrix} = \begin{bmatrix} 1 & 0 & 0 \\ 0 & -1 & 0 \\ 0 & 0 & 1 \end{bmatrix} \begin{bmatrix} x \\ y \\ 1 \end{bmatrix}.
$$

However, to make a reflection about an arbitrary vertical or horizontal axis we need to introduce some more algebraic deception. For example, to make a reflection about the vertical axis $x = 1$, we first subtract 1 from the x-coordinate. This effectively makes the $x = 1$ axis coincident with the major y-axis. Next we perform the reflection by reversing the sign of the modified x-coordinate. And finally, we add 1 to the reflected coordinate to compensate for the original subtraction. Algebraically, the three steps are

$$
\begin{aligned}
x_1 &= x - 1 \\
x_2 &= -(x - 1) \\
x' &= -(x - 1) + 1
\end{aligned}
$$

which simplifies to

$$
\begin{aligned}
x' &= -x + 2 \\
y' &= y
\end{aligned}
$$

or in matrix form

$$\begin{bmatrix} x' \\ y' \\ 1 \end{bmatrix} = \begin{bmatrix} -1 & 0 & 2 \\ 0 & 1 & 0 \\ 0 & 0 & 1 \end{bmatrix} \begin{bmatrix} x \\ y \\ 1 \end{bmatrix}.$$

Figure 7.5 illustrates this process.

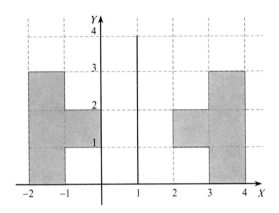

Fig. 7.5 The shape on the right is reflected about the $x = 1$ axis.

In general, to reflect a shape about an arbitrary y-axis, $y = a_x$ the following transform is required:

$$x' = -(x - a_x) + a_x \quad = -x + 2a_x$$
$$y' = y$$

or in matrix form

$$\begin{bmatrix} x' \\ y' \\ 1 \end{bmatrix} = \begin{bmatrix} -1 & 0 & 2a_x \\ 0 & 1 & 0 \\ 0 & 0 & 1 \end{bmatrix} \begin{bmatrix} x \\ y \\ 1 \end{bmatrix}. \qquad (7.3)$$

Similarly, this transform is used for reflections about an arbitrary x-axis $y = a_y$:

$$x' = x$$
$$y' = -(y - a_y) + a_y \quad = -y + 2a_y$$

or in matrix form

$$\begin{bmatrix} x' \\ y' \\ 1 \end{bmatrix} = \begin{bmatrix} 1 & 0 & 0 \\ 0 & -1 & 2a_y \\ 0 & 0 & 1 \end{bmatrix} \begin{bmatrix} x \\ y \\ 1 \end{bmatrix}.$$

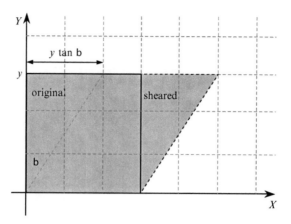

Fig. 7.6 The original square shape is sheared to the right by an angle β, and the horizontal shear is proportional to $y\tan\beta$.

7.4.4 2D Shearing

A shape is sheared by leaning it over at an angle β. Figure 7.6 illustrates the geometry, and we see that the y-coordinates remain unchanged but the x-coordinates are a function of y and $\tan\beta$.

$$x' = x + y\tan\beta$$
$$y' = y$$

or in matrix form

$$\begin{bmatrix} x' \\ y' \\ 1 \end{bmatrix} = \begin{bmatrix} 1 & \tan\beta & 0 \\ 0 & 1 & 0 \\ 0 & 0 & 1 \end{bmatrix} \begin{bmatrix} x \\ y \\ 1 \end{bmatrix}.$$

7.4.5 2D Rotation

Figure 7.7 shows a point $P(x,y)$ which is to be rotated by an angle β about the origin to $P'(x',y')$. It can be seen that

$$x' = R\cos(\theta + \beta)$$
$$y' = R\sin(\theta + \beta)$$

and substituting the identities for $\cos(\theta + \beta)$ and $\sin(\theta + \beta)$ we have

$$x' = R(\cos\theta\cos\beta - \sin\theta\sin\beta)$$

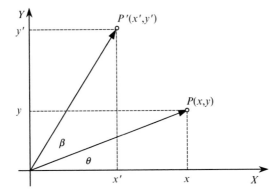

Fig. 7.7 The point $P(x,y)$ is rotated through an angle β to $P'(x',y')$.

$$y' = R(\sin\theta\cos\beta + \cos\theta\sin\beta)$$
$$x' = R\left(\frac{x}{R}\cos\beta - \frac{y}{R}\sin\beta\right)$$
$$y' = R\left(\frac{y}{R}\cos\beta + \frac{x}{R}\sin\beta\right)$$
$$x' = x\cos\beta - y\sin\beta$$
$$y' = x\sin\beta + y\cos\beta$$

or in matrix form

$$\begin{bmatrix} x' \\ y' \\ 1 \end{bmatrix} = \begin{bmatrix} \cos\beta & -\sin\beta & 0 \\ \sin\beta & \cos\beta & 0 \\ 0 & 0 & 1 \end{bmatrix} \begin{bmatrix} x \\ y \\ 1 \end{bmatrix}.$$

For example, to rotate a point by $90°$ the matrix is

$$\begin{bmatrix} x' \\ y' \\ 1 \end{bmatrix} = \begin{bmatrix} 0 & -1 & 0 \\ 1 & 0 & 0 \\ 0 & 0 & 1 \end{bmatrix} \begin{bmatrix} x \\ y \\ 1 \end{bmatrix}.$$

Thus the point $(1,0)$ becomes $(0,1)$. If we rotate through $360°$ the matrix becomes

$$\begin{bmatrix} x' \\ y' \\ 1 \end{bmatrix} = \begin{bmatrix} 1 & 0 & 0 \\ 0 & 1 & 0 \\ 0 & 0 & 1 \end{bmatrix} \begin{bmatrix} x \\ y \\ 1 \end{bmatrix}.$$

Such a matrix has a null effect and is called an *identity matrix*.

To rotate a point (x,y) about an arbitrary point (p_x, p_y) we first, subtract (p_x, p_y) from the coordinates (x,y) respectively. This enables us to perform the rotation about the origin. Second, we perform the rotation, and third, we add (p_x, p_y) to compensate for the original subtraction. Here are the steps:

1. Subtract (p_x, p_y):

$$x_1 = (x - p_x)$$
$$y_1 = (y - p_y).$$

2. Rotate β about the origin:

$$x_2 = (x - p_x)\cos\beta - (y - p_y)\sin\beta$$
$$y_2 = (x - p_x)\sin\beta + (y - p_y)\cos\beta.$$

3. Add (p_x, p_y):

$$x' = (x - p_x)\cos\beta - (y - p_y)\sin\beta + p_x$$
$$y' = (x - p_x)\sin\beta + (y - p_y)\cos\beta + p_y.$$

Simplifying,

$$x' = x\cos\beta - y\sin\beta + p_x(1 - \cos\beta) + p_y\sin\beta$$
$$y' = x\sin\beta + y\cos\beta + p_y(1 - \cos\beta) - p_x\sin\beta$$

and in matrix form

$$\begin{bmatrix} x' \\ y' \\ 1 \end{bmatrix} = \begin{bmatrix} \cos\beta & -\sin\beta & p_x(1 - \cos\beta) + p_y\sin\beta \\ \sin\beta & \cos\beta & p_y(1 - \cos\beta) - p_x\sin\beta \\ 0 & 0 & 1 \end{bmatrix} \begin{bmatrix} x \\ y \\ 1 \end{bmatrix}. \qquad (7.4)$$

If we now consider rotating a point $90°$ about the point $(1,1)$ the matrix operation becomes

$$\begin{bmatrix} x' \\ y' \\ 1 \end{bmatrix} = \begin{bmatrix} 0 & -1 & 2 \\ 1 & 0 & 0 \\ 0 & 0 & 1 \end{bmatrix} \begin{bmatrix} x \\ y \\ 1 \end{bmatrix}.$$

A simple test is to substitute the point $(2,1)$ for (x,y): which is transformed correctly to $(1,2)$.

The algebraic approach in deriving the above transforms is relatively easy. However, it is also possible to use matrices to derive compound transforms, such as a reflection relative to an arbitrary line and scaling and rotation relative to an arbitrary point. These transforms are called *affine*, as parallel lines remain parallel after being transformed. Furthermore, the word 'affine' is used to imply that there is a strong geometric *affinity* between the original and transformed shape. One can not always guarantee that angles and lengths are preserved, as the scaling transform can alter these when different x and y scaling factors are used. For completeness, we will repeat these transforms from a matrix perspective.

7.4.6 2D Scaling

The strategy used to scale a point (x, y) relative to some arbitrary point (p_x, p_y) is to first, translate $(-p_x, -p_y)$; second, perform the scaling; and third translate (p_x, p_y). These three transforms are represented in matrix form as follows:

$$
\begin{bmatrix} x' \\ y' \\ 1 \end{bmatrix} = \begin{bmatrix} \text{translate}(p_x, p_y) \end{bmatrix} \begin{bmatrix} \text{scale}(s_x, s_y) \end{bmatrix} \begin{bmatrix} \text{translate}(-p_x, -p_y) \end{bmatrix} \begin{bmatrix} x \\ y \\ 1 \end{bmatrix}
$$

which expands to

$$
\begin{bmatrix} x' \\ y' \\ 1 \end{bmatrix} = \begin{bmatrix} 1 & 0 & p_x \\ 0 & 1 & p_y \\ 0 & 0 & 1 \end{bmatrix} \begin{bmatrix} s_x & 0 & 0 \\ 0 & s_y & 0 \\ 0 & 0 & 1 \end{bmatrix} \begin{bmatrix} 1 & 0 & -p_x \\ 0 & 1 & -p_y \\ 0 & 0 & 1 \end{bmatrix} \begin{bmatrix} x \\ y \\ 1 \end{bmatrix}.
$$

Note the sequence of the transforms, as this often causes confusion. The first transform acting on the point $(x, y, 1)$ is translate $(-p_x, -p_y)$, followed by scale (s_x, s_y), followed by translate (p_x, p_y). If they are placed in any other sequence, you will discover, like Gauss, that transforms are not commutative!

We can now combine these matrices into a single matrix by multiplying them together. This can be done in any sequence, so long as we preserve the original order. Let's start with scale (s_x, s_y) and translate $(-p_x, -p_y)$ matrices. This produces

$$
\begin{bmatrix} x' \\ y' \\ 1 \end{bmatrix} = \begin{bmatrix} 1 & 0 & p_x \\ 0 & 1 & p_y \\ 0 & 0 & 1 \end{bmatrix} \begin{bmatrix} s_x & 0 & -s_x p_x \\ 0 & s_y & -s_y p_y \\ 0 & 0 & 1 \end{bmatrix} \begin{bmatrix} x \\ y \\ 1 \end{bmatrix}
$$

and finally

$$
\begin{bmatrix} x' \\ y' \\ 1 \end{bmatrix} = \begin{bmatrix} s_x & 0 & p_x(1 - s_x) \\ 0 & s_y & p_y(1 - s_y) \\ 0 & 0 & 1 \end{bmatrix} \begin{bmatrix} x \\ y \\ 1 \end{bmatrix}
$$

which is the same as the previous transform (7.2).

7.4.7 2D Reflection

A reflection about the y-axis is given by

$$
\begin{bmatrix} x' \\ y' \\ 1 \end{bmatrix} = \begin{bmatrix} -1 & 0 & 0 \\ 0 & 1 & 0 \\ 0 & 0 & 1 \end{bmatrix} \begin{bmatrix} x \\ y \\ 1 \end{bmatrix}.
$$

Therefore, using matrices, we can reason that a reflection transform about an arbitrary axis $x = a_x$, parallel with the y-axis, is given by

$$
\begin{bmatrix} x' \\ y' \\ 1 \end{bmatrix} = \begin{bmatrix} \text{translate}(a_x,0) \end{bmatrix} \begin{bmatrix} \text{reflection} \end{bmatrix} \begin{bmatrix} \text{translate}(-a_x,0) \end{bmatrix} \begin{bmatrix} x \\ y \\ 1 \end{bmatrix}
$$

which expands to

$$
\begin{bmatrix} x' \\ y' \\ 1 \end{bmatrix} = \begin{bmatrix} 1 & 0 & a_x \\ 0 & 1 & 0 \\ 0 & 0 & 1 \end{bmatrix} \begin{bmatrix} -1 & 0 & 0 \\ 0 & 1 & 0 \\ 0 & 0 & 1 \end{bmatrix} \begin{bmatrix} 1 & 0 & -a_x \\ 0 & 1 & 0 \\ 0 & 0 & 1 \end{bmatrix} \begin{bmatrix} x \\ y \\ 1 \end{bmatrix}.
$$

We can now combine these matrices into a single matrix by multiplying them together. Let's begin by multiplying the reflection and the translate $(-a_x,0)$ matrices together. This produces

$$
\begin{bmatrix} x' \\ y' \\ 1 \end{bmatrix} = \begin{bmatrix} 1 & 0 & a_x \\ 0 & 1 & 0 \\ 0 & 0 & 1 \end{bmatrix} \begin{bmatrix} -1 & 0 & a_x \\ 0 & 1 & 0 \\ 0 & 0 & 1 \end{bmatrix} \begin{bmatrix} x \\ y \\ 1 \end{bmatrix}
$$

and finally

$$
\begin{bmatrix} x' \\ y' \\ 1 \end{bmatrix} = \begin{bmatrix} -1 & 0 & 2a_x \\ 0 & 1 & 0 \\ 0 & 0 & 1 \end{bmatrix} \begin{bmatrix} x \\ y \\ 1 \end{bmatrix}
$$

which is the same as the previous transform (7.3).

7.4.8 2D Rotation About an Arbitrary Point

A rotation about the origin is given by

$$
\begin{bmatrix} x' \\ y' \\ 1 \end{bmatrix} = \begin{bmatrix} \cos\beta & -\sin\beta & 0 \\ \sin\beta & \cos\beta & 0 \\ 0 & 0 & 1 \end{bmatrix} \begin{bmatrix} x \\ y \\ 1 \end{bmatrix}.
$$

Therefore, using matrices, we can develop a rotation about an arbitrary point (p_x, p_y) as follows:

$$
\begin{bmatrix} x' \\ y' \\ 1 \end{bmatrix} = \begin{bmatrix} \text{translate}(p_x, p_y) \end{bmatrix} \begin{bmatrix} \text{rotate}\beta \end{bmatrix} \begin{bmatrix} \text{translate}(-p_x, -p_y) \end{bmatrix} \begin{bmatrix} x \\ y \\ 1 \end{bmatrix}
$$

which expands to

$$
\begin{bmatrix} x' \\ y' \\ 1 \end{bmatrix} = \begin{bmatrix} 1 & 0 & p_x \\ 0 & 1 & p_y \\ 0 & 0 & 1 \end{bmatrix} \begin{bmatrix} \cos\beta & -\sin\beta & 0 \\ \sin\beta & \cos\beta & 0 \\ 0 & 0 & 1 \end{bmatrix} \begin{bmatrix} 1 & 0 & -p_x \\ 0 & 1 & -p_y \\ 0 & 0 & 1 \end{bmatrix} \begin{bmatrix} x \\ y \\ 1 \end{bmatrix} .
$$

We can now combine these matrices into a single matrix by multiplying them together. Let's begin by multiplying the rotate β and the translate $(-p_x, -p_y)$ matrices together. This produces

$$
\begin{bmatrix} x' \\ y' \\ 1 \end{bmatrix} = \begin{bmatrix} 1 & 0 & p_x \\ 0 & 1 & p_y \\ 0 & 0 & 1 \end{bmatrix} \begin{bmatrix} \cos\beta & -\sin\beta & -p_x\cos\beta + p_y\sin\beta \\ \sin\beta & \cos\beta & -p_x\sin\beta - p_y\cos\beta \\ 0 & 0 & 1 \end{bmatrix} \begin{bmatrix} x \\ y \\ 1 \end{bmatrix}
$$

and finally

$$
\begin{bmatrix} x' \\ y' \\ 1 \end{bmatrix} = \begin{bmatrix} \cos\beta & -\sin\beta & p_x(1 - \cos\beta) + p_y\sin\beta \\ \sin\beta & \cos\beta & p_y(1 - \cos\beta) - p_x\sin\beta \\ 0 & 0 & 1 \end{bmatrix} \begin{bmatrix} x \\ y \\ 1 \end{bmatrix}
$$

which is the same as the previous transform (7.4).

I hope it is now obvious to the reader that one can derive all sorts of transforms either algebraically, or by using matrices – it is just a question of convenience.

7.5 3D Transforms

Now we come to transforms in three dimensions, where we apply the same reasoning as in two dimensions. Scaling and translation are basically the same, but where in 2D we rotated a shape about a point, in 3D we rotate an object about an axis.

7.5.1 3D Translation

The algebra is so simple for 3D translation that we can simply write the homogeneous matrix directly:

$$
\begin{bmatrix} x' \\ y' \\ z' \\ 1 \end{bmatrix} = \begin{bmatrix} 1 & 0 & 0 & t_x \\ 0 & 1 & 0 & t_y \\ 0 & 0 & 1 & t_z \\ 0 & 0 & 0 & 1 \end{bmatrix} \begin{bmatrix} x \\ y \\ z \\ 1 \end{bmatrix} .
$$

7.5.2 3D Scaling

The algebra for 3D scaling is

$$x' = s_x x$$
$$y' = s_y y$$
$$z' = s_z z$$

which in matrix form is

$$
\begin{bmatrix} x' \\ y' \\ z' \\ 1 \end{bmatrix} =
\begin{bmatrix} s_x & 0 & 0 & 0 \\ 0 & s_y & 0 & 0 \\ 0 & 0 & s_z & 0 \\ 0 & 0 & 0 & 1 \end{bmatrix}
\begin{bmatrix} x \\ y \\ z \\ 1 \end{bmatrix}.
$$

The scaling is relative to the origin, but we can arrange for it to be relative to an arbitrary point (p_x, p_y, p_z) with the following algebra:

$$x' = s_x(x - p_x) + p_x$$
$$y' = s_y(y - p_y) + p_y$$
$$z' = s_z(z - p_z) + p_z$$

which in matrix form is

$$
\begin{bmatrix} x' \\ y' \\ z' \\ 1 \end{bmatrix} =
\begin{bmatrix} s_x & 0 & 0 & p_x(1 - s_x) \\ 0 & s_y & 0 & p_y(1 - s_y) \\ 0 & 0 & s_z & p_z(1 - s_z) \\ 0 & 0 & 0 & 1 \end{bmatrix}
\begin{bmatrix} x \\ y \\ z \\ 1 \end{bmatrix}.
$$

7.5.3 3D Rotation

In two dimensions a shape is rotated about a point, whether it be the origin or some arbitrary position. In three dimensions an object is rotated about an axis, whether it be the x-, y- or z-axis, or some arbitrary axis. To begin with, let's look at rotating a vertex about one of the three orthogonal axes; such rotations are called *Euler rotations* after the Swiss mathematician Leonhard Euler (1707–1783).

Recall that a general 2D-rotation transform is given by

$$
\begin{bmatrix} x' \\ y' \\ 1 \end{bmatrix} =
\begin{bmatrix} \cos\beta & -\sin\beta & 0 \\ \sin\beta & \cos\beta & 0 \\ 0 & 0 & 1 \end{bmatrix}
\begin{bmatrix} x \\ y \\ 1 \end{bmatrix}
$$

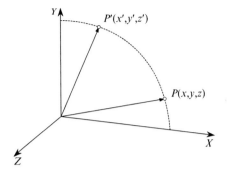

Fig. 7.8 Rotating the point P about the z-axis.

which in 3D can be visualized as rotating a point $P(x,y,z)$ on a plane parallel with the xy-plane as shown in Fig. 7.8. In algebraic terms this can be written as

$$x' = x\cos\beta - y\sin\beta$$
$$y' = x\sin\beta + y\cos\beta$$
$$z' = z.$$

Therefore, the 3D transform can be written as

$$\begin{bmatrix} x' \\ y' \\ z' \\ 1 \end{bmatrix} = \begin{bmatrix} \cos\beta & -\sin\beta & 0 & 0 \\ \sin\beta & \cos\beta & 0 & 0 \\ 0 & 0 & 1 & 0 \\ 0 & 0 & 0 & 1 \end{bmatrix} \begin{bmatrix} x \\ y \\ z \\ 1 \end{bmatrix}$$

which basically rotates a point about the z-axis.

When rotating about the x-axis, the x-coordinates remain constant whilst the y- and z-coordinates are changed. Algebraically, this is

$$x' = x$$
$$y' = y\cos\beta - z\sin\beta$$
$$z' = y\sin\beta + z\cos\beta$$

or in matrix form

$$\begin{bmatrix} x' \\ y' \\ z' \\ 1 \end{bmatrix} = \begin{bmatrix} 1 & 0 & 0 & 0 \\ 0 & \cos\beta & -\sin\beta & 0 \\ 0 & \sin\beta & \cos\beta & 0 \\ 0 & 0 & 0 & 1 \end{bmatrix} \begin{bmatrix} x \\ y \\ z \\ 1 \end{bmatrix}.$$

When rotating about the y-axis, the y-coordinate remains constant whilst the x- and z-coordinates are changed. Algebraically, this is

$$x' = z\sin\beta + x\cos\beta$$
$$y' = y$$
$$z' = z\cos\beta - x\sin\beta$$

or in matrix form

$$\begin{bmatrix} x' \\ y' \\ z' \\ 1 \end{bmatrix} = \begin{bmatrix} \cos\beta & 0 & \sin\beta & 0 \\ 0 & 1 & 0 & 0 \\ -\sin\beta & 0 & \cos\beta & 0 \\ 0 & 0 & 0 & 1 \end{bmatrix} \begin{bmatrix} x \\ y \\ z \\ 1 \end{bmatrix}.$$

Note that the matrix terms do not appear to share the symmetry seen in the previous two matrices. Nothing really has gone wrong, it is just the way the axes are paired together to rotate the coordinates.

The above rotations are also known as *yaw*, *pitch* and *roll*, and great care should be taken with these angles when referring to other books and technical papers. Sometimes a left-handed system of axes is used rather than a right-handed set, and the vertical axis may be the y-axis or the z-axis.

Consequently, the matrices representing the rotations can vary greatly. In this text all Cartesian coordinate systems are right-handed, and the vertical axis is always the y-axis.

The roll, pitch and yaw angles are defined as follows:

- *roll* is the angle of rotation about the z-axis.
- *pitch* is the angle of rotation about the x-axis.
- *yaw* is the angle of rotation about the y-axis.

Figure 7.9 illustrates these rotations and the sign convention. The homogeneous matrices representing these rotations are as follows:

- rotate *roll* about the z-axis:

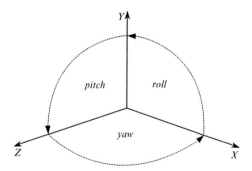

Fig. 7.9 The convention for *roll*, *pitch* and *yaw* angles.

$$\begin{bmatrix} \cos roll & -\sin roll & 0 & 0 \\ \sin roll & \cos roll & 0 & 0 \\ 0 & 0 & 1 & 0 \\ 0 & 0 & 0 & 1 \end{bmatrix}.$$

- rotate *pitch* about the *x*-axis:

$$\begin{bmatrix} 1 & 0 & 0 & 0 \\ 0 & \cos pitch & -\sin pitch & 0 \\ 0 & \sin pitch & \cos pitch & 0 \\ 0 & 0 & 0 & 1 \end{bmatrix}.$$

- rotate *yaw* about the *y*-axis:

$$\begin{bmatrix} \cos yaw & 0 & \sin yaw & 0 \\ 0 & 1 & 0 & 0 \\ -\sin yaw & 0 & \cos yaw & 0 \\ 0 & 0 & 0 & 1 \end{bmatrix}.$$

A common sequence for applying these rotations is *roll, pitch, yaw*, as seen in the following transform:

$$\begin{bmatrix} x' \\ y' \\ z' \\ 1 \end{bmatrix} = \begin{bmatrix} yaw \end{bmatrix} \begin{bmatrix} pitch \end{bmatrix} \begin{bmatrix} roll \end{bmatrix} \begin{bmatrix} x \\ y \\ z \\ 1 \end{bmatrix}$$

and if a translation is involved,

$$\begin{bmatrix} x' \\ y' \\ z' \\ 1 \end{bmatrix} = \begin{bmatrix} translate \end{bmatrix} \begin{bmatrix} yaw \end{bmatrix} \begin{bmatrix} pitch \end{bmatrix} \begin{bmatrix} roll \end{bmatrix} \begin{bmatrix} x \\ y \\ z \\ 1 \end{bmatrix}.$$

When these rotation transforms are applied, the vertex is first rotated about the *z*-axis (*roll*), followed by a rotation about the *x*-axis (*pitch*), followed by a rotation about the *y*-axis (*yaw*). Euler rotations are relative to the fixed frame of reference. This is not always easy to visualize as one's attention is normally with the rotating frame of reference. Let's consider a simple example where an axial system is subjected to a pitch rotation followed by a yaw rotation relative to fixed frame of reference.

We begin with two frames of reference XYZ and $X'Y'Z'$ mutually aligned. Figure 7.10 shows the orientation of $X'Y'Z'$ after it is subjected to a pitch of $90°$ about the x-axis. And Fig. 7.11 shows the final orientation after $X'Y'Z'$ is subjected to a yaw of $90°$ about the y-axis.

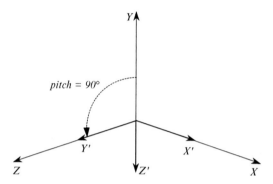

Fig. 7.10 The $X'Y'Z'$ axial system after a *pitch* of $90°$.

7.5.4 Gimbal Lock

Let's take another example starting from the point where the two axial systems are mutually aligned. Figure 7.12 shows the orientation of $X'Y'Z'$ after it is subjected to a roll of $45°$ about the z-axis, and Fig. 7.13 shows the orientation of $X'Y'Z'$ after it is subjected to a pitch of $90°$ about the x-axis. Now the interesting thing about this orientation is that if we now performed a yaw of $45°$ about the z-axis, it would rotate the x'-axis towards the x-axis, counteracting the effect of the original roll. yaw has become a negative roll rotation, caused by the $90°$ pitch. This situation is known as *gimbal lock*, because one degree of rotational freedom has been lost. Quite innocently, we have stumbled across one of the major weaknesses of Euler

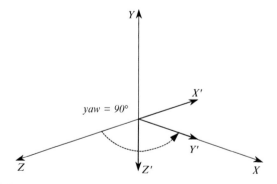

Fig. 7.11 The $X'Y'Z'$ axial system after a *yaw* of $90°$.

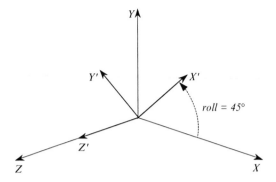

Fig. 7.12 The $X'Y'Z'$ axial system after a *roll* of 45°.

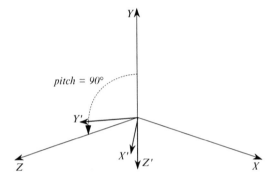

Fig. 7.13 The $X'Y'Z'$ axial system after a *pitch* of 90°.

angles: under certain conditions it is only possible to rotate an object about two axes. One way of preventing this is to create a secondary set of axes constructed from three orthogonal vectors that are also rotated alongside an object or virtual camera. But instead of making the rotations relative to the fixed frame of reference, the roll, pitch and yaw rotations are relative to the rotating frame of reference. Another method is to use quaternions, which will be investigated later in this chapter.

7.5.5 *Rotating About an Axis*

The above rotations were relative to the x-, y-, z-axes. Now let's consider rotations about an axis parallel to one of these axes. To begin with, we will rotate about an axis parallel with the z-axis, as shown in Fig. 7.14. The scenario is very reminiscent of the 2D case for rotating a point about an arbitrary point, and the general transform is given by

$$\begin{bmatrix} x' \\ y' \\ z' \\ 1 \end{bmatrix} = \Big[\, \text{translate}(p_x, p_y, 0) \Big] \Big[\, \text{rotate}\beta \,\Big] \Big[\, \text{translate}(-p_x, -p_y, 0) \Big] \begin{bmatrix} x \\ y \\ z \\ 1 \end{bmatrix}$$

and the matrix is

$$\begin{bmatrix} x' \\ y' \\ z' \\ 1 \end{bmatrix} = \begin{bmatrix} \cos\beta & -\sin\beta & 0 & p_x(1-\cos\beta) + p_y\sin\beta \\ \sin\beta & \cos\beta & 0 & p_y(1-\cos\beta) - p_x\sin\beta \\ 0 & 0 & 1 & 0 \\ 0 & 0 & 0 & 1 \end{bmatrix} \begin{bmatrix} x \\ y \\ z \\ 1 \end{bmatrix}.$$

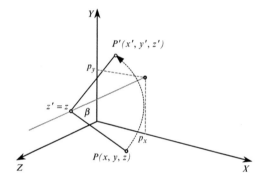

Fig. 7.14 Rotating a point about an axis parallel with the x-axis.

I hope you can see the similarity between rotating in 3D and 2D: the x- and y-coordinates are updated while the z-coordinate is held constant. We can now state the other two matrices for rotating about an axis parallel with the x-axis and parallel with the y-axis:

- rotating about an axis parallel with the x-axis:

$$\begin{bmatrix} x' \\ y' \\ z' \\ 1 \end{bmatrix} = \begin{bmatrix} 1 & 0 & 0 & 0 \\ 0 & \cos\beta & -\sin\beta & p_y(1-\cos\beta) + p_z\sin\beta \\ 0 & \sin\beta & \cos\beta & p_z(1-\cos\beta) - p_y\sin\beta \\ 0 & 0 & 0 & 1 \end{bmatrix} \begin{bmatrix} x \\ y \\ z \\ 1 \end{bmatrix}.$$

- rotating about an axis parallel with the y-axis:

$$\begin{bmatrix} x' \\ y' \\ z' \\ 1 \end{bmatrix} = \begin{bmatrix} \cos\beta & 0 & \sin\beta & p_x(1-\cos\beta) - p_z\sin\beta \\ 0 & 1 & 0 & 0 \\ -\sin\beta & 0 & \cos\beta & p_z(1-\cos\beta) + p_x\sin\beta \\ 0 & 0 & 0 & 1 \end{bmatrix} \begin{bmatrix} x \\ y \\ z \\ 1 \end{bmatrix}.$$

7.5.6 3D Reflections

Reflections in 3D occur with respect to a plane, rather than an axis. The matrix giving the reflection relative to the yz-plane is

$$
\begin{bmatrix} x' \\ y' \\ z' \\ 1 \end{bmatrix} = \begin{bmatrix} -1 & 0 & 0 & 0 \\ 0 & 1 & 0 & 0 \\ 0 & 0 & 1 & 0 \\ 0 & 0 & 0 & 1 \end{bmatrix} \begin{bmatrix} x \\ y \\ z \\ 1 \end{bmatrix}
$$

and the reflection relative to a plane parallel to, and a_x units from the yz-plane is

$$
\begin{bmatrix} x' \\ y' \\ z' \\ 1 \end{bmatrix} = \begin{bmatrix} -1 & 0 & 0 & 2a_x \\ 0 & 1 & 0 & 0 \\ 0 & 0 & 1 & 0 \\ 0 & 0 & 0 & 1 \end{bmatrix} \begin{bmatrix} x \\ y \\ z \\ 1 \end{bmatrix}.
$$

It is left to the reader to develop similar matrices for the other major axial planes.

7.6 Change of Axes

Points in one coordinate system often have to be referenced in another one. For example, to view a 3D scene from an arbitrary position, a virtual camera is positioned in the world space using a series of transforms. An object's coordinates, which are relative to the world frame of reference, are computed relative to the camera's axial system, and then used to develop a perspective projection. Before explaining how this is achieved in 3D, let's examine the simple case of changing axial systems in two dimensions.

7.6.1 2D Change of Axes

Figure 7.15 shows a point $P(x,y)$ relative to the XY-axes, but we require to know the coordinates relative to the $X'Y'$-axes. To do this, we need to know the relationship between the two coordinate systems, and ideally we want to apply a technique that works in 2D and 3D. If the second coordinate system is a simple translation (t_x, t_y) relative to the reference system, as shown in Fig. 7.15, the point $P(x,y)$ has coordinates relative to the translated system $(x - t_x, y - t_y)$:

$$
\begin{bmatrix} x' \\ y' \\ 1 \end{bmatrix} = \begin{bmatrix} 1 & 0 & -t_x \\ 0 & 1 & -t_y \\ 0 & 0 & 1 \end{bmatrix} \begin{bmatrix} x \\ y \\ 1 \end{bmatrix}.
$$

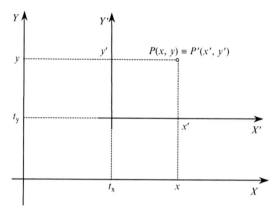

Fig. 7.15 The $X'Y'$ axial system is translated (t_x, t_y).

If the $X'Y'$-axes are rotated β relative to the XY-axes, as shown in Fig. 7.16, a point $P(x, y)$ relative to the XY-axes becomes $P'(x', y')$ relative to the rotated axes is given by

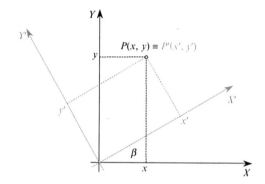

Fig. 7.16 The $X'Y'$ axial system is rotated β.

$$
\begin{bmatrix} x' \\ y' \\ 1 \end{bmatrix} = \begin{bmatrix} \cos(-\beta) & -\sin(-\beta) & 0 \\ \sin(-\beta) & \cos(-\beta) & 0 \\ 0 & 0 & 1 \end{bmatrix} \begin{bmatrix} x \\ y \\ 1 \end{bmatrix}
$$

which simplifies to

$$
\begin{bmatrix} x' \\ y' \\ 1 \end{bmatrix} = \begin{bmatrix} \cos\beta & \sin\beta & 0 \\ -\sin\beta & \cos\beta & 0 \\ 0 & 0 & 1 \end{bmatrix} \begin{bmatrix} x \\ y \\ 1 \end{bmatrix} .
$$

When a coordinate system is rotated and translated relative to the reference system, a point $P(x, y)$ becomes $P'(x', y')$ relative to the new axes given by

$$
\begin{bmatrix} x' \\ y' \\ 1 \end{bmatrix} = \begin{bmatrix} \cos\beta & \sin\beta & 0 \\ -\sin\beta & \cos\beta & 0 \\ 0 & 0 & 1 \end{bmatrix} \begin{bmatrix} 1 & 0 & -t_x \\ 0 & 1 & -t_y \\ 0 & 0 & 1 \end{bmatrix} \begin{bmatrix} x \\ y \\ 1 \end{bmatrix}
$$

which simplifies to

$$
\begin{bmatrix} x' \\ y' \\ 1 \end{bmatrix} = \begin{bmatrix} \cos\beta & \sin\beta & -t_x\cos\beta - t_y\sin\beta \\ -\sin\beta & \cos\beta & t_x\sin\beta - t_y\cos\beta \\ 0 & 0 & 1 \end{bmatrix} \begin{bmatrix} x \\ y \\ 1 \end{bmatrix}.
$$

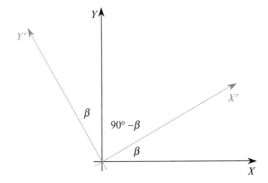

Fig. 7.17 If the X'- and Y'-axes are assumed to be unit vectors, their direction cosines form the elements of the rotation matrix.

7.6.2 Direction Cosines

Direction cosines are the cosines of the angles between a vector and the Cartesian axes, and for unit vectors they are the vector's components. Figure 7.17 shows two unit vectors X' and Y', and by inspection the direction cosines for X' are $\cos\beta$ and $\cos(90° - \beta)$, which can be rewritten as $\cos\beta$ and $\sin\beta$, and the direction cosines for Y' are $\cos(90° + \beta)$ and $\cos\beta$, which can be rewritten as $-\sin\beta$ and $\cos\beta$. But these direction cosines $\cos\beta$, $\sin\beta$, $-\sin\beta$ and $\cos\beta$ are the four elements of the rotation matrix used above

$$
\begin{bmatrix} \cos\beta & \sin\beta \\ -\sin\beta & \cos\beta \end{bmatrix}.
$$

The top row contains the direction cosines for the X'-axis and the bottom row contains the direction cosines for the Y'-axis. This relationship also holds in 3D.

Before exploring changes of axes in 3D let's evaluate a simple example in 2D where a set of axes is rotated 45° as shown in Fig. 7.18. The appropriate transform is

$$
\begin{bmatrix} x' \\ y' \\ 1 \end{bmatrix} = \begin{bmatrix} \cos 45° & \sin 45° & 0 \\ -\sin 45° & \cos 45° & 0 \\ 0 & 0 & 1 \end{bmatrix} \begin{bmatrix} x \\ y \\ 1 \end{bmatrix}
$$

$$
\approx \begin{bmatrix} 0.707 & 0.707 & 0 \\ -0.707 & 0.707 & 0 \\ 0 & 0 & 1 \end{bmatrix} \begin{bmatrix} x \\ y \\ 1 \end{bmatrix}.
$$

The four vertices on a unit square become

$$
\begin{aligned}
(0,0) &\to (0,0) \\
(1,0) &\to (0.707, -0.707) \\
(1,1) &\to (1.1414, 0) \\
(0,1) &\to (0.707, 0.707)
\end{aligned}
$$

which by inspection of Fig. 7.18 are correct.

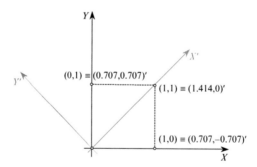

Fig. 7.18 The vertices of a unit square relative to the two axial systems.

7.6.3 3D Change of Axes

The ability to reference a collection of coordinates is fundamental in computer graphics, especially in 3D. And rather than investigate them within this section, let's delay their analysis for the next section, where we see how the technique is used for relating an object's coordinates relative to an arbitrary virtual camera.

7.7 Positioning the Virtual Camera

Four coordinate systems are used in the computer graphics pipeline: *object space*, *world space*, *camera space* and *image space*.

- The object space is a domain where objects are modeled and assembled.

- The world space is where objects are positioned and animated through appropriate transforms. The world space also hosts a virtual camera or observer.

- The camera space is a transform of the world space relative to the camera.

- Finally, the image space is a projection – normally perspective – of the camera space onto an image plane.

The transforms considered so far are used to manipulate and position objects within the world space. What we will consider next is how a virtual camera or observer is positioned in world space, and the process of converting world coordinates to camera coordinates. The procedure used generally depends on the method employed to define the camera's frame of reference within the world space, which may involve the use of direction cosines, Euler angles or quaternions. We will examine how each of these techniques could be implemented.

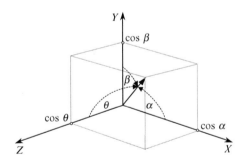

Fig. 7.19 The components of a unit vector are equal to the cosines of the angles between the vector and the axes.

7.7.1 Direction Cosines

A 3D unit vector has three components $[x \quad y \quad z]^T$, which are equal to the cosines of the angles formed between the vector and the three orthogonal axes. These angles are known as *direction cosines* and can be computed taking the dot product of the vector and the Cartesian unit vectors. Figure 7.19 shows the direction cosines and the angles. These direction cosines enable any point $P(x, y, z)$ in one frame of reference to be transformed into $P'(x',y',z')$ in another frame of reference as follows:

$$\begin{bmatrix} x' \\ y' \\ z' \\ 1 \end{bmatrix} = \begin{bmatrix} r_{11} & r_{12} & r_{13} & 0 \\ r_{21} & r_{22} & r_{23} & 0 \\ r_{31} & r_{32} & r_{33} & 0 \\ 0 & 0 & 0 & 1 \end{bmatrix} \begin{bmatrix} x \\ y \\ z \\ 1 \end{bmatrix}$$

where:

- r_{11}, r_{12}, r_{13} are the direction cosines of the secondary x-axis
- r_{21}, r_{22}, r_{23} are the direction cosines of the secondary y-axis
- r_{31}, r_{32}, r_{33} are the direction cosines of the secondary z-axis.

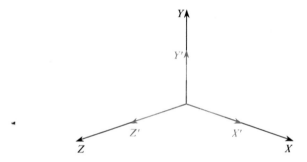

Fig. 7.20 Two axial systems mutually aligned.

To illustrate this operation, consider the scenario shown in Fig. 7.20 which shows two axial systems mutually aligned. Evaluating the direction cosines results in the following matrix transformation:

$$\begin{bmatrix} x' \\ y' \\ z' \\ 1 \end{bmatrix} = \begin{bmatrix} 1 & 0 & 0 & 0 \\ 0 & 1 & 0 & 0 \\ 0 & 0 & 1 & 0 \\ 0 & 0 & 0 & 1 \end{bmatrix} \begin{bmatrix} x \\ y \\ z \\ 1 \end{bmatrix}$$

which is the identity matrix and implies that $(x',y',z') = (x,y,z)$.

Figure 7.21 shows another scenario, and the associated transform is

$$\begin{bmatrix} x' \\ y' \\ z' \\ 1 \end{bmatrix} = \begin{bmatrix} 0 & 1 & 0 & 0 \\ -1 & 0 & 0 & 0 \\ 0 & 0 & 1 & 0 \\ 0 & 0 & 0 & 1 \end{bmatrix} \begin{bmatrix} x \\ y \\ z \\ 1 \end{bmatrix}.$$

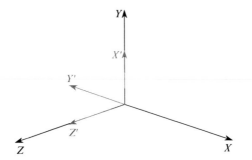

Fig. 7.21 The $X'Y'Z'$ axial system after a roll of $90°$.

Substituting $(1,1,0)$ for (x,y,z) produces $(1,-1,0)$ for (x',y',z') in the new frame of reference, which by inspection, is correct.

If the virtual camera is offset by (t_x,t_y,t_z) the transform relating points in world space to camera space can be expressed as a compound operation consisting of a translation back to the origin, followed by a change of axial systems. This can be expressed as

$$
\begin{bmatrix} x' \\ y' \\ z' \\ 1 \end{bmatrix} = \begin{bmatrix} r_{11} & r_{12} & r_{13} & 0 \\ r_{21} & r_{22} & r_{23} & 0 \\ r_{31} & r_{32} & r_{33} & 0 \\ 0 & 0 & 0 & 1 \end{bmatrix} \begin{bmatrix} 1 & 0 & 0 & -t_x \\ 0 & 1 & 0 & -t_y \\ 0 & 0 & 1 & -t_z \\ 0 & 0 & 0 & 1 \end{bmatrix} \begin{bmatrix} x \\ y \\ z \\ 1 \end{bmatrix}.
$$

As an example, consider the scenario shown in Fig. 7.22. The values of (t_x,t_y,t_z) are $(10,1,1)$, and the direction cosines are as shown in the following matrix operation:

$$
\begin{bmatrix} x' \\ y' \\ z' \\ 1 \end{bmatrix} = \begin{bmatrix} -1 & 0 & 0 & 0 \\ 0 & 1 & 0 & 0 \\ 0 & 0 & -1 & 0 \\ 0 & 0 & 0 & 1 \end{bmatrix} \begin{bmatrix} 1 & 0 & 0 & -10 \\ 0 & 1 & 0 & -1 \\ 0 & 0 & 1 & -1 \\ 0 & 0 & 0 & 1 \end{bmatrix} \begin{bmatrix} x \\ y \\ z \\ 1 \end{bmatrix}
$$

which simplifies to

$$
\begin{bmatrix} x' \\ y' \\ z' \\ 1 \end{bmatrix} = \begin{bmatrix} -1 & 0 & 0 & 10 \\ 0 & 1 & 0 & -1 \\ 0 & 0 & -1 & 1 \\ 0 & 0 & 0 & 1 \end{bmatrix} \begin{bmatrix} x \\ y \\ z \\ 1 \end{bmatrix}.
$$

Substituting $(0,0,0)$ for (x,y,z) in the above transform produces $(10,-1,1)$ for (x',y',z'), which can be confirmed from Fig. 7.22. Similarly, substituting $(0,1,1)$ for (x,y,z) produces $(10,0,0)$ for (x',y',z'), which is also correct.

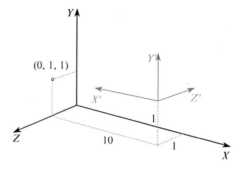

Fig. 7.22 The secondary axial system is subject to a *yaw* of 180° and an offset of $(10, 1, 1)$.

7.7.2 Euler Angles

Another approach for locating the virtual camera involves Euler angles, but we must remember that they suffer from gimbal lock. However, if the virtual camera is located in world space using Euler angles, the transform relating world coordinates to camera coordinates can be derived from the inverse operations. The *yaw*, *pitch*, *roll* matrices described above are called *orthogonal matrices*, as the inverse matrix is the transpose of the original rows and columns. Consequently, to rotate through angles $-roll$, $-pitch$ and $-yaw$, we use

- rotate $-roll$ about the z-axis:

$$\begin{bmatrix} \cos roll & \sin roll & 0 & 0 \\ -\sin roll & \cos roll & 0 & 0 \\ 0 & 0 & 1 & 0 \\ 0 & 0 & 0 & 1 \end{bmatrix}.$$

- rotate $-pitch$ about the x-axis:

$$\begin{bmatrix} 1 & 0 & 0 & 0 \\ 0 & \cos pitch & \sin pitch & 0 \\ 0 & -\sin pitch & \cos pitch & 0 \\ 0 & 0 & 0 & 1 \end{bmatrix}.$$

- rotate $-yaw$ about the y-axis:

$$\begin{bmatrix} \cos yaw & 0 & -\sin yaw & 0 \\ 0 & 1 & 0 & 0 \\ \sin yaw & 0 & \cos yaw & 0 \\ 0 & 0 & 0 & 1 \end{bmatrix}.$$

The same result is obtained by substituting $-roll$, $-pitch$, $-yaw$ in the original matrices. As described above, the virtual camera will normally be translated from the origin by (t_x, t_y, t_z), which implies that the transform from the world space to the camera space must be evaluated as follows:

$$
\begin{bmatrix} x' \\ y' \\ z' \\ 1 \end{bmatrix} = \begin{bmatrix} -roll \end{bmatrix} \begin{bmatrix} -pitch \end{bmatrix} \begin{bmatrix} -yaw \end{bmatrix} \begin{bmatrix} translate(-t_x, -t_y, -t_z) \end{bmatrix} \begin{bmatrix} x \\ y \\ z \\ 1 \end{bmatrix}
$$

which can be represented by a single homogeneous matrix:

$$
\begin{bmatrix} x' \\ y' \\ z' \\ 1 \end{bmatrix} = \begin{bmatrix} T_{11} & T_{12} & T_{13} & T_{14} \\ T_{21} & T_{22} & T_{23} & T_{24} \\ T_{31} & T_{32} & T_{33} & T_{34} \\ T_{41} & T_{42} & T_{43} & T_{44} \end{bmatrix} \begin{bmatrix} x \\ y \\ z \\ 1 \end{bmatrix}
$$

where

$$T_{11} = \cos(yaw)\cos(roll) + \sin(yaw)\sin(pitch)\sin(roll)$$
$$T_{12} = \cos(pitch)\sin(roll)$$
$$T_{13} = -\sin(yaw)\cos(roll) + \cos(yaw)\sin(pitch)\sin(roll)$$
$$T_{14} = -(t_x T_{11} + t_y T_{12} + t_z T_{13})$$
$$T_{21} = -\cos(yaw)\sin(roll) + \sin(yaw)\sin(pitch)\cos(roll)$$
$$T_{22} = \cos(pitch)\cos(roll)$$
$$T_{23} = -\sin(yaw)\sin(roll) + \cos(yaw)\sin(pitch)\cos(roll)$$
$$T_{24} = -(t_x T_{21} + t_y T_{22} + t_z T_{23})$$
$$T_{31} = \sin(yaw)\cos(pitch)$$
$$T_{32} = -\sin(pitch)$$
$$T_{33} = \cos(yaw)\cos(pitch)$$
$$T_{34} = -(t_x T_{31} + t_y T_{32} + t_z T_{33})$$
$$T_{41} = T_{42} = T_{43} = 0$$
$$T_{44} = 1.$$

This, too, can be verified by a simple example. For instance, consider the situation shown in Fig. 7.22 where the following conditions prevail:

$$roll = 0°$$
$$pitch = 0°$$
$$yaw = 180°$$

$$t_x = 10$$
$$t_y = 1$$
$$t_z = 1.$$

The transform is

$$
\begin{bmatrix} x' \\ y' \\ z' \\ 1 \end{bmatrix} =
\begin{bmatrix} -1 & 0 & 0 & 10 \\ 0 & 1 & 0 & -1 \\ 0 & 0 & -1 & 1 \\ 0 & 0 & 0 & 1 \end{bmatrix}
\begin{bmatrix} x \\ y \\ z \\ 1 \end{bmatrix}
$$

which is identical to the equation used for direction cosines. Another example is shown in Fig. 7.23 where the following conditions prevail:

$$roll = 90°$$
$$pitch = 180°$$
$$yaw = 0°$$
$$t_x = 0.5$$
$$t_y = 0.5$$
$$t_z = 11.$$

The transform is

$$
\begin{bmatrix} x' \\ y' \\ z' \\ 1 \end{bmatrix} =
\begin{bmatrix} 0 & -1 & 0 & 0.5 \\ -1 & 0 & 0 & 0.5 \\ 0 & 0 & -1 & 11 \\ 0 & 0 & 0 & 1 \end{bmatrix}
\begin{bmatrix} x \\ y \\ z \\ 1 \end{bmatrix}.
$$

Substituting $(1,1,1)$ for (x,y,z) produces $(-0.5,-0.5,10)$ for (x',y',z'). Similarly, substituting $(0,0,1)$ for (x,y,z) produces $(0.5,0.5,10)$ for (x',y',z'), which can be visually verified from Fig. 7.23.

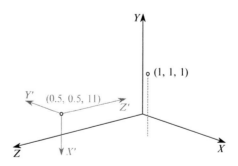

Fig. 7.23 The secondary axial system is subject to a *roll* of 90°, a *pitch* of 180° and a translation of $(0.5,0.5,11)$.

7.8 Rotating a Point About an Arbitrary Axis

7.8.1 Matrices

Let's now consider two ways of developing a matrix for rotating a point about an
arbitrary axis. The first approach employs vector analysis and is quite succinct. The
second technique is less analytical and relies on matrices and trigonometric evalua-
tion and is rather laborious. Fortunately, they both arrive at the same result!

Figure 7.24 shows a view of the geometry associated with the task at hand. For
clarification, Fig. 7.25 shows a cross-sectionand a plan view of the geometry.

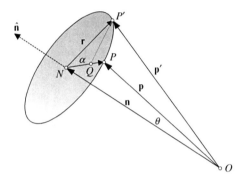

Fig. 7.24 A view of the geometry associated with rotating a point about an arbitrary axis.

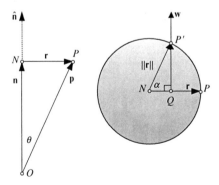

Fig. 7.25 A cross-sectionand plan view of the geometry associated with rotating a point about an
arbitrary axis.

The axis of rotation is given by the unit vector:

$$\hat{\mathbf{v}} = a\mathbf{i} + b\mathbf{j} + c\mathbf{k}.$$

$P(x_p, y_p\, z_p)$ is the point to be rotated by angle α to $P'(x'_p, y'_p, z'_p)$.

O is the origin, whilst $\mathbf{p}$ and $\mathbf{p}'$ are position vectors for P and P' respectively. From Figs. 7.24 and 7.25:

$$\mathbf{p}' = \overrightarrow{ON} + \overrightarrow{NQ} + \overrightarrow{QP'}.$$

To find $\overrightarrow{ON}$:

$$|\mathbf{n}| = |\mathbf{p}| \cos \theta = \hat{\mathbf{n}} \cdot \mathbf{p}$$

therefore,

$$\overrightarrow{ON} = \mathbf{n} = \hat{\mathbf{n}}(\hat{\mathbf{n}} \cdot \mathbf{p}).$$

To find $\overrightarrow{NQ}$:

$$\overrightarrow{NQ} = \frac{NQ}{NP}\mathbf{r} = \frac{NQ}{NP'}\mathbf{r} = \cos \alpha \, \mathbf{r}$$

but

$$\mathbf{p} = \mathbf{n} + \mathbf{r} = \hat{\mathbf{n}}(\hat{\mathbf{n}} \cdot \mathbf{p}) + \mathbf{r}$$

therefore,

$$\mathbf{r} = \mathbf{p} - \hat{\mathbf{n}}(\hat{\mathbf{n}} \cdot \mathbf{p})$$

and

$$\overrightarrow{NQ} = [\mathbf{p} - \hat{\mathbf{n}}(\hat{\mathbf{n}} \cdot \mathbf{p})] \cos \alpha.$$

To find $\overrightarrow{QP'}$:
Let

$$\hat{\mathbf{n}} \times \mathbf{p} = \mathbf{w}$$

where

$$|\mathbf{w}| = |\hat{\mathbf{n}}| \cdot |\mathbf{p}| \sin \theta = |\mathbf{p}| \sin \theta$$

but

$$|\mathbf{r}| = |\mathbf{p}| \sin \theta$$

therefore,

$$|\mathbf{w}| = |\mathbf{r}|.$$

Now

$$\frac{QP'}{NP'} = \frac{QP'}{|\mathbf{r}|} = \frac{QP'}{|\mathbf{w}|} = \sin \alpha$$

therefore,

$$\overrightarrow{QP'} = \mathbf{w} \sin \alpha = (\hat{\mathbf{n}} \times \mathbf{p}) \sin \alpha$$

then

$$\mathbf{p}' = \hat{\mathbf{n}}(\hat{\mathbf{n}} \cdot \mathbf{p}) + [\mathbf{p} - \hat{\mathbf{n}}(\hat{\mathbf{n}} \cdot \mathbf{p}] \cos \alpha + (\hat{\mathbf{n}} \times \mathbf{p}) \sin \alpha$$

and

$$\mathbf{p}' = \mathbf{p} \cos \alpha + \hat{\mathbf{n}}(\hat{\mathbf{n}} \cdot \mathbf{p})(1 - \cos \alpha) + (\hat{\mathbf{n}} \times \mathbf{p}) \sin \alpha.$$

Let

$$K = 1 - \cos \alpha$$

then

$$\mathbf{p}' = \mathbf{p}\cos\alpha + \hat{\mathbf{n}}(\hat{\mathbf{n}}\cdot\mathbf{p})K + (\hat{\mathbf{n}}\times\mathbf{p})\sin\alpha$$

and

$$
\begin{aligned}
\mathbf{p}' ={}& (x_p\mathbf{i}+y_p\mathbf{j}+z_p\mathbf{k})\cos\alpha + (a\mathbf{i}+b\mathbf{j}+c\mathbf{k})(ax_p+by_p+cz_p)K \\
&+ [(bz_p-cy_p)\mathbf{i}+(cx_p-az_p)\mathbf{j}+(ay_p-bx_p)\mathbf{k}]\sin\alpha \\
\mathbf{p}' ={}& [x_p\cos\alpha + a(ax_p+by_p+cz_p)K + (bz_p-cy_p)\sin\alpha]\mathbf{i} \\
&+ [y_p\cos\alpha + b(ax_p+by_p+cz_p)K + (cx_p-az_p)\sin\alpha]\mathbf{j} \\
&+ [z_p\cos\alpha + c(ax_p+by_p+cz_p)K + (ay_p-bx_p)\sin\alpha]\mathbf{k} \\
\mathbf{p}' ={}& [x_p(a^2K+\cos\alpha) + y_p(abK-c\sin\alpha) + z_p(acK+b\sin\alpha)]\mathbf{i} \\
&+ [x_p(abK+c\sin\alpha) + y_p(b^2K+\cos\alpha) + z_p(bcK-a\sin\alpha)]\mathbf{j} \\
&+ [x_p(acK-b\sin\alpha) + y_p(bcK+a\sin\alpha) + z_p(c^2K+\cos\alpha)]\mathbf{k}
\end{aligned}
$$

and the transform is:

$$
\begin{bmatrix} x'_p \\ y'_p \\ z'_p \\ 1 \end{bmatrix}
=
\begin{bmatrix}
a^2K+\cos\alpha & abK-c\sin\alpha & acK+b\sin\alpha & 0 \\
abK+c\sin\alpha & b^2K+\cos\alpha & bcK-a\sin\alpha & 0 \\
acK-b\sin\alpha & bcK+a\sin\alpha & c^2K+\cos\alpha & 0 \\
0 & 0 & 0 & 1
\end{bmatrix}
\begin{bmatrix} x_p \\ y_p \\ z_p \\ 1 \end{bmatrix}
$$

where

$$K = 1 - \cos\alpha.$$

Now let's approach the problem using transforms and trigonometric identities. The following is extremely tedious, but it is a good exercise for improving one's algebraic skills!

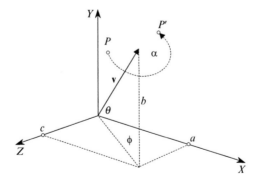

Fig. 7.26 The geometry associated with rotating a point about an arbitrary axis.

Figure 7.26 shows a point $P(x,y,z)$ to be rotated through an angle α to $P'(x',y',z')$ about an axis defined by

$$\mathbf{v} = a\mathbf{i} + b\mathbf{j} + c\mathbf{k}$$

where $|\mathbf{v}| = 1$.

The transforms to achieve this operation can be expressed as follows:

$$\begin{bmatrix} x' \\ y' \\ z' \end{bmatrix} = [T_5]\ [T_4]\ [T_3]\ [T_2]\ [T_1] \begin{bmatrix} x \\ y \\ z \end{bmatrix}$$

which aligns the axis of rotation with the x-axis, performs the rotation of P through an angle α about the x-axis, and returns the axis of rotation back to its original position. Therefore,

$$T_1 \text{ rotates } +\phi \text{ about the } y\text{-axis}$$
$$T_2 \text{ rotates } -\theta \text{ about the } z\text{-axis}$$
$$T_3 \text{ rotates } +\alpha \text{ about the } x\text{-axis}$$
$$T_4 \text{ rotates } +\theta \text{ about the } z\text{-axis}$$
$$T_5 \text{ rotates } -\phi \text{ about the } y\text{-axis}$$

where

$$T_1 = \begin{bmatrix} \cos\phi & 0 & \sin\phi \\ 0 & 1 & 0 \\ -\sin\phi & 0 & \cos\phi \end{bmatrix} \quad T_2 = \begin{bmatrix} \cos\theta & \sin\theta & 0 \\ -\sin\theta & \cos\theta & 0 \\ 0 & 0 & 1 \end{bmatrix}$$

$$T_3 = \begin{bmatrix} 1 & 0 & 0 \\ 0 & \cos\alpha & -\sin\alpha \\ 0 & \sin\alpha & \cos\alpha \end{bmatrix} \quad T_4 = \begin{bmatrix} \cos\theta & -\sin\theta & 0 \\ \sin\theta & \cos\theta & 0 \\ 0 & 0 & 1 \end{bmatrix}$$

$$T_5 = \begin{bmatrix} \cos\phi & 0 & -\sin\phi \\ 0 & 1 & 0 \\ \sin\phi & 0 & \cos\phi \end{bmatrix}.$$

Let

$$[T_5]\ [T_4]\ [T_3]\ [T_2]\ [T_1] = \begin{bmatrix} E_{1,1} & E_{1,2} & E_{1,3} & 0 \\ E_{2,1} & E_{2,2} & E_{2,3} & 0 \\ E_{3,1} & E_{3,2} & E_{3,3} & 0 \\ 0 & 0 & 0 & 1 \end{bmatrix}$$

where by multiplying the matrices together we find that:

$$E_{1,1} = \cos^2\phi \cos^2\theta + \cos^2\phi \sin^2\theta \cos\alpha + \sin^2\phi \cos\alpha$$
$$E_{1,2} = \cos\phi \cos\theta \sin\theta - \cos\phi \sin\theta \cos\theta \cos\alpha - \sin\phi \cos\theta \sin\alpha$$
$$E_{1,3} = \cos\phi \sin\phi \cos^2\theta + \cos\phi \sin\phi \sin^2\theta \cos\alpha + \sin^2\phi \sin\theta \sin\alpha$$
$$\qquad + \cos^2\phi \sin\theta \sin\alpha - \cos\phi \sin\phi \cos\alpha$$

$$E_{2,1} = \sin\theta\cos\theta\cos\phi - \cos\theta\sin\theta\cos\phi\cos\alpha + \cos\theta\sin\phi\sin\alpha$$

$$E_{2,2} = \sin^2\theta + \cos^2\theta\cos\alpha$$

$$E_{2,3} = \sin\theta\cos\theta\sin\phi - \cos\theta\sin\theta\sin\phi\cos\alpha - \cos\theta\cos\phi\sin\alpha$$

$$E_{3,1} = \cos\phi\sin\phi\cos^2\theta + \cos\phi\sin\phi\sin^2\theta\cos\alpha - \cos^2\phi\sin\theta\sin\alpha$$
$$= -\cos\phi\sin\phi\cos\alpha$$

$$E_{3,2} = \sin\phi\cos\theta\sin\theta - \sin\phi\sin\theta\cos\theta\cos\alpha + \cos\phi\cos\theta\sin\alpha$$

$$E_{3,3} = \sin^2\phi\cos^2\theta + \sin^2\phi\sin^2\theta\cos\alpha - \cos\phi\sin\phi\sin\theta\sin\alpha$$
$$+ \cos\phi\sin\phi\sin\theta\sin\alpha + \cos^2\phi\cos\alpha.$$

From Fig. 7.26 we compute the sin and cos of θ and ϕ in terms of a, b and c, and then compute their equivalent $\sin^2$ and $\cos^2$ values:

$$\cos\theta = \sqrt{1-b^2} \Rightarrow \cos^2\theta = 1 - b^2$$

$$\sin\theta = b \Rightarrow \sin^2\theta = b^2$$

$$\cos\phi = \frac{a}{\sqrt{1-b^2}} \Rightarrow \cos^2\phi = \frac{a^2}{1-b^2}$$

$$\sin\phi = \frac{c}{\sqrt{1-b^2}} \Rightarrow \sin^2\phi = \frac{c^2}{1-b^2}$$

To find $E_{1,1}$:

$$E_{1,1} = \cos^2\phi\cos^2\theta + \cos^2\phi\sin^2\theta\cos\alpha + \sin^2\phi\cos\alpha$$

$$= \frac{a^2}{1-b^2}(1-b^2) + \frac{a^2}{1-b^2}b^2\cos\alpha + \frac{c^2}{1-b^2}\cos\alpha$$

$$= a^2 + \frac{a^2b^2}{1-b^2}\cos\alpha + \frac{c^2}{1-b^2}\cos\alpha$$

$$= a^2 + \left(\frac{c^2+a^2b^2}{1-b^2}\right)\cos\alpha$$

but

$$a^2 + b^2 + c^2 = 1 \Rightarrow c^2 = 1 - a^2 - b^2$$

substituting c^2 in $E_{1,1}$

$$E_{1,1} = a^2 + \left(\frac{1-a^2-b^2+a^2b^2}{1-b^2}\right)\cos\alpha$$

$$= a^2 + \left(\frac{(1-a^2)(1-b^2)}{1-b^2}\right)\cos\alpha$$

$$= a^2 + (1-a^2)\cos\alpha$$

$$= a^2(1-\cos\alpha) + \cos\alpha.$$

Let
$$K = 1 - \cos\alpha$$

then
$$E_{1,1} = a^2 K + \cos\alpha.$$

To find $E_{1,2}$:

$$E_{1,2} = \cos\phi\cos\theta\sin\theta - \cos\phi\sin\theta\cos\theta\cos\alpha - \sin\phi\cos\theta\sin\alpha$$
$$= \frac{a}{\sqrt{1-b^2}}\sqrt{1-b^2}b - \frac{a}{\sqrt{1-b^2}}b\sqrt{1-b^2}\cos\alpha - \frac{c}{\sqrt{1-b^2}}\sqrt{1-b^2}\sin\alpha$$
$$= ab - ab\cos\alpha - c\sin\alpha$$
$$= ab(1-\cos\alpha) - c\sin\alpha$$
$$E_{1,2} = abK - c\sin\alpha.$$

To find $E_{1,3}$:

$$E_{1,3} = \cos\phi\sin\phi\cos^2\theta + \cos\phi\sin\phi\sin^2\theta\cos\alpha + \sin^2\phi\sin\theta\sin\alpha$$
$$+ \cos^2\phi\sin\theta\sin\alpha - \cos\phi\sin\phi\cos\alpha$$
$$= \cos\phi\sin\phi\cos^2\theta + \cos\phi\sin\phi\sin^2\theta\cos\alpha + \sin\theta\sin\alpha - \cos\phi\sin\phi\cos\alpha$$
$$= \frac{a}{\sqrt{1-b^2}}\frac{c}{\sqrt{1-b^2}}(1-b^2) + \frac{a}{\sqrt{1-b^2}}\frac{c}{\sqrt{1-b^2}}b^2\cos\alpha + b\sin\alpha$$
$$- \frac{a}{\sqrt{1-b^2}}\frac{c}{\sqrt{1-b^2}}\cos\alpha$$
$$= ac + ac\frac{b^2}{(1-b^2)}\cos\alpha + b\sin\alpha - \frac{ac}{(1-b^2)}\cos\alpha$$
$$= ac + ac\frac{(b^2-1)}{(1-b^2)}\cos\alpha + b\sin\alpha$$
$$= ac(1-\cos\alpha) + b\sin\alpha$$
$$E_{1,3} = acK + b\sin\alpha.$$

Using similar algebraic methods, we discover that:

$$E_{2,1} = abK + c\sin\alpha$$
$$E_{2,2} = b^2 K + \cos\alpha$$
$$E_{2,3} = bcK - a\sin\alpha$$
$$E_{3,1} = acK - b\sin\alpha$$
$$E_{3,2} = bcK + a\sin\alpha$$
$$E_{3,3} = c^2 K + \cos\alpha$$

and our original matrix transform becomes:

$$
\begin{bmatrix} x'_p \\ y'_p \\ z'_p \\ 1 \end{bmatrix} =
\begin{bmatrix}
a^2K+\cos\alpha & abK-c\sin\alpha & acK+b\sin\alpha & 0 \\
abK+c\sin\alpha & b^2K+\cos\alpha & bcK-a\sin\alpha & 0 \\
acK-b\sin\alpha & bcK+a\sin\alpha & c^2K+\cos\alpha & 0 \\
0 & 0 & 0 & 1
\end{bmatrix}
\begin{bmatrix} x_p \\ y_p \\ z_p \\ 1 \end{bmatrix}
$$

where

$$ K = 1 - \cos\alpha. $$

which is identical to the transformation derived from the first approach.

Now let's test the matrix with a simple example that can be easily verified. If we rotate the point $P(10,5,0)$ $360°$ about an axis defined by $\mathbf{v} = \mathbf{i}+\mathbf{j}+\mathbf{k}$, it should return to itself producing $P'(x',y',z')$.

Therefore

$$ \alpha = 360° \quad \cos\alpha = 1 \quad \sin\alpha = 0 \quad K = 0 $$

$$ a = 1 \quad b = 1 \quad c = 1 $$

and

$$
\begin{bmatrix} 10 \\ 5 \\ 0 \\ 1 \end{bmatrix} =
\begin{bmatrix}
1 & 0 & 0 & 0 \\
0 & 1 & 0 & 0 \\
0 & 0 & 1 & 0 \\
0 & 0 & 0 & 1
\end{bmatrix}
\begin{bmatrix} 10 \\ 5 \\ 0 \\ 1 \end{bmatrix}.
$$

As the matrix is an identity matrix $P' = P$.

7.8.2 Quaternions

As mentioned earlier, quaternions were invented by Sir William Rowan Hamilton in the mid-nineteenth century. Sir William was looking for a way to represent complex numbers in higher dimensions, and it took 15 years of toil before he stumbled upon the idea of using a 4D notation – hence the name 'quaternion'.

Knowing that a complex number is the combination of a real and imaginary quantity: $a + ib$, it is tempting to assume that its 3D equivalent is $a + ib + jc$ where $i^2 = j^2 = -1$. Unfortunately, when Hamilton formed the product of two such objects, he could not resolve the dyads ij and ji, and went on to explore an extension $a + ib + jc + kd$ where $i^2 = j^2 = k^2 = -1$. This too, presented problems with the dyads ij, jk, ki and their mirrors ji, kj and ik. But after many years of thought Hamilton stumbled across the rules:

$$ i^2 = j^2 = k^2 = ijk = -1 $$
$$ ij = k, \quad jk = i, \quad ki = j $$
$$ ji = -k, \quad kj = -i, \quad ik = -j. $$

Although quaternions had some enthusiastic supporters, there were many mathematicians and scientists who were suspicious of the need to involve so many imaginary terms.

Towards the end of the nineteenth century Josiah Gibbs resolved the problem by declaring that the three imaginary quantities could be viewed as a 3D vector and changed the $ib + jc + kd$ into $b\mathbf{i} + c\mathbf{j} + d\mathbf{k}$, where $\mathbf{i}, \mathbf{j}$ and $\mathbf{k}$ are unit Cartesian vectors. Today, there are two ways of defining a quaternion:

$$\mathbf{q} = [s, \mathbf{v}]$$
$$\mathbf{q} = [s + \mathbf{v}].$$

The difference is rather subtle: the first separates the scalar and the vector with a comma, whereas the second preserves the '+' sign as used in complex numbers. Although the idea of adding a scalar to a vector seems strange, this notation is used for the rest of this section as it will help us understand the ideas behind geometric algebra, which are introduced later on.

Since Hamilton's invention, mathematicians have shown that quaternions can be used to rotate points about an arbitrary axis, and hence the orientation of objects and the virtual camera. In order to develop the equation that performs this transformation we will have to understand the action of quaternions in the context of rotations.

A quaternion $\mathbf{q}$ is the combination of a scalar and a vector:

$$\mathbf{q} = [s + \mathbf{v}]$$

where s is a scalar and $\mathbf{v}$ is a 3D vector. If we express the vector $\mathbf{v}$ in terms of its components, we have in an algebraic form

$$\mathbf{q} = [s + x\mathbf{i} + y\mathbf{j} + z\mathbf{k}]$$

where s, x, y and z are real numbers.

7.8.3 Adding and Subtracting Quaternions

Given two quaternions $\mathbf{q}_1$ and $\mathbf{q}_2$:

$$\mathbf{q}_1 = [s_1 + \mathbf{v}_1] = [s_1 + x_1\mathbf{i} + y_1\mathbf{j} + z_1\mathbf{k}]$$
$$\mathbf{q}_2 = [s_2 + \mathbf{v}_2] = [s_2 + x_2\mathbf{i} + y_2\mathbf{j} + z_2\mathbf{k}]$$

they are equal if, and only if, their corresponding terms are equal. Furthermore, like vectors, they can be added and subtracted as follows:

$$\mathbf{q}_1 \pm \mathbf{q}_2 = [(s_1 \pm s_2) + (x_1 \pm x_2)\mathbf{i} + (y_1 \pm y_2)\mathbf{j} + (z_1 \pm z_2)\mathbf{k}].$$

7.8.4 Multiplying Quaternions

When multiplying quaternions we must employ the following rules:

$$\mathbf{i}^2 = \mathbf{j}^2 = \mathbf{k}^2 = \mathbf{ijk} = -1$$
$$\mathbf{ij} = \mathbf{k}, \ \mathbf{jk} = \mathbf{i}, \ \mathbf{ki} = \mathbf{j}$$
$$\mathbf{ji} = -\mathbf{k}, \ \mathbf{kj} = -\mathbf{i}, \ \mathbf{ik} = -\mathbf{j}.$$

Note that whilst quaternion addition is commutative, the rules make quaternion products non-commutative.

Given two quaternions $\mathbf{q}_1$ and $\mathbf{q}_2$:

$$\mathbf{q}_1 = [s_1 + \mathbf{v}_1] = [s_1 + x_1\mathbf{i} + y_1\mathbf{j} + z_1\mathbf{k}]$$

$$\mathbf{q}_2 = [s_2 + \mathbf{v}_2] = [s_2 + x_2\mathbf{i} + y_2\mathbf{j} + z_2\mathbf{k}]$$

their product $\mathbf{q}_1\mathbf{q}_2$ is given by:

$$\mathbf{q}_1\mathbf{q}_2 = [(s_1s_2 - x_1x_2 - y_1y_2 - z_1z_2) + (s_1x_2 + s_2x_1 + y_1z_2 - y_2z_1)\mathbf{i}$$
$$+ (s_1y_2 + s_2y_1 + z_1x_2 - z_2x_1)\mathbf{j} + (s_1z_2 + s_2z_1 + x_1y_2 - x_2y_1)\mathbf{k}$$

which can be rewritten using the dot and cross product notation as

$$\mathbf{q}_1\mathbf{q}_2 = [(s_1s_2 - \mathbf{v}_1 \cdot \mathbf{v}_2) + s_1\mathbf{v}_2 + s_2\mathbf{v}_1 + \mathbf{v}_1 \times \mathbf{v}_2]$$

where

$$(s_1s_2 - \mathbf{v}_1 \cdot \mathbf{v}_2)$$

is a scalar, and

$$s_1\mathbf{v}_2 + s_2\mathbf{v}_1 + \mathbf{v}_1 \times \mathbf{v}_2$$

is a vector.

7.8.5 Pure Quaternion

A pure quaternion has a zero scalar term:

$$\mathbf{q} = [\mathbf{v}]$$

which is a vector. Therefore, given two pure quaternions:

$$\mathbf{q}_1 = [\mathbf{v}_1] = [x_1\mathbf{i} + y_1\mathbf{j} + z_1\mathbf{k}]$$
$$\mathbf{q}_2 = [\mathbf{v}_2] = [x_2\mathbf{i} + y_2\mathbf{j} + z_2\mathbf{k}]$$

their product is

$$\mathbf{q}_1\mathbf{q}_2 = [\mathbf{v}_1 \times \mathbf{v}_2].$$

7.8.6 The Inverse Quaternion

Given the quaternion

$$\mathbf{q} = [s + x\mathbf{i} + y\mathbf{j} + z\mathbf{k}]$$

its inverse $\mathbf{q}^{-1}$ is given by

$$\mathbf{q}^{-1} = \frac{s - x\mathbf{i} - y\mathbf{j} - z\mathbf{k}]}{|\mathbf{q}|^2}$$

where $|\mathbf{q}|$ is the magnitude, or modulus of $\mathbf{q}$, and is equal to

$$|\mathbf{q}| = \sqrt{s^2 + x^2 + y^2 + z^2}.$$

It can also be shown that

$$\mathbf{q}\mathbf{q}^{-1} = \mathbf{q}^{-1}\mathbf{q} = 1.$$

7.8.7 Unit Quaternion

A unit quaternion has a magnitude equal to 1:

$$|\mathbf{q}| = \sqrt{s^2 + x^2 + y^2 + z^2} = 1.$$

7.8.8 Rotating Points About an Axis

Basically, quaternions are associated with vectors rather than individual points. Therefore, in order to manipulate a single vertex, it must be turned into a position vector, which has its tail at the origin. A vertex can then be represented in quaternion form by its equivalent position vector with a zero scalar term. For example, a point $P(x, y, z)$ is represented in quaternion form by

$$\mathbf{P} = [0 + x\mathbf{i} + y\mathbf{j} + z\mathbf{k}]$$

which is transformed into another position vector using the process described below. The coordinates of the rotated point are the components of the rotated position vector. This may seem an indirect process, but in reality it turns out to be rather simple. Let's now consider how this is achieved.

It can be shown that a position vector $\mathbf{P}$ can be rotated through an angle θ about an axis using the following operation:

$$\mathbf{P}' = \mathbf{qPq}^{-1}$$

where the axis and angle of rotation are encoded within the unit quaternion $\mathbf{q}$, whose modulus is 1, and $\mathbf{P}'$ is the rotated vector. For example, to rotate a point $P(x,y,z)$ through an angle θ about an axis $\mathbf{u}$, we use the following steps:

1. Convert the point $P(x,y,z)$ to a pure quaternion $\mathbf{P}$:

$$\mathbf{P} = [0 + x\mathbf{i} + y\mathbf{j} + z\mathbf{k}].$$

2. Define the axis of rotation as a unit vector $\hat{\mathbf{u}}$:

$$\hat{\mathbf{u}} = [x_u\mathbf{i} + y_u\mathbf{j} + z_u\mathbf{k}]$$

and

$$|\hat{\mathbf{u}}| = 1.$$

3. Define the transforming quaternion $\mathbf{q}$:

$$\mathbf{q} = [\cos(\theta/2) + \sin(\theta/2)\hat{\mathbf{u}}].$$

4. Define the inverse of the transforming quaternion $\mathbf{q}^{-1}$:

$$\mathbf{q}^{-1} = [\cos(\theta/2) - \sin(\theta/2)\hat{\mathbf{u}}].$$

5. Compute $\mathbf{P}'$:

$$\mathbf{P}' = \mathbf{qPq}^{-1}.$$

6. Unpack (x', y', z'):

$$P'(x', y', z') \quad \Leftarrow \quad \mathbf{P}' = [0 + x'\mathbf{i} + y'\mathbf{j} + z'\mathbf{k}].$$

We can verify the action of the above transform with a simple example. Consider the point $P(0,1,1)$ in Fig. 7.27 which is to be rotated $90°$ about the y-axis. We can see that the rotated point P' has the coordinates $(1,1,0)$ which we will confirm algebraically. The point P is represented by the quaternion $\mathbf{P}$:

$$\mathbf{P} = [0 + 0\mathbf{i} + 1\mathbf{j} + 1\mathbf{k}]$$

and is rotated by evaluating the quaternion $\mathbf{P}'$:

$$\mathbf{P}' = \mathbf{qPq}^{-1}$$

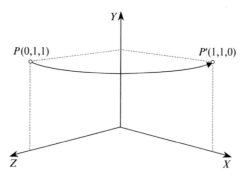

Fig. 7.27 The point $P(0,1,1)$ is rotated to $P'(1,1,0)$ using a quaternion coincident with the y-axis.

which will store the rotated coordinates. The axis of rotation is $\mathbf{j}$, therefore the unit quaternion $\mathbf{q}$ is given by

$$\mathbf{q} = [\cos(90°/2) + \sin(90°/2)[0\mathbf{i} + \mathbf{j} + 0\mathbf{k}]]$$
$$= [\cos 45° + 0\mathbf{i} + \sin 45°\mathbf{j} + 0\mathbf{k}].$$

The inverse quaternion $\mathbf{q}^{-1}$ is given by

$$\mathbf{q}^{-1} = \frac{[\cos(90°/2) - \sin(90°/2)[0\mathbf{i} + \mathbf{j} - 0\mathbf{k}]]}{|\mathbf{q}|^2}$$

but as $\mathbf{q}$ is a unit quaternion, the denominator $|\mathbf{q}|^2$ equals unity and can be ignored. Therefore

$$\mathbf{q}^{-1} = [\cos 45° - 0\mathbf{i} - \sin 45°\mathbf{j} - 0\mathbf{k}].$$

Let's evaluate $\mathbf{qPq}^{-1}$ in two stages: $(\mathbf{qP})\mathbf{q}^{-1}$, and for clarity, zero components will continue to be included.

1.

$$\mathbf{qP} = [\cos 45° + 0\mathbf{i} + \sin 45°\mathbf{j} + 0\mathbf{k}] \, [0 + 0\mathbf{i} + \mathbf{j} + 0\mathbf{k}]$$
$$= [-\sin 45° + \sin 45°\mathbf{i} + \cos 45°\mathbf{j} + \cos 45°\mathbf{k}].$$

2.

$$(\mathbf{qP})\mathbf{q}^{-1} = [-\sin 45° + \sin 45°\mathbf{i} + \cos 45°\mathbf{j} + \cos 45°\mathbf{k}]$$
$$\cdot [\cos 45° - 0\mathbf{i} - \sin 45°\mathbf{j} - 0\mathbf{k}]$$
$$= [0 + 2\cos 45° \sin 45°\mathbf{i} + (\cos^2 45° + \sin^2 45°)\mathbf{j} + (\cos^2 45° - \sin^2 45°)\mathbf{k}]$$
$$\mathbf{P}' = [0 + \mathbf{i} + \mathbf{j} + 0\mathbf{k}]$$

and the vector component of $\mathbf{P}'$ confirms that P is indeed rotated to $(1,1,0)$.

We will evaluate one more example before continuing. Consider a rotation about the z-axis as illustrated in Fig. 7.28. The original point has coordinates $(0,1,1)$ and is rotated $-90°$. From the figure we see that this should finish at $(1,0,1)$. This time the quaternion $\mathbf{q}$ is defined by

$$\begin{aligned}\mathbf{q} &= [\cos(-90°/2) + \sin(-90°/2)[0\mathbf{i} + 0\mathbf{j} + \mathbf{k}]] \\ &= [\cos 45° + 0\mathbf{i} + 0\mathbf{j} - \sin 45°\mathbf{k}]\end{aligned}$$

with its inverse

$$\mathbf{q}^{-1} = [\cos 45° + 0\mathbf{i} + 0\mathbf{j} + \sin 45°\mathbf{k}]$$

and the point to be rotated in quaternion form is

$$\mathbf{P} = [0 + 0\mathbf{i} + \mathbf{i} + \mathbf{k}].$$

Evaluating this in two stages we have
1.

$$\begin{aligned}\mathbf{qP} &= [\cos 45° + 0\mathbf{i} + 0\mathbf{j} - \sin 45°\mathbf{k}] \cdot [0 + 0\mathbf{i} + \mathbf{j} + \mathbf{k}] \\ &= [\sin 45° + \sin 45°\mathbf{i} + \cos 45°\mathbf{j} + \cos 45°\mathbf{k}].\end{aligned}$$

2.

$$\begin{aligned}(\mathbf{qP})\mathbf{q}^{-1} &= [\sin 45° + \sin 45°\mathbf{i} + \cos 45°\mathbf{j} + \cos 45°\mathbf{k}] \\ &\quad \cdot [\cos 45° + 0\mathbf{i} + 0\mathbf{j} + \sin 45°\mathbf{k}] \\ &= [0 + \sin 90°\mathbf{i} + \cos 90°\mathbf{j} + \mathbf{k}] \\ &= [0 + \mathbf{i} + 0\mathbf{j} + \mathbf{k}].\end{aligned}$$

The vector component of P' confirms that P is rotated to $(1,0,1)$.

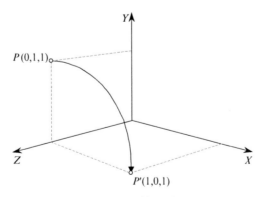

Fig. 7.28 The point $P(0,1,1)$ is rotated $-90°$ to $P'(1,0,1)$ using a quaternion coincident with the z-axis.

7.8.9 Roll, Pitch and Yaw Quaternions

Having already looked at roll, pitch and yaw rotations, we can now define them as quaternions:

$$\mathbf{q}_{roll} = [\cos(\theta/2) + 0\mathbf{i} + 0\mathbf{j} + \sin(\theta/2)\mathbf{k}]$$
$$\mathbf{q}_{pitch} = [\cos(\theta/2) + \sin(\theta/2)\mathbf{i} + 0\mathbf{j} + 0\mathbf{k}]$$
$$\mathbf{q}_{yaw} = [\cos(\theta/2) + 0\mathbf{i} + \sin(\theta/2)\mathbf{j} + 0\mathbf{k}]$$

where θ is the angle of rotation.

These quaternions can be multiplied together to create a single quaternion representing a compound rotation. For example, if the quaternions are defined as

$$\mathbf{q}_{roll} = [\cos(roll/2) + 0\mathbf{i} + 0\mathbf{j} + \sin(roll/2)\mathbf{k}]$$
$$\mathbf{q}_{pitch} = [\cos(pitch/2) + \sin(pitch/2)\mathbf{i} + 0\mathbf{j} + 0\mathbf{k}]$$
$$\mathbf{q}_{yaw} = [\cos(yaw/2) + 0\mathbf{i} + \sin(yaw/2)\mathbf{j} + 0\mathbf{k}]$$

they can be combined to a single quaternion $\mathbf{q}$:

$$\mathbf{q} = \mathbf{q}_{yaw}\mathbf{q}_{pitch}\mathbf{q}_{roll} = [s + x\mathbf{i} + y\mathbf{j} + z\mathbf{k}]$$

where

$$s = \cos(yaw/2)\cos(pitch/2)\cos(roll/2) + \sin(yaw/2)\sin(pitch/2)\sin(roll/2)$$
$$x = \cos(yaw/2)\sin(pitch/2)\cos(roll/2) + \sin(yaw/2)\cos(pitch/2)\sin(roll/2)$$
$$y = \sin(yaw/2)\cos(pitch/2)\cos(roll/2) - \cos(yaw/2)\sin(pitch/2)\sin(roll/2)$$
$$z = \cos(yaw/2)\cos(pitch/2)\sin(roll/2) - \sin(yaw/2)\sin(pitch/2)\cos(roll/2).$$

Let's examine this compound quaternion with an example. For instance, given the following conditions let's derive a single quaternion $\mathbf{q}$ to represent the compound rotation:

$$roll = 90°$$
$$pitch = 180°$$
$$yaw = 0°.$$

The values of s, x, y, z are

$$s = 0$$
$$x = \cos 45°$$
$$y = -\sin 45°$$
$$z = 0$$

and the quaternion **q** is

$$\mathbf{q} = [0 + \cos 45°\mathbf{i} - \sin 45°\mathbf{j} + 0\mathbf{k}].$$

If the point $P(1,1,1)$ is subjected to this compound rotation, the rotated point is computed using the standard quaternion transform:

$$\mathbf{P}' = \mathbf{qPq}^{-1}.$$

Let's evaluate $\mathbf{qPq}^{-1}$ in two stages:
1.

$$\mathbf{qP} = [0 + \cos 45°\mathbf{i} - \sin 45°\mathbf{j} + 0\mathbf{k}] \cdot [0 + \mathbf{i} + \mathbf{j} + \mathbf{k}]$$
$$= [0 - \sin 45°\mathbf{i} - \cos 45°\mathbf{j} + (\sin 45° + \cos 45°)\mathbf{k}].$$

2.

$$(\mathbf{qP})\mathbf{q}^{-1} = [0 - \sin 45°\mathbf{i} - \cos 45°\mathbf{j} + (\sin 45° + \cos 45°)\mathbf{k}]$$
$$\cdot [0 - \cos 45°\mathbf{i} + \sin 45°\mathbf{j} + 0\mathbf{k}]$$
$$\mathbf{P}' = [0 - \mathbf{i} - \mathbf{j} - \mathbf{k}].$$

Therefore, the coordinates of the rotated point are $(-1, -1, -1)$ which can be confirmed from Fig. 7.29.

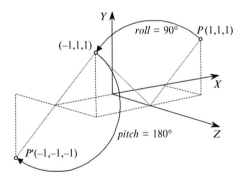

Fig. 7.29 The point $P(1,1,1)$ is subject to a compound roll of 90° to $(-1,1,1)$ and a pitch of 180° and ends up at $P'(-1,-1,-1)$.

7.8.10 Quaternions in Matrix Form

There is a direct relationship between quaternions and matrices. For example, given the quaternion

$$[s + x\mathbf{i} + y\mathbf{j} + z\mathbf{k}]$$

the equivalent matrix is

$$\begin{bmatrix} M_{11} & M_{12} & M_{13} \\ M_{21} & M_{22} & M_{23} \\ M_{31} & M_{32} & M_{33} \end{bmatrix}$$

where

$$M_{11} = 1 - 2(y^2 + z^2)$$
$$M_{12} = 2(xy - sz)$$
$$M_{13} = 2(xz + sy)$$
$$M_{21} = 2(xy + sz)$$
$$M_{22} = 1 - 2(x^2 + z^2)$$
$$M_{23} = 2(yz - sx)$$
$$M_{31} = 2(xz - sy)$$
$$M_{32} = 2(yz + sx)$$
$$M_{33} = 1 - 2(x^2 + y^2).$$

Substituting the following values of s, x, y, z:

$$s = 0$$
$$x = \cos 45°$$
$$y = -\sin 45°$$
$$z = 0$$

the matrix transformation is

$$\begin{bmatrix} x' \\ y' \\ z' \end{bmatrix} = \begin{bmatrix} 0 & -1 & 0 \\ -1 & 0 & 0 \\ 0 & 0 & -1 \end{bmatrix} \begin{bmatrix} x \\ y \\ z \end{bmatrix}.$$

Substituting $(1, 1, 1)$ for (x, y, z) the rotated point (x', y', z') becomes $(-1, -1, -1)$ as shown in Fig. 7.29.

7.8.11 Frames of Reference

A quaternion, or its equivalent matrix, can be used to rotate a vertex or position a virtual camera. If unit quaternions are used, the associated matrix is orthogonal, which means that its transpose is equivalent to rotating the frame of reference in the opposite direction. For example, if the virtual camera is oriented with a yaw rotation of $180°$, i.e., looking along the negative z-axis, the orientation quaternion is $[0 + 0\mathbf{i} + \mathbf{j} + 0\mathbf{k}]$. Therefore $s = 0$, $x = 0$, $y = 1$, $z = 0$. The equivalent matrix is

$$\begin{bmatrix} -1 & 0 & 0 \\ 0 & 1 & 0 \\ 0 & 0 & -1 \end{bmatrix}$$

which is equal to its transpose. Therefore, a vertex (x, y, z) in world space has coordinates (x', y', z') in camera space and the transform is defined by

$$\begin{bmatrix} x' \\ y' \\ z' \end{bmatrix} = \begin{bmatrix} -1 & 0 & 0 \\ 0 & 1 & 0 \\ 0 & 0 & -1 \end{bmatrix} \begin{bmatrix} x \\ y \\ z \end{bmatrix}.$$

If the vertex (x, y, z) is $(1, 1, 0)$, (x', y', z') becomes $(-1, 1, 0)$ which is correct. However, it is unlikely that the virtual camera will only be subjected to a simple rotation, as it will normally be translated from the origin. Consequently, a translation matrix will have to be introduced as described above.

7.9 Transforming Vectors

The transforms described in this chapter have been used to transform single points. However, a geometric database will not only contain pure vertices, but vectors, which must also be subject to any prevailing transform. A generic transform Q of a 3D point can be represented by

$$\begin{bmatrix} x' \\ y' \\ z' \\ 1 \end{bmatrix} = \begin{bmatrix} Q \end{bmatrix} \begin{bmatrix} x \\ y \\ z \\ 1 \end{bmatrix}$$

and as a vector is defined by two points we can write

$$\begin{bmatrix} x' \\ y' \\ z' \\ 1 \end{bmatrix} = \begin{bmatrix} Q \end{bmatrix} \begin{bmatrix} x_2 - x_1 \\ y_2 - y_1 \\ z_2 - z_1 \\ 1 - 1 \end{bmatrix}$$

where we see the homogeneous scaling term collapse to zero. Which implies that any vector $[x \quad y \quad z]^T$ can be transformed using

$$\begin{bmatrix} x' \\ y' \\ z' \\ 0 \end{bmatrix} = [Q] \begin{bmatrix} x \\ y \\ z \\ 0 \end{bmatrix}.$$

Let's put this to the test by using a transform from an earlier example. The problem concerned a change of axial system where a virtual camera was subject to the following:

$$roll = 180°$$
$$pitch = 90°$$
$$yaw = 90°$$
$$t_x = 2$$
$$t_y = 2$$
$$t_z = 0$$

and the transform is

$$\begin{bmatrix} x' \\ y' \\ z' \\ 1 \end{bmatrix} = \begin{bmatrix} 0 & -1 & 0 & 2 \\ 0 & 0 & 1 & 0 \\ -1 & 0 & 0 & 2 \\ 0 & 0 & 0 & 1 \end{bmatrix} \begin{bmatrix} x \\ y \\ z \\ 1 \end{bmatrix}.$$

When the point $(1,1,0)$ is transformed it becomes $(1,0,1)$ as shown in Fig. 7.30. But if we transform the vector $[1 \quad 1 \quad 0]^T$, it becomes $[-1 \quad 0 \quad -1]^T$ using the following transform

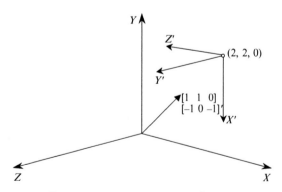

Fig. 7.30 Vector $[1 \quad 1 \quad 0]^T$ is transformed to $[-1 \quad 0 \quad -1]^T$.

$$\begin{bmatrix} -1 \\ 0 \\ -1 \\ 0 \end{bmatrix} = \begin{bmatrix} 0 & -1 & 0 & 2 \\ 0 & 0 & 1 & 0 \\ -1 & 0 & 0 & 2 \\ 0 & 0 & 0 & 1 \end{bmatrix} \begin{bmatrix} 1 \\ 1 \\ 0 \\ 0 \end{bmatrix}$$

which is correct with reference to Fig. 7.30.

7.10 Determinants

Before concluding this chapter I would like to expand upon the role of the determinant in transforms. Normally, determinants arise in the solution of linear equations such as

$$c_1 = a_1 x + b_1 y$$
$$c_2 = a_2 x + b_2 y$$

where values of x and y are defined in terms of the other constants. Without showing the algebra, the values of x and y are given by

$$x = \frac{c_1 b_2 - c_2 b_1}{a_1 b_2 - a_2 b_1} \qquad (7.5)$$

$$y = \frac{a_1 c_2 - a_2 c_1}{a_1 b_2 - a_2 b_1} \qquad (7.6)$$

provided that the denominator $a_1 b_2 - a_2 b_1 \neq 0$.

It is also possible to write the linear equations in matrix form as

$$\begin{bmatrix} c_1 \\ c_2 \end{bmatrix} = \begin{bmatrix} a_1 & b_1 \\ a_2 & b_2 \end{bmatrix} \begin{bmatrix} x \\ y \end{bmatrix}$$

and we notice that the denominator comes from the matrix terms $a_1 b_2 - a_2 b_1$. This is called the *determinant*, and is only valid for square matrices. A determinant is defined as follows:

$$\begin{vmatrix} a_1 & b_1 \\ a_2 & b_2 \end{vmatrix} = a_1 b_2 - a_2 b_1$$

where the terms are cross-multiplied and subtracted. With this notation it is possible to rewrite the original linear equations as

$$\frac{x}{\begin{vmatrix} c_1 & b_1 \\ c_2 & b_2 \end{vmatrix}} = \frac{y}{\begin{vmatrix} a_1 & c_1 \\ a_2 & c_2 \end{vmatrix}} = \frac{1}{\begin{vmatrix} a_1 & b_1 \\ a_2 & b_2 \end{vmatrix}}.$$

With a set of three linear equations:

$$d_1 = a_1 x + b_1 y + c_1 z$$
$$d_2 = a_2 x + b_2 y + c_2 z$$
$$d_3 = a_3 x + b_3 y + c_3 z$$

the value of x is computed using

$$x = \frac{d_1 b_2 c_3 - d_1 b_3 c_2 + d_2 b_3 c_1 - d_2 b_1 c_3 + d_3 b_1 c_2 - d_3 b_2 c_1}{a_1 b_2 c_3 - a_1 b_3 c_2 + a_2 b_3 c_1 - a_2 b_1 c_3 + a_3 b_1 c_2 - a_3 b_2 c_1}$$

with similar expressions for y and z. Once more, the denominator comes from the determinant of the matrix associated with the matrix formulation of the linear equations:

$$\begin{bmatrix} d_1 \\ d_2 \\ d_3 \end{bmatrix} = \begin{bmatrix} a_1 & b_1 & c_1 \\ a_2 & b_2 & c_2 \\ a_3 & b_3 & c_3 \end{bmatrix} \begin{bmatrix} x \\ y \\ z \end{bmatrix}$$

where

$$\begin{vmatrix} a_1 & b_1 & c_1 \\ a_2 & b_2 & c_2 \\ a_3 & b_3 & c_3 \end{vmatrix} = a_1 b_2 c_3 - a_1 b_3 c_2 + a_2 b_3 c_1 - a_2 b_1 c_3 + a_3 b_1 c_2 - a_3 b_2 c_1$$

which can be written as

$$a_1 \begin{vmatrix} b_2 & c_2 \\ b_3 & c_3 \end{vmatrix} - a_2 \begin{vmatrix} b_1 & c_1 \\ b_3 & c_3 \end{vmatrix} + a_3 \begin{vmatrix} b_1 & c_1 \\ b_2 & c_2 \end{vmatrix}.$$

Let's now see what creates a zero determinant. If we write, for example

$$10 = 2x + y$$

there are an infinite number of solutions for x and y, and it is impossible to solve the equation. However, if we introduce a second equation relating x and y:

$$4 = 5x - y$$

we can solve for x and y using (7.5) and (7.6):

$$x = \frac{10 \times (-1) - 4 \times 1}{2 \times (-1) - 5 \times 1} = \frac{-14}{-7} = 2$$
$$y = \frac{2 \times 4 - 5 \times 10}{2 \times (-1) - 5 \times 1} = \frac{-42}{-7} = 6$$

therefore $x = 2$ and $y = 6$, which is correct.

But say the second equation had been

$$20 = 4x + 2y$$

which creates a pair of simultaneous equations:

$$10 = 2x + y \tag{7.7}$$
$$20 = 4x + 2y. \tag{7.8}$$

If we now solve for x and y we get

$$x = \frac{10 \times 2 - 20 \times 1}{2 \times 2 - 4 \times 1} = \frac{0}{0} = \text{undefined}$$
$$y = \frac{2 \times 20 - 4 \times 10}{2 \times 2 - 4 \times 1} = \frac{0}{0} = \text{undefined}$$

which yields undefined results. The reason for this is that (7.7) is the same as (7.8) – the second equation is nothing more than twice the first equation, and therefore brings nothing new to the relationship. When this occurs, the equations are called *linearly dependent*.

Having shown the algebraic origins of the determinant, let us investigate their graphical significance. Consider the transform

$$\begin{bmatrix} x' \\ y' \end{bmatrix} = \begin{bmatrix} a & b \\ c & d \end{bmatrix} \begin{bmatrix} x \\ y \end{bmatrix}.$$

The determinant of the transform is $ad - cb$. If we subject the vertices of a unit-square to this transform, we create the situation shown in Fig. 7.31. The vertices of the unit-square are transformed as follows:

$$(0,0) \Rightarrow (0,0)$$
$$(1,0) \Rightarrow (a,c)$$
$$(1,1) \Rightarrow (a+b,c+d)$$
$$(0,1) \Rightarrow (b,d).$$

From Fig. 7.31 it can be seen that the area of the transformed unit-square A' is given by

$$area = (a+b)(c+d) - B - C - D - E - F - G$$
$$= ac + ad + cb + bd - \frac{1}{2}bd - cb - \frac{1}{2}ac - \frac{1}{2}bd - cb - \frac{1}{2}ac$$
$$= ad - cb$$

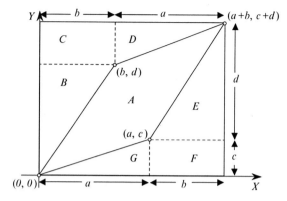

Fig. 7.31 The inner parallelogram is the transformed unit square.

which is the determinant of the transform. But as the area of the original unit-square is 1, the determinant of the transform controls the scaling factor applied to the transformed shape.

Let's examine the determinants of two transforms. The first 2D transform encodes a scaling of 2, and results in an overall area scaling of 4:

$$\begin{bmatrix} 2 & 0 \\ 0 & 2 \end{bmatrix}$$

and the determinant is

$$\begin{vmatrix} 2 & 0 \\ 0 & 2 \end{vmatrix} = 4.$$

The second 2D transform encodes a scaling of 3 and a translation of $(3,3)$, and results in an overall area scaling of 9:

$$\begin{bmatrix} 3 & 0 & 3 \\ 0 & 3 & 3 \\ 0 & 0 & 1 \end{bmatrix}$$

and the determinant is

$$3\begin{vmatrix} 3 & 3 \\ 0 & 1 \end{vmatrix} - 0\begin{vmatrix} 0 & 3 \\ 0 & 1 \end{vmatrix} + 0\begin{vmatrix} 0 & 3 \\ 3 & 3 \end{vmatrix} = 9.$$

These two examples demonstrate the extra role played by the elements of a matrix.

7.11 Perspective Projection

Of all the projections employed in computer graphics, the *perspective projection* is one most widely used. There are two stages to its computation: the first stage involves converting world coordinates to the camera's frame of reference, and the second stage transforms camera coordinates to the projection plane coordinates. We have already looked at the transforms for locating a camera in world space, and the inverse transform for converting world coordinates to the camera's frame of reference. Let's now investigate how these camera coordinates are transformed into a perspective projection.

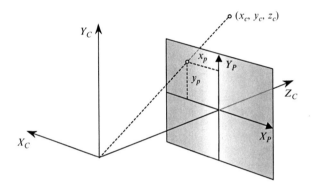

Fig. 7.32 The axial system used to produce a perspective view.

We begin by assuming that the camera is directed along the z-axis as shown in Fig. 7.32. Positioned d units along the z-axis is a projection screen, which is used to capture a perspective projection of an object. Figure 7.32 shows that any point (x_c, y_c, z_c) becomes transformed to (x_p, y_p, d). It also shows that the screen's x-axis is pointing in the opposite direction to the camera's x-axis, which can be compensated for by reversing the sign of x_p when it is computed.

Figure 7.33 shows a plan view of the scenario depicted in Fig. 7.32, and Fig. 7.34 a side view, which permits us to inspect the geometry and make the following observations:

$$\frac{x_c}{z_c} = \frac{-x_p}{d}$$
$$x_p = \frac{-x_c}{z_c/d}$$

and

$$\frac{y_c}{z_c} = \frac{y_p}{d}$$
$$y_p = \frac{y_c}{z_c/d}.$$

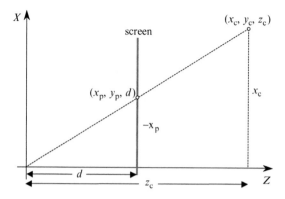

Fig. 7.33 The plan view of the camera's axial system.

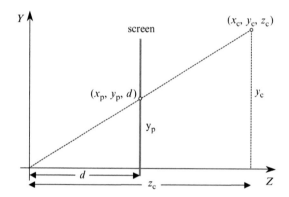

Fig. 7.34 The side view of the camera's axial system.

This can be expressed in matrix form as

$$
\begin{bmatrix} x_p \\ y_p \\ z_p \\ w \end{bmatrix} = \begin{bmatrix} -1 & 0 & 0 & 0 \\ 0 & 1 & 0 & 0 \\ 0 & 0 & 1 & 0 \\ 0 & 0 & 1/d & 0 \end{bmatrix} \begin{bmatrix} x_c \\ y_c \\ z_c \\ 1 \end{bmatrix}.
$$

At first the transform seems strange, but if we multiply this out we get

$$
\begin{bmatrix} x_p & y_p & z_p & w \end{bmatrix}^T = \begin{bmatrix} -x_c & y_c & z_c & z_c/d \end{bmatrix}^T
$$

and if we remember the idea behind homogeneous coordinates, we must divide the terms x_p, y_p, z_p by w to get the scaled terms, which produces

$$
x_p = \frac{-x_c}{z_c/d}
$$

$$y_p = \frac{y_c}{z_c/d}$$

$$z_p = \frac{z_c}{z_c/d} = d$$

which, after all, is rather elegant. Notice that this transform takes into account the sign change that occurs with the x-coordinate. Some books will leave this sign reversal until the mapping is made to screen coordinates.

7.12 Summary

The purpose of this chapter was to introduce the reader to transforms and matrices – I hope this has been achieved. This end of the chapter, is not really the end of the subject, as one can do so much with matrices and quaternions. For example, it would be interesting to see how a matrix behaves when some of its elements are changed dynamically, and what happens when we interpolate between a pair of quaternions. Such topics will be addressed in later chapters.

Chapter 8
Interpolation

8.1 Introduction

Interpolation is not a branch of mathematics but rather a collection of techniques the reader will find useful when solving computer graphics problems. Basically, an *interpolant* is a way of changing one number into another. For example, to change 2 into 4 we simply add 2, which is not very useful. The real function of an interpolant is to change one number into another in, perhaps, 10 equal steps. Thus if we start with 2 and repeatedly added 0.2, it would generate the sequence 2.0, 2.2, 2.4, 2.6, 2.8, 3.0, 3.2, 3.4, 3.6, 3.8, and 4. These numbers could then be used to translate, scale, rotate an object, move a virtual camera, or change the position, color or brightness of a virtual light source.

In order to repeat the above interpolant for different numbers we require a formula, which is one of the first exercises of this chapter. We also need to explore ways of controlling the spacing between the interpolated values. In animation, for example, we often need to move an object very slowly and gradually increase its speed. Conversely, we may want to bring an object to a halt, making its speed less and less.

We start with the simplest of all interpolants: the linear interpolant.

8.2 Linear Interpolation

A *linear interpolant* generates equal spacing between the interpolated values for equal changes in the interpolating parameter. In the introductory example the increment 0.2 is calculated by subtracting the first number from the second and dividing the result by 10, i.e., $(4-2)/10 = 0.2$. Although this works, it is not in a very flexible form, so let's express the problem differently. Given two numbers n_1 and n_2, which represent the start and final values of the interpolant, we require an interpolated value controlled by a parameter t that varies between 0 and 1. When $t = 0$, the result is n_1, and when $t = 1$, the result is n_2. A solution to this problem is given by

J. Vince, *Mathematics for Computer Graphics*, Undergraduate Topics in Computer Science, DOI 10.1007/978-1-84996-023-6_8,

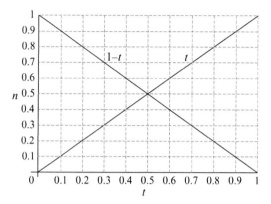

Fig. 8.1 The graphs of $(1-t)$ and t over the range 0 to 1.

$$n = n_1 + t(n_2 - n_1)$$

for when $n_1 = 2$, $n_2 = 4$ and $t = 0.5$:

$$n = 2 + \frac{1}{2}(4 - 2) = 3$$

which is a halfway point. Furthermore, when $t = 0$, $n = n_1$, and when $t = 1$, $n = n_2$, which confirms that we have a sound interpolant. However, it can be expressed differently:

$$n = n_1(1 - t) + n_2 t \tag{8.1}$$

which shows what is really going on, and forms the basis for further development. Figure 8.1 shows the graphs of $(1-t)$ and t over the range 0 to 1. With reference to (8.1), we see that as t changes from 0 to 1, the $(1-t)$ term varies from 1 to 0. This effectively attenuates the value of n_1 to zero over the range of t, while the t term scales n_2 from zero to its actual value. Figure 8.2 illustrates these two actions with $n_1 = 1$ and $n_2 = 5$.

Notice that the terms $(1-t)$ and t sum to unity; this is not a coincidence. This type of interpolant ensures that if it takes a quarter of n_1, it balances it with three-quarters of n_2, and vice versa. Obviously we could design an interpolant that takes arbitrary portions of n_1 and n_2, but that would lead to arbitrary results.

Although this interpolant is extremely simple, it is widely used in computer graphics software. Just to put it into context, consider the task of moving an object between two locations (x_1, y_1, z_1) and (x_2, y_2, z_2). The interpolated position is given by

$$x = x_1(1 - t) + x_2 t$$
$$y = y_1(1 - t) + y_2 t$$
$$z = z_1(1 - t) + z_2 t$$

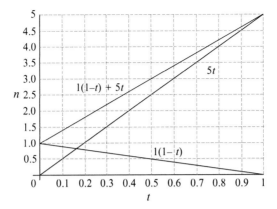

Fig. 8.2 The top line shows the result of linearly interpolating between 1 and 5.

for $0 \le t \le 1$. The parameter t could be generated from two frame values within an animation. What is assured by this interpolant, is that equal steps in t result in equal steps in x, y, and z. Figure 8.3 illustrates this linear spacing with a 2D example where we interpolate between the points $(1, 1)$ and $(4, 5)$. Note the equal spacing between the intermediate interpolated points.

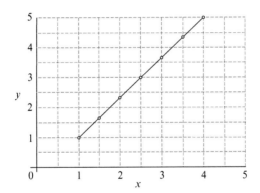

Fig. 8.3 Interpolating between the points $(1, 1)$ and $(4, 5)$.

We can write (8.1) in matrix form as follows:

$$n = \begin{bmatrix} (1-t) & t \end{bmatrix} \begin{bmatrix} n_1 \\ n_2 \end{bmatrix}$$

or as

$$n = \begin{bmatrix} t & 1 \end{bmatrix} \begin{bmatrix} -1 & 1 \\ 1 & 0 \end{bmatrix} \begin{bmatrix} n_1 \\ n_2 \end{bmatrix}.$$

The reader can confirm that this generates identical results to the algebraic form.

8.3 Non-Linear Interpolation

A linear interpolant ensures that equal steps in the parameter t give rise to equal steps in the interpolated values; but it is often required that equal steps in t give rise to unequal steps in the interpolated values. We can achieve this using a variety of mathematical techniques. For example, we could use trigonometric functions or polynomials. To begin with, let's look at a trigonometric solution.

8.3.1 Trigonometric Interpolation

In Chapter 4 we noted that $\sin^2 \beta + \cos^2 \beta = 1$, which satisfies one of the requirements of an interpolant: the terms must sum to 1. If β varies between 0 and $\pi/2$, $\cos^2 \beta$ varies between 1 and 0, and $\sin^2 \beta$ varies between 0 and 1, which can be used to modify the two interpolated values n_1 and n_2 as follows:

$$n = n_1 \cos^2 t + n_2 \sin^2 t \qquad [0 \leq t \leq \pi/2]. \qquad (8.2)$$

The interpolation curves are shown in Fig. 8.4.

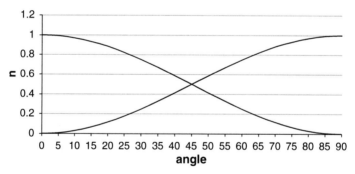

Fig. 8.4 The curves for $\cos^2 \beta$ and $\sin^2 \beta$.

If we make $n_1 = 1$ and $n_2 = 3$ in (8.2), we obtain the curves shown in Fig. 8.5. If we apply this interpolant to two 2D points in space, $(1, 1)$ and $(4, 3)$, we obtain a straight-line interpolation, but the distribution of points is non-linear, as shown in Fig. 8.6. In other words, equal steps in t give rise to unequal distances.

The main problem with this approach is that it is impossible to change the nature of the curve – it is a *sinusoid*, and its slope is determined by the interpolated values. One way of gaining control over the interpolated curve is to use a *polynomial*, which is the subject of the next section.

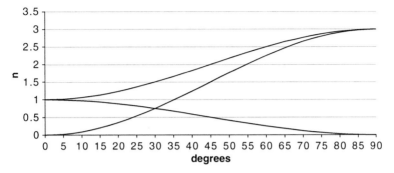

Fig. 8.5 Interpolating between 1 and 3 using a trigonometric interpolant.

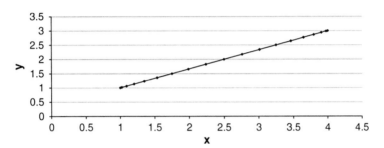

Fig. 8.6 Interpolating between two points $(1,1)$ and $(4,3)$. Note the non-linear distribution of points.

8.3.2 Cubic Interpolation

To begin with, let's develop a cubic blending function that will be similar to the previous sinusoidal one. This can then be extended to provide extra flexibility. A *cubic polynomial* will form the basis of the interpolant:

$$v_1 = at^3 + bt^2 + ct + d$$

and the final interpolant will be of the form

$$n = \begin{bmatrix} v_1 & v_2 \end{bmatrix} \begin{bmatrix} n_1 \\ n_2 \end{bmatrix}.$$

The task is to find the values of the constants associated with the polynomials v_1 and v_2. The requirements are:

1. The cubic function v_2 must grow from 0 to 1 for $0 \leq t \leq 1$.
2. The slope at a point t must equal the slope at the point $(1-t)$. This ensures slope symmetry over the range of the function.

3. The value v_2 at any point t must also produce $(1 - v_2)$ at $(1 - t)$. This ensures curve symmetry.
- To satisfy the first requirement:

$$v_2 = at^3 + bt^2 + ct + d$$

and when $t = 0$, $v_2 = 0$ and $d = 0$. Similarly, when $t = 1$, $v_2 = a + b + c$.
- To satisfy the second requirement, we differentiate v_2 to obtain the slope

$$\frac{dv_2}{dt} = 3at^2 + 2bt + c = 3a(1 - t)^2 + 2b(1 - t) + c$$

and equating constants we discover $c = 0$ and $0 = 3a + 2b$.
- To satisfy the third requirement:

$$at^3 + bt^2 = 1 - [a(1 - t)^3 + b(1 - t)^2]$$

where we discover $1 = a + b$. But $0 = 3a + 2b$, therefore $a = 2$ and $b = 3$.
Therefore,

$$v_2 = -2t^3 + 3t^2. \tag{8.3}$$

To find the curve's mirror curve, which starts at 1 and collapses to 0 as t moves from 0 to 1, we subtract (8.3) from 1:

$$v_1 = 2t^3 - 3t^2 + 1.$$

Therefore, the two polynomials are

$$v_1 = 2t^3 - 3t^2 + 1 \tag{8.4}$$

$$v_2 = -2t^3 + 3t^2 \tag{8.5}$$

and are shown in Fig. 8.7. They can be used as interpolants as follows:

$$n = v_1 n_1 + v_2 n_2$$

which in matrix form is

$$n = [2t^3 - 3t^2 + 1 \quad -2t^3 + 3t^2] \begin{bmatrix} n_1 \\ n_2 \end{bmatrix}$$

$$n = [t^3 \quad t^2 \quad t \quad 1] \begin{bmatrix} 2 & -2 \\ -3 & 3 \\ 0 & 0 \\ 1 & 0 \end{bmatrix} \begin{bmatrix} n_1 \\ n_2 \end{bmatrix}. \tag{8.6}$$

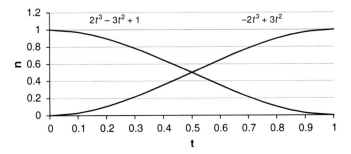

Fig. 8.7 Two cubic interpolants.

If we let $n_1 = 1$ and $n_2 = 3$ we obtain the curves shown in Fig. 8.8. And if we apply the interpolant to the points $(1,1)$ and $(4,3)$ we obtain the curves shown in Fig. 8.9. This interpolant can be used to blend any pair of numbers together. But say we wished to associate other qualities with the numbers n_1 and n_2, such as their tangent vectors s_1 and s_2. Perhaps we could interpolate these alongside n_1 and n_2. In fact this can be done, as we shall see.

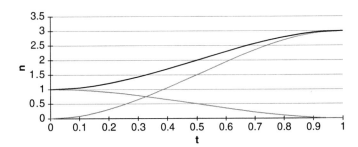

Fig. 8.8 Interpolating between 1 and 3 using a cubic interpolant.

The requirement is to modulate the interpolating curve in Fig. 8.8 with two further cubic curves. One that blends out the tangent vector s_1 associated with n_1, and the other that blends in the tangent vector s_2 associated with n_2. Let's begin with a cubic polynomial to blend s_1 to zero:

$$v_{out} = at^3 + bt^2 + ct + d.$$

v_{out} must equal zero when $t = 0$ and $t = 1$, otherwise it will disturb the start and end values. Therefore $d = 0$, and

$$a + b + c = 0.$$

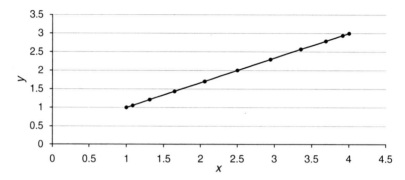

Fig. 8.9 A cubic interpolant between points $(1,1)$ and $(4,3)$.

The rate of change of v_{out} relative to t (i.e., $\frac{dv_{out}}{dt}$) must equal 1 when $t = 0$, so it can be used to multiply s_1. When $t = 1$, $\frac{dv_{out}}{dt}$ must equal 0 to attenuate any trace of s_1:

$$\frac{dv_{out}}{dt} = 3at^2 + 2bt + c$$

but $\frac{dv_{out}}{dt} = 1$ when $t = 0$, and $\frac{dv_{out}}{dt} = 0$ when $t = 1$. Therefore, $c = 1$, and

$$3a + 2b + 1 = 0.$$

Using (8.6) implies that $b = -2$ and $a = 1$. Therefore, the polynomial v_{out} has the form

$$v_{out} = t^3 - 2t^2 + t. \tag{8.7}$$

Using a similar argument, one can prove that the function to blend in s_2 equals

$$v_{in} = t^3 - t^2. \tag{8.8}$$

Graphs of (8.4), (8.5), (8.6) and (8.7) are shown in Fig. 8.10. The complete interpolating function looks like

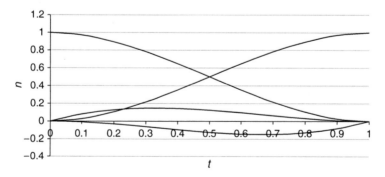

Fig. 8.10 The four Hermite interpolating curves.

$$n = [2t^3 - 3t^2 + 1 \quad -2t^3 + 3t^2 \quad t^3 - 2t^2 + t \quad t^3 - t^2] \begin{bmatrix} n_1 \\ n_2 \\ s_1 \\ s_2 \end{bmatrix}$$

and unpacking the constants and polynomial terms we obtain

$$n = [t^3 \quad t^2 \quad t^1 \quad 1] \begin{bmatrix} 2 & -2 & 1 & 1 \\ -3 & 3 & -2 & -1 \\ 0 & 0 & 1 & 0 \\ 1 & 0 & 0 & 0 \end{bmatrix} \begin{bmatrix} n_1 \\ n_2 \\ s_1 \\ s_2 \end{bmatrix}.$$

This type of interpolation is called *Hermite interpolation*, after the French mathematician Charles Hermite (1822–1901). Hermite also proved in 1873 that e is transcendental.

This interpolant can be used as shown above to blend a pair of numerical values and their tangent vectors, or it can be used to interpolate between points in space. To demonstrate the latter we will explore a 2D example, and it is very easy to implement the technique in 3D.

Figure 8.11 shows how two points $(0,0)$ and $(1,1)$ are to be connected by a cubic curve that responds to the initial and final tangent vectors. At the start point $(0,1)$ the tangent vector is $[-5 \quad 0]^T$, and at the final point $(1,1)$ the tangent vector is $[0 \quad -5]^T$. The x and y interpolants are

$$x = [t^3 \quad t^2 \quad t^1 \quad 1] \begin{bmatrix} 2 & -2 & 1 & 1 \\ -3 & 3 & -2 & -1 \\ 0 & 0 & 1 & 0 \\ 1 & 0 & 0 & 0 \end{bmatrix} \begin{bmatrix} 0 \\ 1 \\ -5 \\ 0 \end{bmatrix}$$

$$y = [t^3 \quad t^2 \quad t^1 \quad 1] \begin{bmatrix} 2 & -2 & 1 & 1 \\ -3 & 3 & -2 & -1 \\ 0 & 0 & 1 & 0 \\ 1 & 0 & 0 & 0 \end{bmatrix} \begin{bmatrix} 0 \\ 1 \\ 0 \\ -5 \end{bmatrix}$$

which become

$$x = [t^3 \quad t^2 \quad t^1 \quad 1] \begin{bmatrix} -7 \\ 13 \\ -5 \\ 0 \end{bmatrix} = -7t^3 + 13t^2 - 5t$$

$$y = \begin{bmatrix} t^3 & t^2 & t^1 & 1 \end{bmatrix} \begin{bmatrix} -7 \\ 8 \\ 0 \\ 0 \end{bmatrix} = -7t^3 + 8t^2.$$

When these polynomials are plotted over the range $0 \le t \le 1$ we obtain the curve shown in Fig. 8.11.

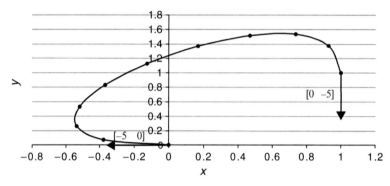

Fig. 8.11 A Hermite curve between the points $(0,0)$ and $(1,1)$ with tangent vectors $\begin{bmatrix} -5 & 0 \end{bmatrix}^T$ and $\begin{bmatrix} 0 & -5 \end{bmatrix}^T$.

We have now reached a point where we are starting to discover how parametric polynomials can be used to generate space curves, which is the subject of the next chapter. So, to conclude this chapter on interpolants, we will take a look at interpolating vectors.

8.4 Interpolating Vectors

So far we have been interpolating between a pair of numbers. Now the question arises: can we use the same interpolants for vectors? Perhaps not, because a vector contains both magnitude and direction, and when we interpolate between two vectors, both quantities must be preserved. For example, if we interpolated the x- and y-components of the vectors $\begin{bmatrix} 2 & 3 \end{bmatrix}^T$ and $\begin{bmatrix} 4 & 7 \end{bmatrix}^T$, the in-between vectors would carry the change of orientation but ignore the change in magnitude. To preserve both, we must understand how the interpolation should operate.

Figure 8.12 shows two unit vectors $\mathbf{v}_1$ and $\mathbf{v}_2$ separated by an angle θ. The interpolated vector $\mathbf{v}$ can be defined as a proportion of $\mathbf{v}_1$ and a proportion of $\mathbf{v}_2$:

$$\mathbf{v} = a\mathbf{v}_1 + b\mathbf{v}_2.$$

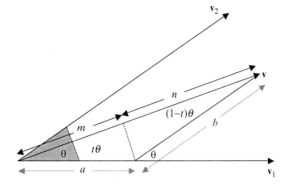

Fig. 8.12 Vector $\mathbf{v}$ is derived from a part of $\mathbf{v}_1$ and b part of $\mathbf{v}_2$.

Let's define the values of a and b such that they are a function of the separating angle θ. Vector $\mathbf{v}$ is $t\theta$ from $\mathbf{v}_1$ and $(1-t)\theta$ from $\mathbf{v}_2$, and it is evident from Fig. 8.12 that using the sine rule

$$\frac{a}{\sin(1-t)\theta} = \frac{b}{\sin t\theta} \qquad (8.9)$$

and furthermore

$$m = a\cos t\theta$$
$$n = b\cos(1-t)\theta$$

where

$$m+n = 1. \qquad (8.10)$$

From (8.9),

$$b = \frac{a\sin t\theta}{\sin(1-t)\theta}$$

and from (8.10) we get

$$a\cos\theta + \frac{a\sin t\theta\cos(1-t)\theta}{\sin(1-t)\theta} = 1.$$

Solving for a we find

$$a = \frac{\sin(1-t)\theta}{\sin\theta}$$
$$b = \frac{\sin t\theta}{\sin\theta}.$$

Therefore, the final interpolant is

$$\mathbf{v} = \frac{\sin(1-t)\theta}{\sin\theta}\mathbf{v}_1 + \frac{\sin t\theta}{\sin\theta}\mathbf{v}_2. \qquad (8.11)$$

To see how this operates, let's consider a simple exercise of interpolating between two unit vectors $[1 \quad 0]^T$ and $[-\frac{1}{\sqrt{2}} \quad \frac{1}{\sqrt{2}}]^T$. The angle between the vectors θ is 135°. (8.11) is used to interpolate individually the x- and the y-components individually:

$$v_x = \frac{\sin(1-t)135°}{\sin 135°} \times (1) + \frac{\sin t135°}{\sin 135°} \times \left(-\frac{1}{\sqrt{2}}\right)$$

$$v_y = \frac{\sin(1-t)135°}{\sin 135°} \times (0) + \frac{\sin t135°}{\sin 135°} \times \left(\frac{1}{\sqrt{2}}\right).$$

Figure 8.13 shows the interpolating curves and Fig. 8.14 shows the positions of the interpolated vectors, and a trace of the interpolated vectors.

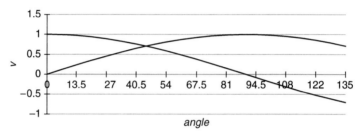

Fig. 8.13 Curves of the two parts of (8.11).

Two observations to note with (8.11):

- The angle θ is the angle between the two vectors, which, if not known, can be computed using the dot product.
- Secondly, the range of θ is given by $0 \leq \theta \leq 180°$, but when $\theta = 180°$ the denominator collapses to zero. To illustrate this we will repeat (8.11) for $\theta = 179°$.

The result is shown in Fig. 8.15, which reveals clearly that the interpolant works normally over this range. One more degree, however, and it fails! Nevertheless, one could still leave the range equal to $180°$ and test for the conditions $t = 0$ then $\mathbf{v} = \mathbf{v}_1$ and when $t = 180°$ then $\mathbf{v} = \mathbf{v}_2$.

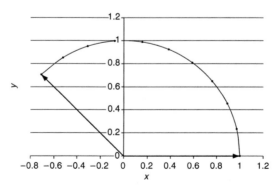

Fig. 8.14 A trace of the interpolated vectors between $[1 \quad 0]^T$ and $[-\frac{1}{\sqrt{2}} \quad \frac{1}{\sqrt{2}}]^T$.

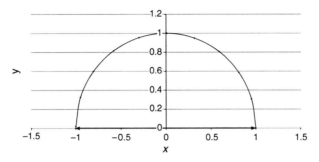

Fig. 8.15 Interpolating between two unit vectors 179° apart.

So far, we have only considered unit vectors. Now let's see how the interpolant responds to vectors of different magnitudes. As a test, we can input the following vectors to (8.11):

$$\mathbf{v}_1 = \begin{bmatrix} 2 \\ 0 \end{bmatrix} \quad \text{and} \quad \mathbf{v}_2 = \begin{bmatrix} 0 \\ 1 \end{bmatrix}.$$

The separating angle $\theta = 90°$, and the result is shown in Fig. 8.16. Note how the initial length of $\mathbf{v}_1$ reduces from 2 to 1 over 90°. It is left to the reader to examine other combinations of vectors. But there is one more application for this interpolant, and that is with quaternions.

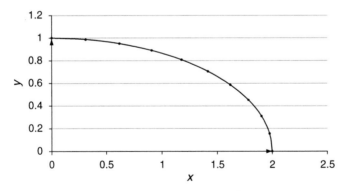

Fig. 8.16 Interpolating between the vectors $[2 \quad 0]^T$ and $[0 \quad 1]^T$.

8.5 Interpolating Quaternions

It just so happens that the interpolant used for vectors also works with quaternions. Which means that, given two quaternions $\mathbf{q}_1$ and $\mathbf{q}_2$, the interpolated quaternion $\mathbf{q}$ is given by

$$q = \frac{\sin(1-t)\theta}{\sin\theta}q_1 + \frac{\sin t\theta}{\sin\theta}q_2. \tag{8.12}$$

The interpolant is applied individually to the four terms of the quaternion.

When interpolating vectors, θ is the angle between the two vectors. If this is not known, it can be derived using the dot product formula:

$$\cos\theta = \frac{v_1 \cdot v_2}{|v_1||v_2|}$$

$$\cos\theta = \frac{x_1 x_2 + y_1 y_2 + z_1 z_2}{|v_1||v_2|}.$$

Similarly, when interpolating quaternions, θ is computed by taking the 4D dot product of the two quaternions:

$$\cos\theta = \frac{q_1 \cdot q_2}{|q_1||q_2|}$$

$$\cos\theta = \frac{s_1 s_2 + x_1 x_2 + y_1 y_2 + z_1 z_2}{|q_1||q_2|}.$$

If we are using unit quaternions

$$\cos\theta = s_1 s_2 + x_1 x_2 + y_1 y_2 + z_1 z_2. \tag{8.13}$$

We are now in a position to demonstrate how to interpolate between a pair of quaternions. For example, say we have two quaternions q_1 and q_2 that rotate $0°$ and $90°$ about the z-axis respectively:

$$q_1 = [\cos(0°/2) + \sin(0°/2)[0i + 0j + 1k]]$$
$$q_2 = [\cos(90°/2) + \sin(90°/2)[0i + 0j + 1k]]$$

which become

$$q_1 = [1 + 0i + 0j + 0k]$$
$$q_2 \approx [0.7071 + 0i + 0j + 0.7071k].$$

Any interpolated quaternion can be found by the application of (8.12). But first, we need to find the value of θ using (8.13):

$$\cos\theta \approx 0.7071$$
$$\theta = 45°.$$

Now when $t = 0.5$, the interpolated quaternion is given by

$$q \approx \frac{\sin(45°/2)}{\sin 45°}[1 + 0i + 0j + 0k] + \frac{\sin(45°/2)}{\sin 45°}[0.7071 + 0i + 0j + 0.7071k]$$
$$\approx 0.541196[1 + 0i + 0j + 0k] + 0.541196[0.7071 + 0i + 0j + 0.7071k]$$
$$\approx [0.541196 + 0i + 0j + 0k] + [0.382683 + 0i + 0j + 0.382683k]$$
$$\approx [0.923879 + 0i + 0j + 0.382683k].$$

Although it is not obvious, this interpolated quaternion is also a unit quaternion, as the square root of the sum of the squares is 1. It should rotate a point about the z-axis, halfway between $0°$ and $90°$, i.e., $45°$. We can test that this works with a simple example.

Take the point $(1,0,0)$ and subject it to the standard quaternion operation:

$$\mathbf{P}' = \mathbf{q}\mathbf{P}\mathbf{q}^{-1}.$$

To keep the arithmetic work to a minimum, we substitute $a = 0.923879$ and $b = 0.382683$. Therefore,

$$\mathbf{q} = [a + 0\mathbf{i} + 0\mathbf{j} + b\mathbf{k}]$$
$$\mathbf{q}^{-1} = [a - 0\mathbf{i} - 0\mathbf{j} - b\mathbf{k}]$$
$$\mathbf{P}' = [a + 0\mathbf{i} + 0\mathbf{j} + b\mathbf{k}] \times [0 + 1\mathbf{i} + 0\mathbf{j} + 0\mathbf{k}] \times [a - 0\mathbf{i} - 0\mathbf{j} - b\mathbf{k}]$$
$$= [0 + a\mathbf{i} + b\mathbf{j} + 0\mathbf{k}] \times [a - 0\mathbf{i} - 0\mathbf{j} - b\mathbf{k}]$$
$$= [0 + (a^2 - b^2)\mathbf{i} + 2ab\mathbf{j} + 0\mathbf{k}]$$
$$\mathbf{P}' \approx [0 + 0.7071\mathbf{i} + 0.7071\mathbf{j} + 0\mathbf{k}].$$

Therefore, $(1,0,0)$ is rotated to $(0.7071, 0.7071, 0)$, which is correct!

8.6 Summary

This chapter has covered some very interesting, yet simple ideas about changing one number into another. In the following chapter we will develop these ideas and see how we design algebraic solutions to curves and surfaces.

Chapter 9
Curves and Patches

9.1 Introduction

In this chapter we investigate the foundations of curves and surface patches. This is a very large and complex subject and it will be impossible for us to delve too deeply. However, we can explore many of the ideas that are essential to understanding the mathematics behind 2D and 3D curves and how they are developed to produce surface patches. Once you have understood these ideas you will be able to read more advanced texts and develop a wider knowledge of the subject.

In the previous chapter we saw how polynomials are used as interpolants and blending functions. We will now see how these can form the basis of parametric curves and patches. To begin with, let's start with the humble circle.

9.2 The Circle

The circle has a very simple equation:

$$x^2 + y^2 = r^2$$

where r is the radius and (x, y) is a point on the circumference. Although this equation has its uses, it is not very convenient for drawing the curve. What we really want are two functions that generate the coordinates of any point on the circumference in terms of some parameter t. Figure 9.1 shows a scenario where the x- and y-coordinates are given by

$$x = r\cos t$$
$$y = r\sin t \qquad [\,0 \le t \le 2\pi\,].$$

By varying the parameter t over the range 0 to 2π we trace out the curve of the circumference. In fact, by selecting a suitable range of t we can isolate any portion of the circle's circumference.

J. Vince, *Mathematics for Computer Graphics*, Undergraduate Topics in Computer Science, DOI 10.1007/978-1-84996-023-6_9,
© Springer-Verlag London Limited 2010

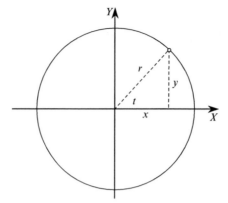

Fig. 9.1 The circle can be drawn by tracing out a series of points on the circumference.

9.3 The Ellipse

The equation for an ellipse is

$$\frac{x^2}{r_{maj}^2} + \frac{y^2}{r_{min}^2} = 1$$

and its parametric form is

$$x = r_{maj} \cos t$$
$$y = r_{min} \sin t \qquad [\, 0 \leq t \leq 2\pi \,]$$

where r_{maj} and r_{min} are the major and minor radii respectively, and (x, y) is a point on the circumference, as shown in Fig. 9.2.

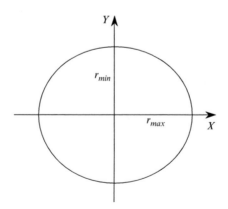

Fig. 9.2 An ellipse showing the major and minor radii.

In the previous chapter we saw how a Hermite curve could be developed using cubic polynomials and tangent slope vectors:

$$n = \begin{bmatrix} t^3 & t^2 & t^1 & 1 \end{bmatrix} \begin{bmatrix} 2 & -2 & 1 & 1 \\ -3 & 3 & -2 & -1 \\ 0 & 0 & 1 & 0 \\ 1 & 0 & 0 & 0 \end{bmatrix} \begin{bmatrix} n_1 \\ n_2 \\ s_1 \\ s_2 \end{bmatrix}$$

which give the x- and y-coordinates for a 2D curve, and there is no reason why it can not be extended to give the z-coordinate for a 3D curve. The tangent slope vectors would also have to be modified to form the end conditions in three dimensions.

We will now examine a very useful parametric curve called a Bézier curve, named after its inventor Pierre Bézier.

9.4 Bézier Curves

Two people, working for competing French car manufacturers, are associated with what are now called *Bézier curves*: Paul de Casteljau, who worked for Citröen, and Pierre Bézier, who worked for Rénault. De Casteljau's work was slightly ahead of Bézier's, but because of Citröen's policy of secrecy it was never published, so Bézier's name has since been associated with the theory of polynomial curves and surfaces. Casteljau started his research work in 1959, but his reports were only discovered in 1975, by which time Bézier had become known for his special curves and surfaces.

9.4.1 Bernstein Polynomials

Bézier curves employ *Bernstein polynomials*, which were described by S. Bernstein in 1912. They are expressed as follows:

$$B_i^n(t) = \binom{n}{i} t^i (1-t)^{n-1} \tag{9.1}$$

where $\binom{n}{i}$ is shorthand for the number of selections of i different items from n distinguishable items when the order of selection is ignored, and equals

$$\binom{n}{i} = \frac{n!}{(n-i)!i!} \tag{9.2}$$

where, for example, 3! (factorial 3) is shorthand for $3 \times 2 \times 1$. When (9.2) is evaluated for different values of i and n, we discover the pattern of numbers shown in Table 9.1. This pattern of numbers is known as *Pascal's triangle*. In western countries they are named after a seventeenth century French mathematician, even though they had been described in China as early as 1303 in *Precious Mirror of the Four Elements* by the Chinese mathematician Chu Shih-chieh. The pattern represents the coefficients found in binomial expansions. For example, the expansion of $(x+a)^n$ for different values of n is

$$(x+a)^0 = 1$$
$$(x+a)^1 = 1x + 1a$$
$$(x+a)^2 = 1x^2 + 2ax + 1a^2$$
$$(x+a)^3 = 1x^3 + 3ax^2 + 3a^2x + 1a^3$$
$$(x+a)^4 = 1x^4 + 4ax^3 + 6a^2x^2 + 4a^3x + 1a^4$$

which reveals Pascal's triangle as coefficients of the polynomial terms.

Table 9.1 Pascal's triangle

		i					
n	0	1	2	3	4	5	6
0	1						
1	1	1					
2	1	2	1				
3	1	3	3	1			
4	1	4	6	4	1		
5	1	5	10	10	5	1	
6	1	6	15	20	15	6	1

Pascal, however, recognized other qualities in the numbers, in that they describe the odds governing combinations. For example, to determine the probability of any girl–boy combination in a family of six children, we sum the numbers in the 6th row of Pascal's triangle:

$$1 + 6 + 15 + 20 + 15 + 6 + 1 = 64.$$

The number (1) at the start and end of the 6th row represent the chances of getting six boys or six girls, i.e., 1 in 64. The next number (6) represents the next most likely combination: five boys and one girl, or five girls and one boy, i.e., 6 in 64. The center number (20) applies to three boys and three girls, for which the chances are 20 in 64.

Thus the $\binom{n}{i}$ term in (9.1) is nothing more than a generator for Pascal's triangle. The powers of t and $(1-t)$ in (9.1) appear as shown in Table 9.2 for different values of n and i. When the two sets of results are combined we get the complete Bernstein polynomial terms shown in Table 9.3. One very important property of these terms is that they sum to unity, which is an important feature of any interpolant.

Table 9.2 Expansion of the terms t and $(1-t)$

			i		
n	0	1	2	3	4
1	t	$(1-t)$			
2	t^2	$t(1-t)$	$(1-t)^2$		
3	t^3	$t^2(1-t)$	$t(1-t)^2$	$(1-t)^3$	
4	t^4	$t^3(1-t)$	$t^2(1-t)^2$	$t(1-t)^3$	$(1-t)^4$

Table 9.3 The Bernstein polynomial terms

			i		
n	0	1	2	3	4
1	$1t$	$1(1-t)$			
2	$1t^2$	$2t(1-t)$	$1(1-t)^2$		
3	$1t^3$	$3t^2(1-t)$	$3t(1-t)^2$	$1(1-t)^3$	
4	$1t^4$	$4t^3(1-t)$	$6t^2(1-t)^2$	$4t(1-t)^3$	$1(1-t)^4$

As the sum of $(1-t)$ and t is 1,

$$[(1-t)+t]^n = 1 \tag{9.3}$$

which is why we can use the binomial expansion of $(1-t)$ and t as interpolants. For example, when $n = 2$ we obtain the quadratic form

$$(1-t)^2 + 2t(1-t) + t^2 = 1. \tag{9.4}$$

Figure 9.3 shows the graphs of the three polynomial terms of (9.4). The $(1-t)^2$ graph starts at 1 and decays to zero, whereas the t^2 graph starts at zero and rises to 1. The $2t(1-t)$ graph starts at zero reaches a maximum of 0.5 and returns to zero. Thus the central polynomial term has no influence at the end points where $t = 0$ and $t = 1$. We can use these three terms to interpolate between a pair of values as follows

$$v = v_1(1-t)^2 + 2t(1-t) + v_2 t^2.$$

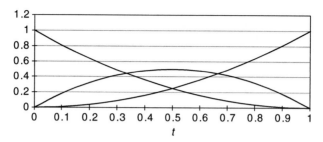

Fig. 9.3 The graphs of the quadratic Bernstein polynomials.

If $v_1 = 1$ and $v_2 = 3$ we obtain the curve shown in Fig. 9.4. But there is nothing preventing us from multiplying the middle term $2t(1-t)$ by any arbitrary number v_c:

$$v = v_1(1-t)^2 + v_c 2t(1-t) + v_2 t^2. \tag{9.5}$$

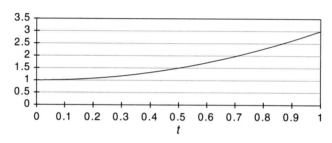

Fig. 9.4 Bernstein interpolation between the values 1 and 3.

For example, if $v_c = 3$ we obtain the graph shown in Fig. 9.5, which is totally different from Fig. 9.4. As Bézier observed, the value of v_c provides an excellent mechanism for determining the shape of the curve between two values. Figure 9.6 shows a variety of graphs for different values of v_c. A very interesting effect occurs when the value of v_c is set midway between v_1 and v_2. For example, when $v_1 = 1$, $v_2 = 3$ and $v_c = 2$, we obtain linear interpolation between v_1 and v_2, as shown in Fig. 9.7.

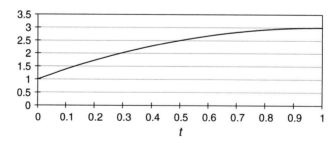

Fig. 9.5 Bernstein interpolation between the values 1 and 3 with $v_c = 3$.

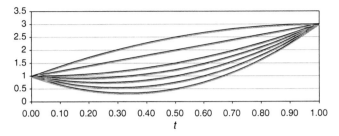

Fig. 9.6 Bernstein interpolation between the values 1 for different values of v_c.

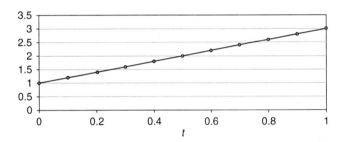

Fig. 9.7 Linear interpolation using a quadratic Bernstein interpolant.

9.4.2 Quadratic Bézier Curves

Quadratic Bézier curves are formed by using Bernstein polynomials to interpolate between the x-, y- and z-coordinates associated with the start- and end-points forming the curve. For example, we can draw a 2D quadratic Bézier curve between $(1,1)$ and $(4,3)$ using the following equations:

$$x = 1(1-t)^2 + x_c 2t(1-t) + 4t^2 \tag{9.6}$$

$$y = 1(1-t)^2 + y_c 2t(1-t) + 3t^2. \tag{9.7}$$

But what should be the values of (x_c, y_c)? Well, this is entirely up to us. The position of this *control vertex* determines how the curve moves between $(1,1)$ and $(4,3)$.

A Bézier curve possesses interpolating and approximating qualities: the interpolating feature ensures that the curve passes through the end points, while the approximating feature shows how the curve passes close to the control point. To illustrate this, if we make $x_c = 3$ and $y_c = 4$ we obtain the curve shown in Fig. 9.8, which shows how the curve intersects the end-points, but misses the control point. It also highlights two important features of Bézier curves: the *convex hull* property, and the end slopes of the curve.

The convex hull property implies that the curve is always contained within the polygon connecting the start, end and control points. In this case the curve is inside the triangle formed by the vertices $(1,1)$, $(3,4)$ and $(4,3)$. The slope of the curve at

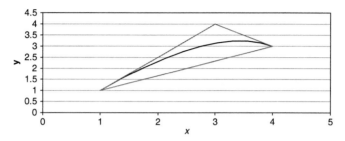

Fig. 9.8 Quadratic Bézier curve between (1, 1) and (4,3), with (3, 4) as the control.

$(1,1)$ is equal to the slope of the line connecting the start point to the control point $(3,4)$, and the slope of the curve at $(4,3)$ is equal to the slope of the line connecting the control point $(3,4)$ to the end point $(4,3)$. Naturally, these two qualities of Bézier curves can be proved mathematically.

9.4.3 Cubic Bernstein Polynomials

Before moving on, there are two further points to note:
- No restrictions are placed upon the position of (x_c, y_c) – it can be anywhere.
- Simply including z-coordinates for the start, end and control vertices creates 3D curves.

One of the problems with quadratic curves is that they are so simple. If we want to construct a complex curve with several peaks and valleys, we would have to join together a large number of such curves. A *cubic curve*, on the other hand, naturally supports one peak and one valley, which simplifies the construction of more complex curves.

When $n = 3$ in (9.3) we obtain the following terms:

$$[(1-t)+t]^3 = (1-t)^3 + 3t(1-t)^2 + 3t^2(1-t) + t^3$$

which can be used as a cubic interpolant, as

$$v = v_1(1-t)^3 + v_{c1}3t(1-t)^2 + v_{c2}3t^2(1-t) + v_2t^3.$$

Once more the terms sum to unity, and the convex hull and slope properties also hold. Figure 9.9 shows the graphs of the four polynomial terms.

This time we have two control values v_{c1} and v_{c2}. These can be set to any value, independent of the values chosen for v_1 and v_2. To illustrate this, let's consider an example of blending between values 1 and 3, with v_{c1} and v_{c2} set to 2.5 and -2.5 respectively. The blending curve is shown in Fig. 9.10.

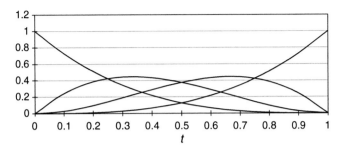

Fig. 9.9 The cubic Bernstein polynomial curves.

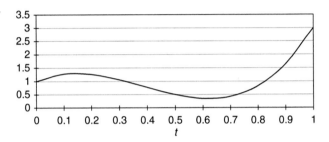

Fig. 9.10 The cubic Bernstein polynomial through the values 1, 2.5, −2.5, 3.

The next step is to associate the blending polynomials with x- and y-coordinates:

$$x = x_1(1-t)^3 + x_{c1}3t(1-t)^2 + x_{c2}3t^2(1-t) + x_2 t^3 \qquad (9.8)$$

$$y = y_1(1-t)^3 + y_{c1}3t(1-t)^2 + y_{c2}3t^2(1-t) + y_2 t^3. \qquad (9.9)$$

Evaluating (9.8) and (9.9) with the following points:

$$(x_1, y_1) = (1, 1) \quad (x_2, y_2) = (4, 3)$$
$$(x_{c1}, y_{c1}) = (2, 3) \quad (x_{c2}, y_{c2}) = (3, -2)$$

we obtain the cubic Bézier curve as shown in Fig. 9.11, which also shows the guide-lines between the end and control points.

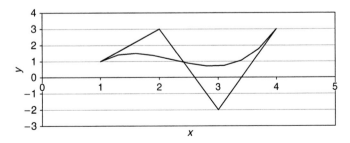

Fig. 9.11 A cubic Bézier curve.

Just to show how consistent Bernstein polynomials are, let's set the values to

$$(x_1,\, y_1) = (1,1) \qquad (x_2,\, y_2) = (4,3)$$
$$(x_{c1},\, y_{c1}) = (2, 1.666) \quad (x_{c2},\, y_{c2}) = (3, 2.333)$$

where $(x_{c1},\, y_{c1})$ and $(x_{c2},\, y_{c2})$ are points one-third and two-thirds respectively, between the start and final values. As we found in the quadratic case, where the single control point was halfway between the start and end values, we obtain linear interpolation as shown in Fig. 9.12.

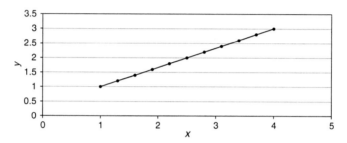

Fig. 9.12 A cubic Bézier line.

Mathematicians are always interested in finding how to express formulae in compact and precise forms, so they have devised an elegant way of abbreviating Bernstein polynomials. Equations (9.6) and (9.7) describe the three polynomial terms for generating a quadratic Bézier curve and (9.8) and (9.9) describe the four polynomial terms for generating a cubic Bézier curve. To begin with, quadratic equations are called *second-degree equations*, and cubics are called *third-degree equations*. In the original Bernstein formulation,

$$B_i^n(t) = \binom{n}{i} t^i (1-t)^{n-1} \tag{9.10}$$

n represents the degree of the polynomial, and i, which has values between 0 and n, creates the individual polynomial terms. These terms are then used to multiply the coordinates of the end and control points. If these points are stored as a vector $\mathbf{P}$, the position vector $\mathbf{p}(t)$ for a point on the curve can be written as

$$\mathbf{p}(t) = \binom{n}{i} t^i (1-t)^{n-i} \mathbf{P}_i \quad \text{for} \quad [0 \le i \le n]$$

or

$$\mathbf{p}(t) = \sum_{i=0}^{n} \binom{n}{i} t^i (1-t)^{n-i} \mathbf{P}_i \quad \text{for} \quad [0 \le i \le n] \tag{9.11}$$

or

$$\mathbf{p}(t) = \sum_{i=0}^{n} B_i^n(t)\mathbf{P}_i \qquad \text{for} \quad [0 \le i \le n]. \qquad (9.12)$$

For example, a point $\mathbf{p}(t)$ on a quadratic curve is represented by

$$\mathbf{p}(t) = 1t^0(1-t)^2\mathbf{P}_0 + 2t^1(1-t)^1\mathbf{P}_1 + 1t^2(1-t)^0\mathbf{P}_2.$$

You will discover (9.11) and (9.12) used in more advanced texts to describe Bézier curves. Although they initially appear intimidating, you should now find them relatively easy to understand.

9.5 A Recursive Bézier Formula

Note that (9.11) explicitly describes the polynomial terms needed to construct the blending terms. With the use of *recursive functions* (a recursive function is a function that calls itself), it is possible to arrive at another formulation that leads towards an understanding of *B-splines*. To begin, we need to express $\binom{n}{i}$ in terms of lower terms, and because the coefficients of any row in Pascal's triangle are the sum of the two coefficients immediately above, we can write

$$\binom{n}{i} = \binom{n-1}{i} + \binom{n-1}{i-1}.$$

Therefore, we can write

$$B_i^n(t) = \binom{n-1}{i}t^i(1-t)^{n-i} + \binom{n-1}{i-1}t^i(1-t)^{n-i}$$
$$B_i^n(t) = (1-t)B_i^{n-1}(t) + tB_{i-1}^{n-1}(t).$$

As with all recursive functions, some condition must terminate the process: in this case it is when the degree is zero. Consequently, $B_0^0(t) = 1$ and $B_j^n(t) = 0$ for $j < 0$.

9.6 Bézier Curves Using Matrices

As we have already seen, matrices provide a very compact notation for algebraic formulae. So let's see how Bernstein polynomials lend themselves to this form of notation. Recall (9.4) which defines the three terms associated with a quadratic Bernstein polynomial. These can be expanded to

$$(1 - 2t + t^2) \quad (2t - 2t^2) \quad (t^2)$$

and can be written as the product:

$$
\begin{bmatrix} t^2 & t & 1 \end{bmatrix}
\begin{bmatrix} 1 & -2 & 1 \\ -2 & 2 & 0 \\ 1 & 0 & 0 \end{bmatrix}.
$$

This means that (9.5) can be expressed as

$$
v = \begin{bmatrix} t^2 & t & 1 \end{bmatrix} =
\begin{bmatrix} 1 & -2 & 1 \\ -2 & 2 & 0 \\ 1 & 0 & 0 \end{bmatrix}
\begin{bmatrix} v_1 \\ v_c \\ v_2 \end{bmatrix}
$$

or

$$
\mathbf{p}(t) = \begin{bmatrix} t^2 & t & 1 \end{bmatrix} =
\begin{bmatrix} 1 & -2 & 1 \\ -2 & 2 & 0 \\ 1 & 0 & 0 \end{bmatrix}
\begin{bmatrix} \mathbf{P}_1 \\ \mathbf{P}_c \\ \mathbf{P}_2 \end{bmatrix}
$$

where $\mathbf{p}(t)$ points to any point on the curve, and $\mathbf{P}_1$, $\mathbf{P}_c$ and $\mathbf{P}_2$ point to the start, control and end points respectively.

A similar development can be used for a cubic Bézier curve, which has the following matrix formulation:

$$
\mathbf{p}(t) = \begin{bmatrix} t^3 & t^2 & t & 1 \end{bmatrix} =
\begin{bmatrix} -1 & 3 & -3 & 1 \\ 3 & -6 & 3 & 0 \\ -3 & 3 & 0 & 0 \\ 1 & 0 & 0 & 0 \end{bmatrix}
\begin{bmatrix} \mathbf{P}_1 \\ \mathbf{P}_{c1} \\ \mathbf{P}_{c2} \\ \mathbf{P}_2 \end{bmatrix}.
$$

There is no doubt that Bézier curves are very useful, and they find their way into all sorts of applications. But, perhaps their one weakness is that whenever an end or control vertex is repositioned, the entire curve is modified. So let's examine another type of curve that prevents this from happening – B-splines. But before we consider this form, let's revisit linear interpolation between multiple values.

9.6.1 Linear Interpolation

To interpolate linearly between two values v_0 and v_1 we use the following interpolant:

$$
v(t) = v_0(1-t) + v_1 t \qquad \text{for} \quad [0 \le t \le 1].
$$

But say we have to interpolate continuously between three values on a linear basis, i.e., v_0, v_1, v_2, with the possibility of extending the technique to any number of values. One solution is to use a sequence of parameter values t_1, t_2, t_3 that are associated with the given values of v, as shown in Fig. 9.13. For the sake of symmetry:

> v_0 is associated with the parameter range t_0 to t_2.
> v_1 is associated with the parameter range t_1 to t_3.
> v_2 is associated with the parameter range t_2 to t_4.

This sequence of parameters is called a *knot vector*. The only assumption we make about the knot vector is that $t_0 \leq t_1 \leq t_2 \leq$, etc.

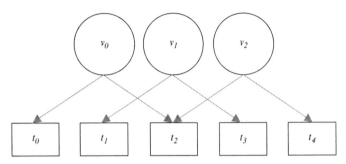

Fig. 9.13 Linearly interpolating between several values.

Now let's invent a linear blending function $B_i^1(t)$ whose subscript i is used to reference values in the knot vector. We want to use the blending function to compute the influence of the three values on any interpolated value $v(t)$ as follows:

$$v(t) = B_0^1(t)v_0 + B_1^1(t)v_1 + B_2^1(t)v_2. \tag{9.13}$$

It's obvious from this arrangement that v_0 will influence $v(t)$ only when t is between t_0 and t_2. Similarly, v_1 and v_2 will influence $v(t)$ only when t is between t_1 and t_3, and t_2 and t_4 respectively.

To understand the action of the blending function let's concentrate upon one particular value $B_1^1(t)$. When t is less than t_1 or greater than t_3, the function $B_1^1(t)$ must be zero. When $t_1 \leq t \leq t_3$, the function must return a value reflecting the proportion of v_1 that influences $v(t)$. During the span $t_1 \leq t \leq t_2$, v_1 has to be blended in, and during the span $t_1 \leq t \leq t_3$, v_1 has to be blended out. The blending in is effected by the ratio

$$\left(\frac{t - t_1}{t_2 - t_1} \right)$$

and the blending out is effected by the ratio

$$\left(\frac{t_3 - t}{t_3 - t_2} \right).$$

Thus $B_1^1(t)$ has to incorporate both ratios, but it must ensure that they only become active during the appropriate range of t. Let's remind ourselves of this requirement by subscripting the ratios accordingly:

$$B_1^1(t) = \left(\frac{t - t_1}{t_2 - t_1}\right)_{1,2} + \left(\frac{t_3 - t}{t_3 - t_2}\right)_{2,3}.$$

We can now write the other two blending terms $B_0^1(t)$ and $B_2^1(t)$ as

$$B_0^1(t) = \left(\frac{t - t_0}{t_1 - t_0}\right)_{0,1} + \left(\frac{t_2 - t}{t_2 - t_1}\right)_{1,2}$$

$$B_2^1(t) = \left(\frac{t - t_2}{t_3 - t_2}\right)_{2,3} + \left(\frac{t_4 - t}{t_4 - t_3}\right)_{3,4}.$$

You should be able to see a pattern linking the variables with their subscripts, and the possibility of writing a general linear blending term $B_i^1(t)$ as

$$B_i^1(t) = \left(\frac{t - t_i}{t_{i+1} - t_i}\right)_{i,i+1} + \left(\frac{t_{i+2} - t}{t_{i+2} - t_{i+1}}\right)_{i+1,i+2}.$$

This enables us to write (9.13) in a general form as

$$v(t) = \sum_{i=0}^{2} B_i^1(t)v_i.$$

But there is still a problem concerning the values associated with the knot vector. Fortunately, there is an easy solution. One simple approach is to keep the differences between t_1, t_2 and t_3 whole numbers, e.g., 0, 1 and 2. But what about the end conditions t_0 and t_4? To understand the resolution of this problem let's examine the action of the three terms over the range of the parameter t. The three terms are

$$\left[\left(\frac{t - t_0}{t_1 - t_0}\right)_{0,1} + \left(\frac{t_2 - t}{t_2 - t_1}\right)_{1,2}\right] v_0 \qquad (9.14)$$

$$\left[\left(\frac{t - t_1}{t_2 - t_1}\right)_{1,2} + \left(\frac{t_3 - t}{t_3 - t_2}\right)_{2,3}\right] v_1 \qquad (9.15)$$

$$\left[\left(\frac{t - t_2}{t_3 - t_2}\right)_{2,3} + \left(\frac{t_4 - t}{t_4 - t_3}\right)_{3,4}\right] v_2 \qquad (9.16)$$

and I propose that the knot vector be initialized with the following values:

t_0	t_1	t_2	t_3	t_4
0	0	1	2	2

- Remember that the subscripts of the ratios are the subscripts of t, not the values of t.
- Over the range $t_0 \leq t \leq t_1$, i.e., 0 to 0. Only the first ratio in (9.14) is active and returns $\frac{0}{0}$. The algorithm must detect this condition and take no action.
- Over the range $t_1 \leq t \leq t_2$. i.e., 0 to 1. The first ratio of (9.14) is active again, and over the range of t blends out v_0. The first ratio of (9.15) is also active, and over the range of t blends in v_1.
- Over the range $t_2 \leq t \leq t_3$. i.e., 1 to 2. The second ratio of (9.15) is active, and over the range of t blends out v_1. The first ratio of (9.16) is also active, and over the range of t blends in v_2.
- Finally, over the range $t_3 \leq t \leq t_4$. i.e., 2 to 2. The second ratio of (9.16) is active and returns $\frac{0}{0}$. The algorithm must detect this condition and take no action.

This process results in a linear interpolation between v_0, v_1 and v_2. If (9.14), (9.15) and (9.16) are applied to coordinate values, the result is two straight lines. This seems like a lot of work just to draw two lines, but the beauty of the technique is that it will work with any number of points, and can be developed for quadratic and higher interpolations.

A. Aitken developed the following recursive interpolant:

$$\mathbf{p}_i^r(t) = \left(\frac{t_{i+r} - t}{t_{i+r} - t_i} \right) \mathbf{p}_i^{r-1}(t) + \left(\frac{t - t_i}{t_{i+r} - t_i} \right) \mathbf{p}_{i+1}^{r-1}(t);$$

$$\begin{cases} r = 1, .. \ n; \\ i = 0, .. \ n - r; \end{cases}$$

which interpolates between a series of points using repeated linear interpolation.

9.7 B-Splines

B-splines, like Bézier curves, use polynomials to generate a curve segment. But, unlike Bézier curves, B-splines employ a series of control points that determine the curve's local geometry. This feature ensures that only a small portion of the curve is changed when a control point is moved.

There are two types of B-splines: *rational* and *non-rational* splines, which divide into two further categories: *uniform* and *non-uniform*. Rational B-splines are formed from the ratio of two polynomials such as

$$x(t) = \frac{X(t)}{W(t)}, \quad y(t) = \frac{Y(t)}{W(t)}, \quad z(t) = \frac{Z(t)}{W(t)}.$$

Although this appears to introduce an unnecessary complication, the division by a second polynomial brings certain advantages:

- They describe perfect circles, ellipses, parabolas and hyperbolas, whereas non-rational curves can only approximate these curves.

- They are invariant of their control points when subjected to rotation, scaling, translation and perspective transformations, whereas non-rational curves lose this geometric integrity.
- They allow weights to be used at the control points to push and pull the curve.

An explanation of uniform and non-uniform types is best left until you understand the idea of splines. So, without knowing the meaning of uniform, let's begin with uniform B-splines.

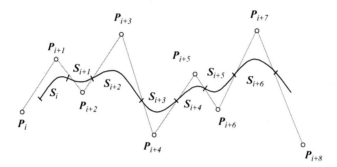

Fig. 9.14 The construction of a uniform non-rational B-spline curve.

9.7.1 Uniform B-Splines

A B-spline is constructed from a string of curve segments whose geometry is determined by a group of local control points. These curves are known as *piecewise polynomials*. A curve segment does not have to pass through a control point, although this may be desirable at the two end points.

Cubic B-splines are very common, as they provide a geometry that is one step away from simple quadratics, and possess continuity characteristics that make the joins between the segments invisible. In order to understand their construction consider the scenario in Fig. 9.14. Here we see a group of $(m+1)$ control points P_0, P_1, P_2, ..., P_m which determine the shape of a cubic curve constructed from a series of curve segments S_0, S_1, S_2, ..., S_{m-3}.

As the curve is cubic, curve segment S_i is influenced by P_i, P_{i+1}, P_{i+2}, P_{i+3}, and curve segment S_{i+1} is influenced by P_{i+1}, P_{i+2}, P_{i+3}, P_{i+4}. And as there are $(m+1)$ control points, there are $(m-2)$ curve segments.

A single segment $S_i(t)$ of a B-spline curve is defined by

$$S_i(t) = \sum_{r=0}^{3} P_{i+r} B_r(t) \quad \text{for} \quad [0 \le t \le 1]$$

where

$$B_0(t) = \frac{-t^3 + 3t^2 - 3t + 1}{6} = \frac{(1-t)^3}{6} \tag{9.17}$$

$$B_1(t) = \frac{3t^3 - 6t^2 + 4}{6} \tag{9.18}$$

$$B_2(t) = \frac{-3t^3 + 3t^2 + 3t + 1}{6} \tag{9.19}$$

$$B_3(t) = \frac{t^3}{6}. \tag{9.20}$$

These are the B-spline *basis functions* and are shown in Fig. 9.15.

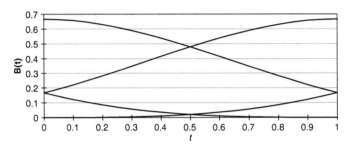

Fig. 9.15 The B-spline basis functions.

Although it is not apparent, these four curve segments are part of one curve. The basis function $B_3(t)$ starts at zero and rises to 0.1666 at $t = 1$. It is taken over by $B_2(t)$ at $t = 0$, which rises to 0.666 at $t = 1$. The next segment is $B_1(t)$ and takes over at $t = 0$ and falls to 0.1666 at $t = 1$. Finally, $B_0(t)$ takes over at 0.1666 and falls to zero at $t = 1$. Equations (9.17)–(9.20) are represented in matrix form by

$$\mathbf{Q}_1(t) = \begin{bmatrix} t^3 & t^2 & t & 1 \end{bmatrix} \frac{1}{6} \begin{bmatrix} -1 & 3 & -3 & 1 \\ 3 & -6 & 3 & 0 \\ -3 & 0 & 3 & 0 \\ 1 & 4 & 1 & 0 \end{bmatrix} \begin{bmatrix} \mathbf{P}_i \\ \mathbf{P}_{i+1} \\ \mathbf{P}_{i+2} \\ \mathbf{P}_{i+3} \end{bmatrix}. \tag{9.21}$$

Let's now illustrate how (9.21) works. We first identify the control points $\mathbf{P}_i$, $\mathbf{P}_{i+1}$, $\mathbf{P}_{i+2}$, etc. Let these be $(0,1)$, $(1,3)$, $(2,0)$, $(4,1)$, $(4,3)$, $(2,2)$ and $(2,3)$. They can be seen in Fig. 9.16 connected together by straight lines. If we take the first four control points: $(0,1), (1,3), (2,0), (4,1)$, and subject the x- and y-coordinates to the matrix in (9.21) over the range $0 \le t \le 1$ we obtain the first B-spline curve segment shown in Fig. 9.16. If we move along one control point and take the next group of control points $(1,3), (2,0), (4,1), (4,3)$, we obtain the second B-spline curve segment. This is repeated a further two times.

Figure 9.16 shows the four curve segments using two gray scales, and it is obvious that even though there are four discrete segments, they join together perfectly. This is no accident. The slopes at the end points of the basis curves are designed to match the slopes of their neighbours and ultimately keep the geometric curve continuous.

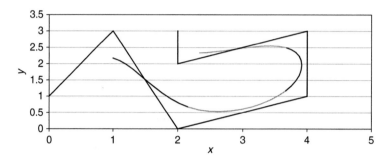

Fig. 9.16 Four curve segments forming a B-spline curve.

9.7.2 Continuity

Constructing curves from several segments can only succeed if the slope of the abutting curves match. As we are dealing with curves whose slopes are changing everywhere, it will be necessary to ensure that even the rate of change of slopes is matched at the join. This aspect of curve design is called *geometric continuity* and is determined by the continuity properties of the basis function. Let's explore such features.

The *first level* of curve continuity C^0, ensures that the physical end of one basis curve corresponds with the following, e.g., $S_i(1) = S_{i+1}(0)$. We know that this occurs from the basis graphs shown in Fig. 9.15. The *second level* of curve continuity C^1, ensures that the slope at the end of one basis curve matches that of the following curve. This can be confirmed by differentiating the basis functions (9.17)–(9.20):

$$B'_0(t) = \frac{-3t^2 + 6t - 3}{6} \tag{9.22}$$

$$B'_1(t) = \frac{9t^2 - 12t}{6} \tag{9.23}$$

$$B'_2(t) = \frac{-9t^2 + 6t + 3}{6} \tag{9.24}$$

$$B'_3(t) = \frac{3t^2}{6}. \tag{9.25}$$

Evaluating (9.22)–(9.25) for $t = 0$ and $t = 1$, we discover the slopes 0.5, 0, −0.5, 0 for the joins between B_3, B_2, B_1, B_0. The *third level* of curve continuity C^2, ensures that the rate of change of slope at the end of one basis curve matches that of the following curve. This can be confirmed by differentiating (9.22)–(9.25):

$$B_0''(t) = -t + 1 \tag{9.26}$$
$$B_1''(t) = 3t - 2 \tag{9.27}$$
$$B_2''(t) = -3t + 1 \tag{9.28}$$
$$B_3''(t) = t. \tag{9.29}$$

Evaluating (9.26)–(9.29) for $t = 0$ and $t = 1$, we discover the values 1, 2, 1, 0 for the joins between B_3, B_2, B_1, B_0. These combined continuity results are tabulated in Table 9.4.

Table 9.4 Continuity properties of cubic B-splines

	t			t			t	
C^0	0	1	C^1	0	1	C^2	0	1
$B_3(t)$	0	1/6	$B_3'(t)$	0	0.5	$B_3''(t)$	0	1
$B_2(t)$	1/6	2/3	$B_2'(t)$	0.5	0	$B_2''(t)$	1	−2
$B_1(t)$	2/3	1/6	$B_1'(t)$	0	−0.5	$B_1''(t)$	−2	1
$B_0(t)$	1/6	0	$B_0'(t)$	−0.5	0	$B_0''(t)$	1	0

9.7.3 Non-uniform B-Splines

Uniform B-splines are constructed from curve segments where the parameter spacing is at equal intervals. *Non-uniform B-splines*, with the support of a knot vector, provide extra shape control and the possibility of drawing periodic shapes. Unfortunately an explanation of the underlying mathematics would take us beyond the introductory nature of this text, and readers are advised to seek out other books dealing in such matters.

9.7.4 Non-uniform Rational B-Splines

Non-uniform rational B-splines (NURBS) combine the advantages of non-uniform B-splines and rational polynomials: they support periodic shapes such as circles, and they accurately describe curves associated with the conic sections. They also play a very important role in describing geometry used in the modeling of computer animation characters.

NURBS surfaces also have a patch formulation and play a very important role in surface modelling in computer animation and CAD. However, tempting though it is to give a description of NURBS surfaces here, they have been omitted because their inclusion would unbalance the introductory nature of this text.

9.8 Surface Patches

9.8.1 Planar Surface Patch

The simplest form of surface geometry consists of a patchwork of polygons or triangles, where three or more vertices provide the basis for describing the associated planar surface. For example, given four vertices $P_{00}, P_{10}, P_{01}, P_{11}$ as shown in Fig. 9.17, a point P_{uv} can be defined as follows. To begin with, a point along the edge $P_{00} - P_{10}$ is defined as is defined as

$$P_{u1} = (1-u)P_{00} + uP_{10}$$

and a point along the edge $P_{01} - P_{11}$ is defined as

$$P_{u2} = (1-u)P_{01} + uP_{11}.$$

Therefore, any point P_{uv} is defined as

$$P_{uv} = (1-v)P_{u1} + vP_{u2}$$
$$P_{uv} = (1-v)[(1-u)P_{00} + uP_{10}] + v[(1-u)P_{01} + uP_{11}]$$
$$P_{uv} = (1-u)(1-v)P_{00} + u(1-v)P_{10} + v(1-u)P_{01} + uvP_{11}.$$

This, however, can be written in matrix form as

$$P_{uv} = [(1-u) \quad u] \begin{bmatrix} P_{00} & P_{01} \\ P_{10} & P_{11} \end{bmatrix} \begin{bmatrix} (1-v) \\ v \end{bmatrix}$$

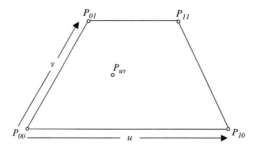

Fig. 9.17 A flat patch defined by u and v parameters.

which expands to

$$P_{uv} = \begin{bmatrix} u & 1 \end{bmatrix} \begin{bmatrix} -1 & 1 \\ 1 & 0 \end{bmatrix} \begin{bmatrix} P_{00} & P_{01} \\ P_{10} & P_{11} \end{bmatrix} \begin{bmatrix} -1 & 1 \\ 1 & 0 \end{bmatrix} \begin{bmatrix} v \\ 1 \end{bmatrix}.$$

Let's illustrate this with an example. Given the following four points: $P_{00} = (0,0,0), P_{10} = (0,0,4), P_{01} = (2,2,1), P_{11} = (2,2,3)$, we can write the coordinates of any point on the patch as

$$x_{uv} = \begin{bmatrix} u & 1 \end{bmatrix} \begin{bmatrix} -1 & 1 \\ 1 & 0 \end{bmatrix} \begin{bmatrix} 0 & 2 \\ 0 & 2 \end{bmatrix} \begin{bmatrix} -1 & 1 \\ 1 & 0 \end{bmatrix} \begin{bmatrix} v \\ 1 \end{bmatrix}$$

$$y_{uv} = \begin{bmatrix} u & 1 \end{bmatrix} \begin{bmatrix} -1 & 1 \\ 1 & 0 \end{bmatrix} \begin{bmatrix} 0 & 2 \\ 0 & 2 \end{bmatrix} \begin{bmatrix} -1 & 1 \\ 1 & 0 \end{bmatrix} \begin{bmatrix} v \\ 1 \end{bmatrix}$$

$$z_{uv} = \begin{bmatrix} u & 1 \end{bmatrix} \begin{bmatrix} -1 & 1 \\ 1 & 0 \end{bmatrix} \begin{bmatrix} 0 & 1 \\ 4 & 3 \end{bmatrix} \begin{bmatrix} -1 & 1 \\ 1 & 0 \end{bmatrix} \begin{bmatrix} v \\ 1 \end{bmatrix}$$

$$x_{uv} = 2v \tag{9.30}$$
$$y_{uv} = 2v \tag{9.31}$$
$$z_{uv} = u(4 - 2v) + v. \tag{9.32}$$

By substituting values of u and v in (9.30)–(9.32) between the range $0 \le (u, v) \le 1$ we obtain the coordinates of any point on the surface of the patch.

If we now introduce the ideas of Bézier control points into a surface patch definition, we provide a very powerful way of creating smooth 3D surface patches.

9.8.2 Quadratic Bézier Surface Patch

Bézier proposed a matrix of nine control points to determine the geometry of a quadratic patch, as shown in Fig. 9.18. Any point on the patch is defined by

$$P_{uv} = \begin{bmatrix} u^2 & u & 1 \end{bmatrix} \begin{bmatrix} 1 & -2 & 1 \\ -2 & 2 & 0 \\ 1 & 0 & 0 \end{bmatrix} \begin{bmatrix} P_{00} & P_{01} & P_{02} \\ P_{10} & P_{11} & P_{12} \\ P_{20} & P_{21} & P_{22} \end{bmatrix} \begin{bmatrix} 1 & -2 & 1 \\ -2 & 2 & 0 \\ 1 & 0 & 0 \end{bmatrix} \begin{bmatrix} v^2 \\ v \\ 1 \end{bmatrix}.$$

The individual x-, y- and z-coordinates are obtained by substituting the x-, y- and z-values for the central P matrix.

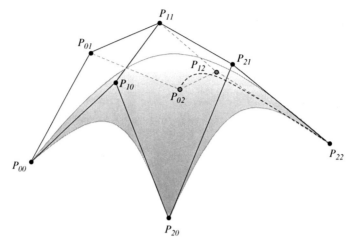

Fig. 9.18 A quadratic Bézier surface patch.

Let's illustrate the process with an example. Given the following points:

$$P_{00} = (0,0,0) \quad P_{01} = (1,1,0) \quad P_{02} = (2,0,0)$$
$$P_{10} = (0,1,1) \quad P_{11} = (1,2,1) \quad P_{12} = (2,1,1)$$
$$P_{20} = (0,0,2) \quad P_{21} = (1,1,2) \quad P_{22} = (2,0,2)$$

we can write

$$x_{uv} = \begin{bmatrix} u^2 & u & 1 \end{bmatrix} \begin{bmatrix} 1 & -2 & 1 \\ -2 & 2 & 0 \\ 1 & 0 & 0 \end{bmatrix} \begin{bmatrix} 0 & 1 & 2 \\ 0 & 1 & 2 \\ 0 & 1 & 2 \end{bmatrix} \begin{bmatrix} 1 & -2 & 1 \\ -2 & 2 & 0 \\ 1 & 0 & 0 \end{bmatrix} \begin{bmatrix} v^2 \\ v \\ 1 \end{bmatrix}$$

$$x_{uv} = \begin{bmatrix} u^2 & u & 1 \end{bmatrix} \begin{bmatrix} 0 & 0 & 0 \\ 0 & 0 & 0 \\ 0 & 2 & 0 \end{bmatrix} \begin{bmatrix} v^2 \\ v \\ 1 \end{bmatrix}$$

$$x_{uv} = 2v$$

$$y_{uv} = \begin{bmatrix} u^2 & u & 1 \end{bmatrix} \begin{bmatrix} 1 & -2 & 1 \\ -2 & 2 & 0 \\ 1 & 0 & 0 \end{bmatrix} \begin{bmatrix} 0 & 1 & 0 \\ 1 & 2 & 1 \\ 0 & 1 & 0 \end{bmatrix} \begin{bmatrix} 1 & -2 & 1 \\ -2 & 2 & 0 \\ 1 & 0 & 0 \end{bmatrix} \begin{bmatrix} v^2 \\ v \\ 1 \end{bmatrix}$$

$$y_{uv} = \begin{bmatrix} u^2 & u & 1 \end{bmatrix} \begin{bmatrix} 0 & 0 & -2 \\ 0 & 0 & 2 \\ -2 & 2 & 0 \end{bmatrix} \begin{bmatrix} v^2 \\ v \\ 1 \end{bmatrix}$$

$$y_{uv} = 2(u + v - u^2 - v^2)$$

$$z_{uv} = \begin{bmatrix} u^2 & u & 1 \end{bmatrix} \begin{bmatrix} 1 & -2 & 1 \\ -2 & 2 & 0 \\ 1 & 0 & 0 \end{bmatrix} \begin{bmatrix} 0 & 0 & 0 \\ 1 & 1 & 1 \\ 2 & 2 & 2 \end{bmatrix} \begin{bmatrix} 1 & -2 & 1 \\ -2 & 2 & 0 \\ 1 & 0 & 0 \end{bmatrix} \begin{bmatrix} v^2 \\ v \\ 1 \end{bmatrix}$$

$$z_{uv} = \begin{bmatrix} u^2 & u & 1 \end{bmatrix} \begin{bmatrix} 0 & 0 & 0 \\ 0 & 0 & 2 \\ 0 & 0 & 0 \end{bmatrix} \begin{bmatrix} v^2 \\ v \\ 1 \end{bmatrix}$$

$$z_{uv} = 2u.$$

Therefore, any point on the surface patch has coordinates

$$x_{uv} = 2v, \quad y_{uv} = 2(u + v - u^2 - v^2), \quad z_{uv} = 2u.$$

Table 9.5 shows the coordinate values for different values of u and v. In this example, the y-coordinates provide the surface curvature, which could be enhanced by modifying the y-coordinates of the control points.

Table 9.5 The x-, y-, z-coordinates for different values of u and v

		v		
		0	0.5	1
u	0	(0,0,0)	(1,0.5,0)	(2,0,0)
	0.5	(0,0.5,1)	(1,0.5,1)	(2,0.5,1)
	1	(0,0,2)	(1,0.5,2)	(2,0,2)

9.8.3 Cubic Bézier Surface Patch

As we saw earlier in this chapter, cubic Bézier curves require two end-points, and two central control points. In the surface patch formulation a 4×4 matrix is required as follows:

$$P_{uv} = \begin{bmatrix} u^3 & u^2 & u & 1 \end{bmatrix} \begin{bmatrix} -1 & 3 & -3 & 1 \\ 3 & -6 & 3 & 0 \\ -3 & 3 & 0 & 0 \\ 1 & 0 & 0 & 0 \end{bmatrix} \begin{bmatrix} P_{00} & P_{01} & P_{02} & P_{03} \\ P_{10} & P_{11} & P_{12} & P_{13} \\ P_{20} & P_{21} & P_{22} & P_{23} \\ P_{30} & P_{31} & P_{32} & P_{33} \end{bmatrix}$$
$$\begin{bmatrix} -1 & 3 & -3 & 1 \\ 3 & -6 & 3 & 0 \\ -3 & 3 & 0 & 0 \\ 1 & 0 & 0 & 0 \end{bmatrix} \begin{bmatrix} v^3 \\ v^2 \\ v \\ 1 \end{bmatrix}$$

which can be illustrated with an example:

Given the points:

$$P_{00} = (0,0,0) \quad P_{01} = (1,1,0) \quad P_{02} = (2,1,0) \quad P_{03} = (3,0,0)$$
$$P_{10} = (0,1,1) \quad P_{11} = (1,2,1) \quad P_{12} = (2,2,1) \quad P_{13} = (3,1,1)$$
$$P_{20} = (0,1,2) \quad P_{21} = (1,2,2) \quad P_{22} = (2,2,2) \quad P_{23} = (3,1,2)$$
$$P_{30} = (0,0,3) \quad P_{31} = (1,1,3) \quad P_{32} = (2,1,3) \quad P_{33} = (3,0,3)$$

we can write the following matrix equations:

$$x_{uv} = \begin{bmatrix} u^3 & u^2 & u & 1 \end{bmatrix} \begin{bmatrix} -1 & 3 & -3 & 1 \\ 3 & -6 & 3 & 0 \\ -3 & 3 & 0 & 0 \\ 1 & 0 & 0 & 0 \end{bmatrix} \begin{bmatrix} 0 & 1 & 2 & 3 \\ 0 & 1 & 2 & 3 \\ 0 & 1 & 2 & 3 \\ 0 & 1 & 2 & 3 \end{bmatrix}$$

$$\begin{bmatrix} -1 & 3 & -3 & 1 \\ 3 & -6 & 3 & 0 \\ -3 & 3 & 0 & 0 \\ 1 & 0 & 0 & 0 \end{bmatrix} \begin{bmatrix} v^3 \\ v^2 \\ v \\ 1 \end{bmatrix}$$

$$x_{uv} = \begin{bmatrix} u^3 & u^2 & u & 1 \end{bmatrix} \begin{bmatrix} 0 & 0 & 0 & 0 \\ 0 & 0 & 0 & 0 \\ 0 & 0 & 0 & 0 \\ 0 & 0 & 3 & 0 \end{bmatrix} \begin{bmatrix} v^3 \\ v^2 \\ v \\ 1 \end{bmatrix}$$

$$x_{uv} = 3v$$

$$y_{uv} = \begin{bmatrix} u^3 & u^2 & u & 1 \end{bmatrix} \begin{bmatrix} -1 & 3 & -3 & 1 \\ 3 & -6 & 3 & 0 \\ -3 & 3 & 0 & 0 \\ 1 & 0 & 0 & 0 \end{bmatrix} \begin{bmatrix} 0 & 1 & 1 & 0 \\ 1 & 2 & 2 & 1 \\ 1 & 2 & 2 & 1 \\ 0 & 1 & 1 & 0 \end{bmatrix}$$

$$\begin{bmatrix} -1 & 3 & -3 & 1 \\ 3 & -6 & 3 & 0 \\ -3 & 3 & 0 & 0 \\ 1 & 0 & 0 & 0 \end{bmatrix} \begin{bmatrix} v^3 \\ v^2 \\ v \\ 1 \end{bmatrix}$$

$$y_{uv} = \begin{bmatrix} u^3 & u^2 & u & 1 \end{bmatrix} \begin{bmatrix} 0 & 0 & 0 & 0 \\ 0 & 0 & 0 & -3 \\ 0 & 0 & 0 & 3 \\ 0 & -3 & 3 & 0 \end{bmatrix} \begin{bmatrix} v^3 \\ v^2 \\ v \\ 1 \end{bmatrix}$$

$$y_{uv} = 3(u + v - u^2 - v^2)$$

$$z_{uv} = \begin{bmatrix} u^3 & u^2 & u & 1 \end{bmatrix} \begin{bmatrix} -1 & 3 & -3 & 1 \\ 3 & -6 & 3 & 0 \\ -3 & 3 & 0 & 0 \\ 1 & 0 & 0 & 0 \end{bmatrix} \begin{bmatrix} 0 & 0 & 0 & 0 \\ 1 & 1 & 1 & 1 \\ 2 & 2 & 2 & 2 \\ 3 & 3 & 3 & 3 \end{bmatrix}$$

$$\begin{bmatrix} -1 & 3 & -3 & 1 \\ 3 & -6 & 3 & 0 \\ -3 & 3 & 0 & 0 \\ 1 & 0 & 0 & 0 \end{bmatrix} \begin{bmatrix} v^3 \\ v^2 \\ v \\ 1 \end{bmatrix}$$

$$z_{uv} = \begin{bmatrix} u^3 & u^2 & u & 1 \end{bmatrix} \begin{bmatrix} 0 & 0 & 0 & 0 \\ 0 & 0 & 0 & 0 \\ 0 & 0 & 0 & 3 \\ 0 & 0 & 0 & 0 \end{bmatrix} \begin{bmatrix} v^3 \\ v^2 \\ v \\ 1 \end{bmatrix}$$

$$z_{uv} = 3u.$$

Therefore, any point on the surface patch has coordinates

$$x_{uv} = 3v, \quad y_{uv} = 3(u + v - u^2 - v^2), \quad z_{uv} = 3u.$$

Table 9.6 shows the coordinate values for different values of u and v. In this example, the y-coordinates provide the surface curvature, which could be enhanced by modifying the y-coordinates of the control points.

Complex 3D surfaces are readily modeled using Bézier patches. One simply creates a mesh of patches such that their control points are shared at the joins. Surface continuity is controlled using the same mechanism for curves. But where the slopes of trailing and starting control edges apply for curves, the corresponding slopes of control tiles apply for patches.

Table 9.6 The x-, y-, z-coordinates for different values of u and v

		v		
		0	0.5	1
	0	$(0,0,0)$	$(1.5,0.75,0)$	$(3,0,0)$
u	0.5	$(0,0.75,1.5)$	$(1.5,1.5,1.5)$	$(3,0.75,1.5)$
	1	$(0,0,3)$	$(1.5,0.75,3)$	$(3,0,3)$

9.9 Summary

This subject has been the most challenging one to describe. On the one hand, the subject is vital to every aspect of computer graphics, and on the other, the reader is required to wrestle with cubic polynomials and a little calculus. However, I do hope that I have managed to communicate some essential concepts behind curves and surfaces, and that you will be tempted to implement some of the mathematics.

Chapter 10
Analytic Geometry

10.1 Introduction

This chapter explores some basic elements of geometry and analytic geometry that are frequently encountered in computer graphics. For completeness, I have included a short review of important elements of Euclidean geometry with which you should be familiar. Perhaps the most important topics that you should try to understand concern the definitions of straight lines in space, 3D planes, and how points of intersection are computed. Another useful topic is the role of parameters in describing lines and line segments, and their intersection.

10.2 Review of Geometry

In the third century BCE Euclid laid the foundations of geometry that have been taught in schools for centuries. In the nineteenth century, mathematicians such as Bernhard Riemann (1809 –1900) and Nicolai Lobachevsky (1793–1856) transformed this Euclidean geometry with ideas such as curved space and spaces with higher dimensions. Although none of these developments affect computer graphics, they do place Euclid's theorems in a specific context: a set of axioms that apply to flat surfaces. We have probably all been taught that parallel lines don't meet, and that the internal angles of a triangle sum to 180°, but these are only true in specific situations. As soon as the surface or space becomes curved, such rules break down. So let's review some rules and observations that apply to shapes drawn on a flat surface.

10.2.1 Angles

By definition, 360° or 2π [radians] measure one revolution. You should be familiar with both units of measurement, and how to convert from one to the other.

J. Vince, *Mathematics for Computer Graphics*, Undergraduate Topics
in Computer Science, DOI 10.1007/978-1-84996-023-6_10,

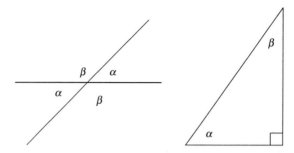

Fig. 10.1 Examples of adjacent, supplementary, opposite and complementary angles.

Figure 10.1 shows examples of *adjacent / supplementary* angles (sum to 180°), *opposite* angles (equal), and *complementary* angles (sum to 90°).

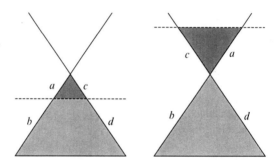

Fig. 10.2 The first intercept theorem.

10.2.2 Intercept Theorems

Figures 10.2 and 10.3 show scenarios involving intersecting lines and parallel lines that give rise to the following observations:

- First intercept theorem:

$$\frac{a+b}{a} = \frac{c+d}{c}, \quad \frac{b}{a} = \frac{d}{c}.$$

- Second intercept theorem:

$$\frac{a}{b} = \frac{c}{d}.$$

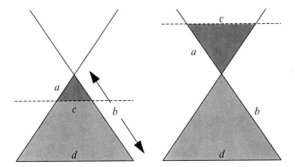

Fig. 10.3 The second intercept theorem.

10.2.3 Golden Section

The *golden section* is widely used in art and architecture to represent an 'ideal' ratio for the height and width of an object. Its origins stem from the interaction between a circle and triangle and give rise to the following relationship:

$$b = \frac{a}{2}\left(\sqrt{5} - 1\right) \approx 0.618a.$$

The rectangle in Fig. 10.4 has proportions:

$$height = 0.618 \times width.$$

However, it is interesting to note that the most widely observed rectangle – the television screen – bears no relation to this ratio.

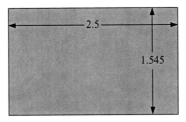

Fig. 10.4 A rectangle with a height to width ratio equal to the golden section.

10.2.4 Triangles

The rules associated with *interior* and *exterior* angles of a triangle are very useful in solving all sorts of geometric problems. Figure 10.5 shows two diagrams identifying interior and exterior angles. We can see that the sum of the interior angles is

180°, and that the exterior angles of a triangle are equal to the sum of the opposite angles:

$$\alpha + \beta + \theta = 180°$$
$$\alpha' = \theta + \beta$$
$$\beta' = \alpha + \theta$$
$$\theta' = \alpha + \beta.$$

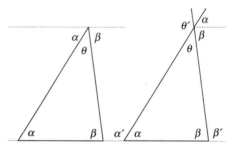

Fig. 10.5 Relationship between interior and exterior angles.

10.2.5 Centre of Gravity of a Triangle

A *median* is a straight line joining a vertex of a triangle to the mid-point of the opposite side. When all three medians are drawn, they intersect at a common point, which is also the triangle's *centre of gravity*. The centre of gravity divides all the medians in the ratio 2 : 1. Figure 10.6 illustrates this arrangement.

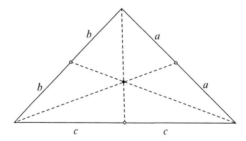

Fig. 10.6 The three medians of a triangle intersect at its centre of gravity.

10.2.6 Isosceles Triangle

Figure 10.7 shows an *isosceles* triangle, which has two equal sides of length l and equal base angles α. The triangle's altitude and area are

$$h = \sqrt{l^2 - \left(\frac{c}{2}\right)^2} \qquad A = \frac{ch}{2}.$$

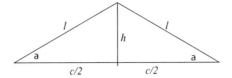

Fig. 10.7 An isosceles triangle.

10.2.7 Equilateral Triangle

An *equilateral* triangle has three equal sides of length l and equal angles of 60°. The triangle's altitude and area are

$$h = \frac{\sqrt{3}}{2}l \qquad A = \frac{\sqrt{3}}{4}l^2.$$

10.2.8 Right Triangle

Figure 10.8 shows a right triangle with its obligatory right angle. The triangle's altitude and area are

$$h = \frac{ab}{c} \qquad A = \frac{ab}{2}.$$

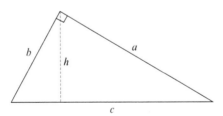

Fig. 10.8 A right triangle.

10.2.9 Theorem of Thales

Figure 10.9 illustrates the Theorem of Thales, which states that the right angle of a right triangle lies on the circumcircle over the hypotenuse.

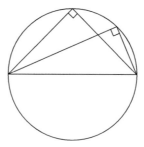

Fig. 10.9 The Theorem of Thales states that the right angle of a right triangle lies on the circumcircle over the hypotenuse.

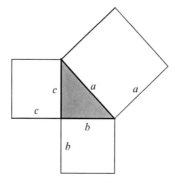

Fig. 10.10 The Theorem of Pythagoras states that $a^2 = b^2 + c^2$.

10.2.10 Theorem of Pythagoras

Although this theorem is named after Pythagoras, there is substantial evidence to show that it was known by the Babylonians a millennium earlier. However, Pythagoras is credited with its proof. Figure 10.10 illustrates the well-known relationship

$$a^2 = b^2 + c^2$$

from which one can show that

$$\sin^2 \alpha + \cos^2 \alpha = 1.$$

10.2.11 Quadrilaterals

Quadrilaterals have four sides and include the square, rectangle, trapezoid, parallelogram and rhombus, whose interior angles sum to 360°. As the square and rectangle are familiar shapes, we will only consider the other three.

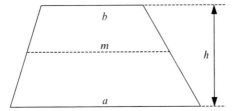

Fig. 10.11 A trapezoid with one pair of parallel sides.

10.2.12 Trapezoid

Figure 10.11 shows a *trapezoid* which has one pair of parallel sides h apart. The mid-line m and area are given by

$$m = \frac{a+b}{2}$$
$$A = mh.$$

10.2.13 Parallelogram

Figure 10.12 shows a *parallelogram*, which is formed from two pairs of intersecting parallel lines, so it has equal opposite sides and equal opposite angles. The altitude, diagonal lengths and area are given by

$$h = b\sin\alpha$$
$$d_{1,2} = \sqrt{a^2 + b^2 \pm 2a\sqrt{b^2 - h^2}}$$
$$A = ah.$$

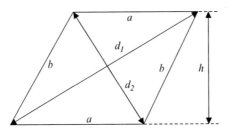

Fig. 10.12 A parallelogram formed by two pairs of parallel lines.

10.2.14 Rhombus

Figure 10.13 shows a *rhombus*, which is a parallelogram with four sides of equal length a. The area is given by

$$A = a^2 \sin \alpha = \frac{d_1 d_2}{2}.$$

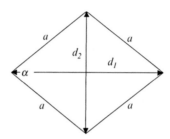

Fig. 10.13 A rhombus is a parallelogram with four equal sides.

10.2.15 Regular Polygon (n-gon)

Figure 10.14 shows part of a regular n-gon with outer radius R_o, inner radius R_i and edge length a_n. Table 10.1 shows the relationship between the area, a_n, R_i and R_o for different polygons.

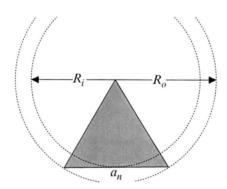

Fig. 10.14 Part of a regular gon showing the inner and outer radii and the edge length.

10.2.16 Circle

The circumference C and area A of a circle are given by

$$C = \pi d = 2\pi r$$

Table 10.1 The area A_n, edge length a_n, inner radius R_i, and outer radius R_o for different polygons

n	$a_n = 2R_i \tan(180°/n)$	$R_i = R_o \cos(180°/n)$	$R_o^2 = R_i^2 + \frac{1}{4}a_n^2$
n	$A_n = \frac{n}{4}a_n^2 \cot(180°/n)$	$A_n = \frac{n}{2}R_o^2 \sin(360°/n)$	$A_n = nR_i^2 \tan(180°/n)$
5	$a_5 = 2R_i\sqrt{5 - 2\sqrt{5}}$	$R_i = \frac{R_o}{4}(\sqrt{5}+1)$	$R_o = R_i(\sqrt{5}-1)$
5	$A_5 = \frac{a_5^2}{4}\sqrt{25 + 10\sqrt{5}}$	$A_5 = \frac{5}{8}R_o^2\sqrt{10 + 2\sqrt{5}}$	$A_5 = 5R_i^2\sqrt{5 - 2\sqrt{5}}$
6	$a_6 = \frac{2}{3}R_i\sqrt{3}$	$R_i = \frac{R_o}{2}\sqrt{3}$	$R_o = \frac{2}{3}R_i\sqrt{3}$
6	$A_6 = \frac{3}{2}a_6^2\sqrt{3}$	$A_6 = \frac{3}{2}R_o^2\sqrt{3}$	$A_6 = 2R_i^2\sqrt{3}$
8	$a_8 = 2R_i(\sqrt{2}-1)$	$R_i = \frac{R_o}{2}\sqrt{2+\sqrt{2}}$	$R_o = R_i\sqrt{4 - 2\sqrt{2}}$
8	$A_8 = 2a_8^2(\sqrt{2}+1)$	$A_8 = 2R_o^2\sqrt{2}$	$A_8 = 8R_i^2(\sqrt{2}-1)$
10	$a_{10} = \frac{2}{5}R_i\sqrt{25 - 10\sqrt{5}}$	$R_i = \frac{R_o}{4}\sqrt{10 + 2\sqrt{5}}$	$R_o = \frac{R_i}{5}(\sqrt{50 - 10\sqrt{5}})$
10	$A_{10} = \frac{5}{2}a_{10}^2\sqrt{5 + 2\sqrt{5}}$	$A_{10} = \frac{5}{4}R_o^2\sqrt{10 - 2\sqrt{5}}$	$A_{10} = 2R_i^2\sqrt{25 - 10\sqrt{5}}$

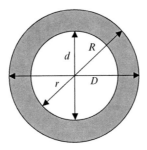

Fig. 10.15 An annulus formed from two concentric circles.

$$A = \pi r^2 = \pi\frac{d^2}{4}$$

where the diameter $d = 2r$.

An *annulus* is the area between two concentric circles as shown in Fig. 10.15, and its area A is given by

$$A = \pi(R^2 - r^2) = \frac{\pi}{4}(D^2 - d^2)$$

where $D = 2R$ and $d = 2r$.

Figure 10.16 shows a sector of a circle, whose area is given by

$$A = \frac{\alpha°}{360°}\pi r^2.$$

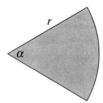

Fig. 10.16 A sector of a circle defined by the angle α.

Figure 10.17 shows a *segment* of a circle, whose area is given by

$$A = \frac{r^2}{2}(\alpha - \sin \alpha)$$

where α is in radians.

The area of an *ellipse* with major and minor radii a and b is given by

$$A = \pi ab.$$

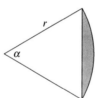

Fig. 10.17 A segment of a circle defined by the angle α.

10.3 2D Analytic Geometry

In this section we briefly examine familiar descriptions of geometric elements and ways of computing intersections.

10.3.1 Equation of a Straight Line

The well-known equation of a line is

$$y = mx + c$$

where m is the slope and c the intersection with the y-axis, as shown in Fig. 10.18. This is called the *normal form*.

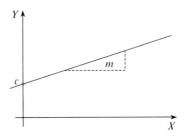

Fig. 10.18 The normal form of the straight line is $y = mx + c$.

Given two points (x_1, y_1) and (x_2, y_2) we can state that for any other point (x, y)

$$\frac{y - y_1}{x - x_1} = \frac{y_2 - y_1}{x_2 - x_1}$$

which yields

$$y = (x - x_1)\frac{y_2 - y_1}{x_2 - x_1} + y_1.$$

Although these equations have their uses, the more general form is much more convenient:

$$ax + by + c = 0.$$

As we shall see, this equation possesses some interesting qualities.

10.3.2 The Hessian Normal Form

Figure 10.19 shows a line whose orientation is controlled by a normal unit vector $\mathbf{n} = \begin{bmatrix} a & b \end{bmatrix}^T$. If $P(x, y)$ is any point on the line, then $\mathbf{p}$ is a position vector where $\mathbf{p} = \begin{bmatrix} x & y \end{bmatrix}^T$ and d is the perpendicular distance from the origin to the line.

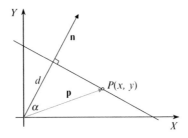

Fig. 10.19 The orientation of a line can be controlled by a normal vector $\mathbf{n}$ and a distance d.

Therefore,

$$\frac{d}{|\mathbf{p}|} = \cos\alpha$$

and

$$d = |\mathbf{p}|\cos\alpha.$$

But the dot product $\mathbf{n}\cdot\mathbf{p}$ is given by

$$\mathbf{n}\cdot\mathbf{p} = |\mathbf{n}||\mathbf{p}|\cos\alpha = ax + by$$

which implies that

$$ax + by = d|\mathbf{n}|$$

and because $|\mathbf{n}| = 1$ we can write

$$ax + by - d = 0$$

where $(x,\ y)$ is a point on the line, a and b are the components of a unit vector normal to the line, and d is the perpendicular distance from the origin to the line. The distance d is positive when the normal vector points away from the origin, otherwise it is negative.

Let's consider two examples:

• *Example 1*

Find the equation of a line whose normal vector is $[3 \quad 4]^T$ and the perpendicular distance from the origin to the line is 1.

We begin by normalizing the normal vector to its unit form.

Therefore, if $\mathbf{n} = [3 \quad 4]^T$, $\quad |\mathbf{n}| = \sqrt{3^2 + 4^2} = 5$ The equation of the line is

$$\frac{3}{5}x + \frac{4}{5}y - 1 = 0.$$

• *Example 2*

Find the Hessian normal form of $y = 2x + 1$

Rearranging the equation we get

$$2x - y + 1 = 0.$$

If we want the normal vector to point away from the origin we multiply by -1:

$$-2x + y - 1 = 0.$$

Normalize the normal vector to a unit form

$$\text{i.e.} \quad \sqrt{(-2)^2 + 1^2} = \sqrt{5}$$

$$-\frac{2}{\sqrt{5}}x + \frac{1}{\sqrt{5}}y - \frac{1}{\sqrt{5}} = 0.$$

Therefore, the perpendicular distance from the origin to the line, and the unit normal vector are respectively

$$\frac{1}{\sqrt{5}} \quad \text{and} \quad \begin{bmatrix} \dfrac{-2}{\sqrt{5}} & \dfrac{1}{\sqrt{5}} \end{bmatrix}^T.$$

The two signs from the square root provide the alternate directions of the vector, and sign of d.

As the Hessian normal form involves a unit normal vector, we can incorporate the vector's direction cosines within the equation:

$$x\cos\alpha + y\sin\alpha - d = 0$$

where α is the angle between the normal vector and the x-axis.

10.3.3 Space Partitioning

The Hessian normal form provides a very useful way of partitioning space into two zones: the partition that includes the normal vector, and the opposite partition. This is illustrated in Fig. 10.20.

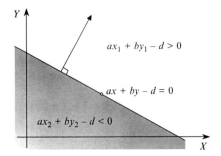

Fig. 10.20 The Hessian normal form of the line equation partitions space into two zones.

Given the equation

$$ax + by - d = 0$$

a point (x, y) on the line satisfies the equation. But if we substitute another point (x_1, y_1) which is in the partition in the direction of the normal vector, it creates the inequality

$$ax_1 + by_1 - d > 0.$$

Conversely, a point (x_2, y_2) which is in the partition opposite to the direction of the normal vector creates the inequality

$$ax_2 + by_2 - d < 0.$$

This space-partitioning feature of the Hessian normal form is useful in clipping lines against polygonal windows.

10.3.4 The Hessian Normal Form from Two Points

Given two points (x_1, y_1) and (x_2, y_2) we can compute the values of a, b and d for the Hessian normal form as follows. To begin, we observe:

$$\frac{y - y_1}{x - x_1} = \frac{y_2 - y_1}{x_2 - x_1} = \frac{\Delta y}{\Delta x}$$

therefore,

$$(y - y_1)\Delta x = (x - x_1)\Delta y$$

and

$$x\Delta y - y\Delta x - (x_1\Delta y - y_1\Delta x) = 0 \qquad (10.1)$$

which is the general equation of a straight line. For the Hessian normal form:

$$\sqrt{\Delta x^2 + \Delta y^2} = 1.$$

Therefore, the Hessian normal form is given by

$$\frac{x\Delta y - y\Delta x - (x_1\Delta y - y_1\Delta x)}{\sqrt{\Delta x^2 + \Delta y^2}} = 0.$$

Let's test this with an example. Given the following points: $(x_1, y_1) = (0, 1)$ and $(x_2, y_2) = (1, 0)$; $\Delta x = 1, \Delta y = -1$. Therefore, using (10.1)

$$x(-1) - y(1) - (0 \times -1 - 1 \times 1) = 0$$
$$-x - y + 1 = 0$$

which is the general equation for the line. We now convert it to the Hessian normal form:

$$\frac{-x - y + 1}{\sqrt{1^2 + (-1)^2}} = 0$$

$$\frac{-x - y + 1}{\sqrt{2}} = 0$$

$$-\frac{x}{\sqrt{2}} - \frac{y}{\sqrt{2}} + \frac{1}{\sqrt{2}} = 0.$$

The choice of sign in the denominator anticipates the two directions for the normal vector, and sign of d.

10.4 Intersection Points

10.4.1 Intersection Point of Two Straight Lines

Given two line equations of the form

$$a_1 x + b_1 y + d_1 = 0$$
$$a_2 x + b_2 y + d_2 = 0$$

the intersection point (x_i, y_i) is given by

$$x_i = \frac{b_1 d_2 - b_2 d_1}{a_1 b_2 - a_2 b_1}$$
$$y_i = \frac{d_1 a_2 - d_2 a_1}{a_1 b_2 - a_2 b_1}$$

or using determinants:

$$x_i = \frac{\begin{vmatrix} b_1 & d_1 \\ b_2 & d_2 \end{vmatrix}}{\begin{vmatrix} a_1 & b_1 \\ a_2 & b_2 \end{vmatrix}}$$

$$y_i = \frac{\begin{vmatrix} d_1 & a_1 \\ d_2 & a_2 \end{vmatrix}}{\begin{vmatrix} a_1 & b_1 \\ a_2 & b_2 \end{vmatrix}}.$$

If the denominator is zero, the equations are linearly dependent, indicating that there is no intersection.

10.4.2 Intersection Point of Two Line Segments

We are often concerned with line segments in computer graphics as they represent the edges of shapes and objects. So let's investigate how to compute the intersection of two 2D-line segments. Figure 10.21 shows two line segments defined by their end points P_1, P_2 and P_3, P_4. If we locate position vectors to these points, we can write the following vector equations to identify the point of intersection:

$$\mathbf{p}_i = \mathbf{p}_1 + t(\mathbf{p}_2 - \mathbf{p}_1) \tag{10.2}$$

$$\mathbf{p}_i = \mathbf{p}_3 + s(\mathbf{p}_4 - \mathbf{p}_3) \tag{10.3}$$

where parameters s and t vary between 0 and 1. For the point of intersection, we can write

$$\mathbf{p}_1 + t(\mathbf{p}_2 - \mathbf{p}_1) = \mathbf{p}_3 + s(\mathbf{p}_4 - \mathbf{p}_3).$$

Therefore, the parameters s and t are given by

$$s = \frac{(\mathbf{p}_1 - \mathbf{p}_3) + t(\mathbf{p}_2 - \mathbf{p}_1)}{\mathbf{p}_4 - \mathbf{p}_3} \tag{10.4}$$

$$t = \frac{(\mathbf{p}_3 - \mathbf{p}_1) + s(\mathbf{p}_4 - \mathbf{p}_3)}{\mathbf{p}_2 - \mathbf{p}_1}. \tag{10.5}$$

From (10.5) we can write

$$t = \frac{(x_3 - x_1) + s(x_4 - x_3)}{x_2 - x_1}$$

$$t = \frac{(y_3 - y_1) + s(y_4 - y_3)}{y_2 - y_1}$$

which yields

$$s = \frac{x_1(y_3 - y_2) + x_2(y_3 - y_1) + x_3(y_2 - y_1)}{(x_2 - x_1)(y_4 - y_3) - (x_4 - x_3)(y_2 - y_1)} \tag{10.6}$$

similarly,

$$t = \frac{x_1(y_4 - y_3) + x_3(y_1 - y_4) + x_4(y_3 - y_1)}{(x_4 - x_3)(y_2 - y_1) - (x_2 - x_1)(y_4 - y_3)}. \tag{10.7}$$

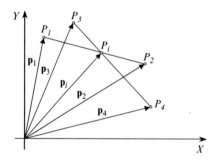

Fig. 10.21 Two line segments with their associated position vectors.

Let's test (10.6) and (10.7) with two examples to illustrate how the equations are used in practice. The first example demonstrates an intersection condition, and the second demonstrates a touching condition.

- *Example 1*

Figure 10.22a shows two line segments intersecting, with an obvious intersection point of $(1.5, 0)$. The coordinates of the line segments are

$$(x_1, y_1) = (1, 0) \qquad (x_2, y_2) = (2, 0)$$
$$(x_3, y_3) = (1.5, -1) \qquad (x_4, y_4) = (1.5, 1)$$

therefore,

$$t = \frac{1(1-(-1)) + 1.5(0-1) + 1.5(-1-0)}{(0-0)(1.5-1.5) - (2-1)(1-(-1))} = 0.5$$

and

$$s = \frac{1(-1-0) + 2(0-(-1)) + 1.5(0-0)}{(1-(-1))(2-1) - (1.5-1.5)(0-0)} = 0.5.$$

Substituting s and t in (10.2) and (10.3) we get $(x_i, y_i) = (1.5, 0)$ as predicted.

- *Example 2*

Figure 10.22b shows two line segments touching at $(1.5,0)$. The coordinates of the line segments are

$$(x_1, y_1) = (1, 0) \qquad (x_2, y_2) = (2, 0)$$
$$(x_3, y_3) = (1.5, 0) \qquad (x_4, y_4) = (1.5, 1)$$

therefore,

$$t = \frac{1(1-0) + 1.5(0-1) + 1.5(0-0)}{(0-0)(1.5-1.5) - (2-1)(1-0)} = 0.5$$

and

$$s = \frac{1(0-0) + 2(0-0) + 1.5(0-0)}{(1-0)(2-1) - (1.5-1.5)(0-0)} = 0.$$

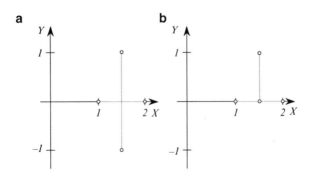

Fig. 10.22 (a) Shows two line segments intersecting. (b) Shows two line segments touching.

The zero value of s confirms that the lines touch, rather than intersect, and $t = 0.5$ confirms that the touching takes place halfway along the line segment.

10.5 Point Inside a Triangle

We often require to test whether a point is inside, outside or touching a triangle. Let's examine two ways of performing this operation. The first is related to finding the area of a triangle.

10.5.1 Area of a Triangle

Let's declare a triangle formed by the anti-clockwise points $(x_1, y_1), (x_2, y_2)$ and (x_3, y_3) as shown in Fig. 10.23. The area of the triangle is given by:

$$A = (x_2 - x_1)(y_3 - y_1) - \frac{(x_2 - x_1)(y_2 - y_1)}{2} - \frac{(x_2 - x_3)(y_3 - y_2)}{2} - \frac{(x_3 - x_1)(y_3 - y_1)}{2}$$

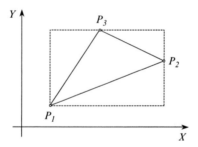

Fig. 10.23 The area of the triangle is computed by subtracting the smaller triangles from the rectangular area.

which simplifies to

$$A = \frac{1}{2}[x_1(y_2 - y_3) + x_2(y_3 - y_1) + x_3(y_1 - y_2)]$$

and this can be further simplified to

$$A = \frac{1}{2}\begin{vmatrix} x_1 & y_1 & 1 \\ x_2 & y_2 & 1 \\ x_3 & y_3 & 1 \end{vmatrix}.$$

Figure 10.24 shows two triangles with opposing vertex sequences. If we calculate the area of the top triangle with anticlockwise vertices, we obtain

$$A = \frac{1}{2}[1(2-4) + 3(4-2) + 2(2-2)] = 2$$

whereas the area of the bottom triangle with clockwise vertices is

$$A = \frac{1}{2}[1(2-0) + 3(0-2) + 2(2-2)] = -2.$$

So the technique is sensitive to vertex direction. We can exploit this sensitivity to test if a point is inside or outside a triangle.

Consider the scenario shown in Fig. 10.25, where the point P_t is inside the triangle (P_1, P_2, P_3).

- If the area of triangle (P_1, P_2, P_t) is positive, P_t must be to the left of the line (P_1, P_2).
- If the area of triangle (P_2, P_3, P_t) is positive, P_t must be to the left of the line (P_2, P_3).
- If the area of triangle (P_3, P_1, P_t) is positive, P_t must be to the left of the line (P_3, P_1).

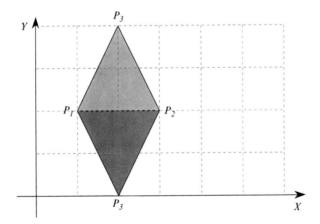

Fig. 10.24 The top triangle has anti-clockwise vertices, and the bottom triangle clockwise vertices.

If all the above tests are positive, P_t is inside the triangle. Furthermore, if one area is zero and the other areas are positive, the point is on the boundary, and if two areas are zero and the other positive, the point is on a vertex.

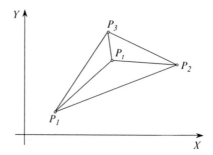

Fig. 10.25 If the point P_t is inside the triangle, it is always to the left as the boundary is traversed in an anti-clockwise direction.

Let's now investigate how the Hessian normal form provides a similar function.

10.5.2 Hessian Normal Form

We can determine whether a point is inside, touching or outside a triangle by representing the triangle's edges in the Hessian normal form, and testing in which partition the point is located. If we arrange that the normal vectors are pointing towards the inside of the triangle, any point inside the triangle will create a positive result when tested against the edge equation. In the following calculations there is no need to ensure that the normal vector is a unit vector. To illustrate this, consider the scenario shown in Fig. 10.26 where we see a triangle formed by the points $(1, 1), (3, 1)$ and $(2, 3)$. With reference to (10.1) we compute the three line equations:

1: The line between $(1, 1)$ and $(3, 1)$:

$$0(x - 1) + 2(1 - y) = 0$$
$$-2y + 2 = 0.$$

We now multiply by -1 to reverse the normal vector:

$$2y - 2 = 0.$$

2: The line between $(3, 1)$ and $(2, 3)$:

$$2(x - 3) - 1(1 - y) = 0$$
$$2x + y - 7 = 0.$$

We now multiply by -1 to reverse the normal vector:

$$-2x - y + 7 = 0.$$

3: The line between $(2, 3)$ and $(1, 1)$:

$$-2(x-2) - 1(3-y) = 0.$$
$$-2x + y + 1 = 0.$$

We now multiply by -1 to reverse the normal vector:

$$2x - y - 1 = 0.$$

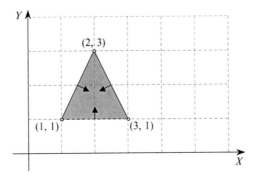

Fig. 10.26 The triangle is represented by three line equations expressed in the Hessian normal form. Any point inside the triangle can be found by evaluating the equations.

Thus the three line equations for the triangle are

$$2y - 2 = 0$$
$$-2x - y + 7 = 0$$
$$2x - y - 1 = 0.$$

We are only interested in the sign of the left-hand expressions:

$$2y - 2 \tag{10.8}$$
$$-2x - y + 7 \tag{10.9}$$
$$2x - y - 1 \tag{10.10}$$

which can be tested for any arbitrary point (x, y). If they are all positive, the point is inside the triangle. If one expression is negative, the point is outside. If one expression is zero, the point is on an edge, and if two expressions are zero, the point is on a vertex.

Just as a quick test, consider the point $(2, 2)$. The three expressions (10.8) to (10.10) are positive, which confirms that the point is inside the triangle. The point $(3, 3)$ is obviously outside the triangle, which is confirmed by two positive results and one negative. Finally, the point $(2, 3)$, which is a vertex, creates one positive result and two zero results.

10.6 Intersection of a Circle with a Straight Line

The equation of a circle has already been given in the previous chapter, so we will now consider how to compute its intersection with a straight line. We begin by testing the equation of a circle with the normal form of the line equation:

$$x^2 + y^2 = r^2 \quad \text{and} \quad y = mx + c.$$

By substituting the line equation in the circle's equation we discover the two intersection points:

$$x_{1,2} = \frac{-mc \pm \sqrt{r^2(1 + m^2) - c^2}}{1 + m^2} \qquad (10.11)$$

$$y_{1,2} = \frac{c \pm m\sqrt{r^2(1 + m^2) - c^2}}{1 + m^2}. \qquad (10.12)$$

Let's test this result with the scenario shown in Fig. 10.27. Using the normal form of the line equation we have

$$y = x + 1, \quad m = 1 \quad \text{and} \quad c = 1.$$

Substituting these values in (10.11) and (10.12) yields

$$x_{1,2} = -1, 0 \quad y_{1,2} = 0, 1.$$

The actual points of intersection are $(-1, 0)$ and $(0, 1)$.

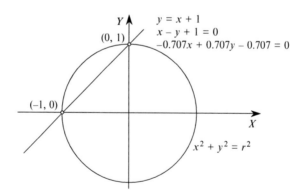

Fig. 10.27 The intersection of a circle with a line defined in its normal form, general form, and the Hessian normal form.

Testing the equation of the circle with the general equation of the line $ax + by + c = 0$ yields intersections given by

$$x_{1,2} = \frac{-ac \pm b\sqrt{r^2(a^2 + b^2) - c^2}}{a^2 + b^2} \qquad (10.13)$$

$$y_{1,2} = \frac{-bc \pm a\sqrt{r^2(a^2 + b^2) - c^2}}{a^2 + b^2}. \tag{10.14}$$

From Fig. 10.27, the general form of the line equation is

$$x - y + 1 = 0 \quad \text{where} \quad a = 1, \, b = -1 \quad \text{and} \quad c = 1.$$

Substituting these values in (10.13) and (10.14) yields

$$x_{1,2} = -1, \, 0 \quad \text{and} \quad y_{1,2} = 0, \, 1$$

which gives the same intersection points found above.

Finally, using the Hessian normal form of the line $ax + by - d = 0$ yields intersections given by

$$x_{1,2} = ad \pm b\sqrt{r^2 - d^2} \tag{10.15}$$

$$y_{1,2} = bd \pm a\sqrt{r^2 - d^2}. \tag{10.16}$$

From Fig. 10.27 the Hessian normal form of the line equation is

$$-0.707x + 0.707y - 0.707 \approx 0$$

where $a \approx -0.707, b \approx 0.707$ and $d \approx 0.707$. Substituting these values in (10.15) and (10.16) yields

$$x_{1,2} = -1, \, 0 \quad \text{and} \quad y_{1,2} = 0, \, 1$$

which gives the same intersection points found above. One can readily see the computational benefits of using the Hessian normal form over the other forms of equations.

10.7 3D Geometry

3D straight lines are best described using vector notation, and readers are urged to develop strong skills in these techniques if they wish to solve problems in 3D geometry. Let's begin this short survey of 3D analytic geometry by describing the equation of a straight line.

10.7.1 Equation of a Straight Line

We start by using a vector **b** to define the orientation of the line, and a point a in space through which the line passes. This scenario is shown in Fig. 10.28. Given

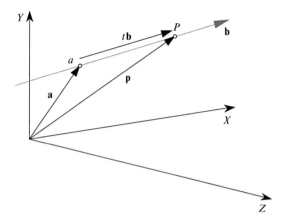

Fig. 10.28 The line equation is based upon the point a and the vector **b**.

another point P on the line we can define a vector t**b** between a and P, where t is a scalar. The position vector **p** for P is given by

$$\mathbf{p} = \mathbf{a} + t\mathbf{b}$$

from which we can obtain the coordinates of the point P:

$$x_p = x_a + tx_b$$
$$y_p = y_a + ty_b$$
$$z_p = z_a + tz_b.$$

For example, if $\mathbf{b} = \begin{bmatrix} 1 & 2 & 3 \end{bmatrix}^T$ and $a = (2, 3, 4)$, then by setting $t = 1$ we can identify a second point on the line:

$$x_p = 2 + 1 = 3$$
$$y_p = 3 + 2 = 5$$
$$z_p = 4 + 3 = 7.$$

In fact, by using different values of t we can slide up and down the line with ease.

If we have two points P_1 and P_2, such as the vertices of an edge, we can represent the line equation using the above vector technique:

$$\mathbf{p} = \mathbf{p}_1 + t(\mathbf{p}_2 - \mathbf{p}_1)$$

where $\mathbf{p}_1$ and $\mathbf{p}_2$ are position vectors to their respective points. Once more, we can write the coordinates of any point P as follows:

$$x_p = x_1 + t(x_2 - x_1)$$
$$y_p = y_1 + t(y_2 - y_1)$$
$$z_p = z_1 + t(z_2 - z_1).$$

10.7.2 Point of Intersection of Two Straight Lines

Given two straight lines we can test for a point of intersection, but must be prepared for three results:

- A real intersection point
- No intersection point
- An infinite number of intersections (identical lines)

If the line equations are of the form

$$\mathbf{p} = \mathbf{a}_1 + r\mathbf{b}_1$$
$$\mathbf{p} = \mathbf{a}_2 + s\mathbf{b}_2$$

for an intersection we can write

$$\mathbf{a}_1 + r\mathbf{b}_1 = \mathbf{a}_2 + s\mathbf{b}_2$$

which yields

$$x_{a1} + rx_{b1} = x_{a2} + sx_{b2} \tag{10.17}$$
$$y_{a1} + ry_{b1} = y_{a2} + sy_{b2} \tag{10.18}$$
$$z_{a1} + rz_{b1} = z_{a2} + sz_{b2}. \tag{10.19}$$

We now have three equations in two unknowns, and any value of r and s must hold for all three equations. We begin by selecting two equations that are linearly independent (i.e., one equation is not a scalar multiple of the other) and solve for r and s, which must then satisfy the third equation. If this final substitution fails, then there is no intersection. If all three equations are linearly dependent, they describe two parallel lines, which can never intersect.

To check for linear dependency we rearrange (10.17) to (10.19) as follows:

$$rx_{b1} - sx_{b2} = x_{a2} - x_{a1} \tag{10.20}$$
$$ry_{b1} - sy_{b2} = y_{a2} - y_{a1} \tag{10.21}$$
$$rz_{b1} - sz_{b2} = z_{a2} - z_{a1}. \tag{10.22}$$

If the determinant Δ of any pair of these equations is zero, then they are dependent. For example, (10.20) and (10.21) form the determinant

$$\Delta = \begin{vmatrix} x_{b1} & -x_{b2} \\ y_{b1} & -y_{b2} \end{vmatrix}$$

which, if zero, implies that the two equations can not yield a solution. As it is impossible to predict which pair of equations from (10.20) to (10.22) will be independent, let's express two independent equations as follows:

$$ra_{11} - sa_{12} = b_1$$
$$ra_{21} - sa_{22} = b_2$$

which yields

$$r = \frac{a_{22}b_1 - a_{12}b_2}{\Delta}$$

$$s = \frac{a_{21}b_1 - a_{11}b_2}{\Delta}$$

where

$$\Delta = \begin{vmatrix} a_{11} & a_{12} \\ a_{21} & a_{22} \end{vmatrix}.$$

Solving for r and s we obtain

$$r = \frac{y_{b2}(x_{a2} - x_{a1}) - x_{b2}(y_{a2} - y_{a1})}{x_{b1}y_{b2} - y_{b1}x_{b2}} \tag{10.23}$$

$$s = \frac{y_{b1}(x_{a2} - x_{a1}) - x_{b1}(y_{a2} - y_{a1})}{x_{b1}y_{b2} - y_{b1}x_{b2}}. \tag{10.24}$$

As a quick test, consider the intersection of the lines encoded by the following vectors:

$$\mathbf{a}_1 = \begin{bmatrix} 0 \\ 1 \\ 0 \end{bmatrix} \quad \mathbf{b}_1 = \begin{bmatrix} 3 \\ 3 \\ 3 \end{bmatrix} \quad \mathbf{a}_2 = \begin{bmatrix} 0 \\ 0.5 \\ 0 \end{bmatrix} \quad \mathbf{b}_2 = \begin{bmatrix} 2 \\ 3 \\ 2 \end{bmatrix}.$$

Substituting the x and y components in (10.23) and (10.24) we discover

$$r = \frac{1}{3} \quad \text{and} \quad s = \frac{1}{2}$$

but for these to be consistent, they must satisfy the z-component of the original equation:

$$rz_{b1} = sz_{b2} = z_{a2} - z_{a1}$$

$$\frac{1}{3} \times 3 - \frac{1}{2} \times 2 = 0$$

which is correct. Therefore, the point of intersection is given by either

$$\mathbf{p}_i = \mathbf{a}_1 + r\mathbf{b}_1 \quad \text{or}$$
$$\mathbf{p}_i = \mathbf{a}_2 + s\mathbf{b}_2.$$

Let's try both, just to prove the point:

$$x_i = 0 + \frac{1}{3}3 = 1 \quad x_i = 0 + \frac{1}{2}2 = 1$$

$$y_i = 1 + \frac{1}{3}3 = 2 \quad y_i = \frac{1}{2} + \frac{1}{2}3 = 2$$

$$z_i = 0 + \frac{1}{3}3 = 1 \quad z_i = 0 + \frac{1}{2}2 = 1.$$

Therefore, the point of intersection point is $(1,2,1)$.

Now let's take two lines that don't intersect, and also exhibit some linear dependency:

$$\mathbf{a}_1 = \begin{bmatrix} 0 \\ 1 \\ 0 \end{bmatrix} \quad \mathbf{b}_1 = \begin{bmatrix} 2 \\ 2 \\ 0 \end{bmatrix} \quad \mathbf{a}_2 = \begin{bmatrix} 0 \\ 2 \\ 0 \end{bmatrix} \quad \mathbf{b}_2 = \begin{bmatrix} 2 \\ 2 \\ 1 \end{bmatrix}.$$

Taking the x and y-components we discover that the determinant Δ is zero, which has identified the linear dependency. Taking the y and z-components the determinant is non-zero, which permits us to compute r and s using

$$r = \frac{z_{b2}(y_{a2} - y_{a1}) - y_{b2}(z_{a2} - z_{a1})}{y_{b1}z_{b2} - z_{b1}y_{b2}}$$

$$s = \frac{z_{b1}(y_{a2} - y_{a1}) - y_{b1}(z_{a2} - z_{a1})}{y_{b1}z_{b2} - z_{b1}y_{b2}}$$

$$r = \frac{1(2-1) - 2(0-0)}{2 \times 1 - 0 \times 2} = \frac{1}{2}$$

$$s = \frac{0(2-1) - 2(0-0)}{2 \times 1 - 0 \times 2} = 0.$$

But these values of r and s must also apply to the x-components:

$$r x_{b1} - s x_{b2} = x_{a2} - x_{a1}$$

$$\frac{1}{2} \times 2 - 0 \times 2 \neq 0$$

which they clearly do not, therefore the lines do not intersect.

Now let's proceed with the equation of a plane, and then look at how to compute the intersection of a line with a plane using a similar technique.

10.8 Equation of a Plane

We now consider four ways of representing a plane equation: the Cartesian form, general form, parametric form and a plane from three points.

10.8.1 Cartesian Form of the Plane Equation

One popular method of representing a plane equation is the Cartesian form, which employs a vector normal to the plane's surface and a point on the plane. The equation is derived as follows.

Let $\mathbf{n}$ be a nonzero vector normal to the plane and $P_0(x_0,\ y_0,\ z_0)$ a point on the plane. $P(x,\ y,\ z)$ is any other point on the plane. Figure 10.29 illustrates the scenario. The normal vector is defined as

$$\mathbf{n} = a\mathbf{i} + b\mathbf{j} + c\mathbf{k}$$

and the position vectors for P_0 and P are

$$\mathbf{p}_0 = x_0\mathbf{i} + y_0\mathbf{j} + z_0\mathbf{k}$$
$$\mathbf{p} = x\mathbf{i} + y\mathbf{j} + z\mathbf{k}$$

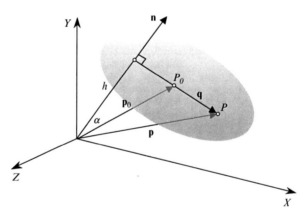

Fig. 10.29 The vector $\mathbf{n}$ is normal to the plane, which also contains a point $P_0(x_0,\ y_0,\ z_0)$. $P(x,\ y,\ z)$ is any other point on the plane.

respectively. From Fig. 10.29 we observe that

$$\mathbf{q} = \mathbf{p} - \mathbf{p}_0$$

and as $\mathbf{n}$ is orthogonal to $\mathbf{q}$

$$\mathbf{n} \cdot \mathbf{q} = 0$$

therefore,

$$\mathbf{n} \cdot (\mathbf{p} - \mathbf{p}_0) = 0$$

which expands into

$$\mathbf{n} \cdot \mathbf{p} = \mathbf{n} \cdot \mathbf{p}_0. \tag{10.25}$$

Writing (10.25) in its Cartesian form we obtain

$$ax + by + cz = ax_0 + by_0 + cz_0$$

but $ax_0 + by_0 + cz_0$ is a scalar quantity associated with the plane and can be replaced by d. Therefore,

$$ax + by + cz = d \qquad (10.26)$$

which is the Cartesian form of the plane equation.

The value of d has the following geometric interpretation.

In Fig. 10.29 the perpendicular distance from the origin to the plane is

$$h = |\mathbf{p}_0| \cos \alpha$$

therefore,

$$\mathbf{n} \cdot \mathbf{p}_0 = |\mathbf{n}| \, |\mathbf{p}_0| \cos \alpha = h|\mathbf{n}|$$

therefore, the plane equation can be also expressed as

$$ax + by + cz = h|\mathbf{n}|. \qquad (10.27)$$

Dividing (10.27) by $|\mathbf{n}|$ we obtain

$$\frac{a}{|\mathbf{n}|}x + \frac{b}{|\mathbf{n}|}y + \frac{c}{|\mathbf{n}|}z = h$$

where

$$|\mathbf{n}| = \sqrt{a^2 + b^2 + c^2}.$$

This means that when a unit normal vector is used, h is the perpendicular distance from the origin to the plane. Let's investigate this equation with an example.

Figure 10.30 shows a plane represented by the normal vector $\mathbf{n} = \mathbf{j} + \mathbf{k}$ and a point on the plane $P_0(0, 1, 0)$. Using (10.26) we have

$$0x + 1y + 1z = 0 \times 0 + 1 \times 1 + 1 \times 0 = 1$$

therefore, the plane equation is

$$y + z = 1.$$

If we normalize the equation to create a unit normal vector, we have

$$\frac{y}{\sqrt{2}} + \frac{z}{\sqrt{2}} = \frac{1}{\sqrt{2}}$$

where the perpendicular distance from the origin to the plane is $\dfrac{1}{\sqrt{2}}$.

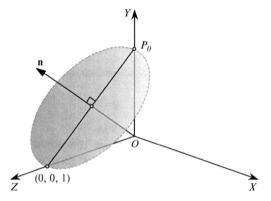

Fig. 10.30 A plane represented by the normal vector **n** and a point $P_0(0, 1, 0)$.

10.8.2 General Form of the Plane Equation

The general form of the equation of a plane is expressed as

$$Ax + By + Cz + D = 0$$

which means that the Cartesian form is translated into the general form by making

$$A = a, \quad B = b, \quad C = c, \quad D = -d.$$

10.8.3 Parametric Form of the Plane Equation

Another method of representing a plane is to employ two vectors and a point that lie on the plane. Figure 10.31 illustrates a scenario where vectors **a** and **b**, and the point $T(x_T, y_T, z_T)$ lie on a plane. We now identify any other point on the plane $P(x, y, z)$ with its associated position vector **p**. The point T also has its associated position vector **t**.

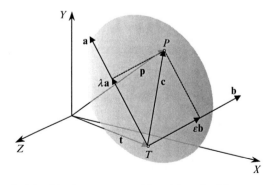

Fig. 10.31 A plane is defined by the vectors **a** and **b** and the point $T(x_T, y_T, z_T)$.

Using vector addition we can write

$$c = \lambda a + \varepsilon b$$

where λ and ε are two scalars such that c locates the point P. We can now write

$$p = t + c \qquad (10.28)$$

therefore,

$$x_P = x_T + \lambda x_a + \varepsilon x_b$$
$$y_P = y_T + \lambda y_a + \varepsilon y_b$$
$$z_P = z_T + \lambda z_a + \varepsilon z_b$$

which means that the coordinates of any point on the plane are formed from the coordinates of the known point on the plane, and a linear mixture of the components of the two vectors. Let's illustrate this vector approach with an example.

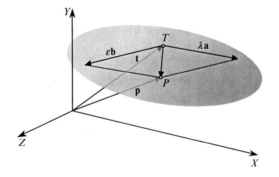

Fig. 10.32 A plane is defined by the vectors **a** and **b** and the point $T(1, 1, 1)$.

Figure 10.32 shows a plane containing the vectors $a = i$ and $b = k$, and the point $T(1, 1, 1)$ with its position vector $t = i + j + k$. By inspection, the plane is parallel with the xz-plane and intersects the y-axis at $y = 1$.

From (10.28) we can write

$$p = t + \lambda a + \varepsilon b$$

where λ and ε are arbitrary scalars.

For example, if $\lambda = 2$ and $\varepsilon = 1$

$$x_P = 1 + 2 \times 1 + 1 \times 0 = 3$$
$$y_P = 1 + 2 \times 0 + 1 \times 0 = 1$$
$$z_P = 1 + 2 \times 0 + 1 \times 1 = 2.$$

Therefore, the point $(3, 1, 2)$ is on the plane.

10.8.4 Converting from the Parametric to the General Form

It is possible to convert from the parametric form to the general form of the plane equation using the following formulae:

$$\lambda = \frac{(\mathbf{a} \cdot \mathbf{b})(\mathbf{b} \cdot \mathbf{t}) - (\mathbf{a} \cdot \mathbf{t})|\mathbf{b}|^2}{|\mathbf{a}|^2 |\mathbf{b}|^2 - (\mathbf{a} \cdot \mathbf{b})^2}$$

$$\varepsilon = \frac{(\mathbf{a} \cdot \mathbf{b})(\mathbf{a} \cdot \mathbf{t}) - (\mathbf{b} \cdot \mathbf{t})|\mathbf{a}|^2}{|\mathbf{a}|^2 |\mathbf{b}|^2 - (\mathbf{a} \cdot \mathbf{b})^2}.$$

The resulting point $P(x_P, y_P, z_P)$ is perpendicular to the origin.

If vectors $\mathbf{a}$ and $\mathbf{b}$ are unit vectors, λ and ε become

$$\lambda = \frac{(\mathbf{a} \cdot \mathbf{b})(\mathbf{b} \cdot \mathbf{t}) - \mathbf{a} \cdot \mathbf{t}}{1 - (\mathbf{a} \cdot \mathbf{b})^2} \tag{10.29}$$

$$\varepsilon = \frac{(\mathbf{a} \cdot \mathbf{b})(\mathbf{a} \cdot \mathbf{t}) - \mathbf{b} \cdot \mathbf{t}}{1 - (\mathbf{a} \cdot \mathbf{b})^2}. \tag{10.30}$$

P's position vector $\mathbf{p}$ is also the plane's normal vector. Then

$$x_P = x_T + \lambda x_a + \varepsilon x_b$$
$$y_P = y_T + \lambda y_a + \varepsilon y_b$$
$$z_P = z_T + \lambda z_a + \varepsilon z_b.$$

The normal vector is

$$\mathbf{p} = x_P \mathbf{i} + y_P \mathbf{j} + z_P \mathbf{k}$$

and because $|\mathbf{p}|$ is the perpendicular distance from the plane to the origin we can state

$$\frac{x_P}{|\mathbf{p}|} x + \frac{y_P}{|\mathbf{p}|} y + \frac{z_P}{|\mathbf{p}|} z = |\mathbf{p}|$$

or in the general form of the plane equation:

$$Ax + By + Cz + D = 0$$

where

$$A = \frac{x_P}{|\mathbf{p}|}, \quad B = \frac{y_P}{|\mathbf{p}|}, \quad C = \frac{z_P}{|\mathbf{p}|}, \quad D = -|\mathbf{p}|.$$

Figure 10.33 illustrates a plane inclined $45°$ to the $y-$ and z-axes and parallel with the x-axis. The vectors for the parametric equation are

$$\mathbf{a} = \mathbf{j} - \mathbf{k}$$
$$\mathbf{b} = \mathbf{i}$$
$$\mathbf{t} = \mathbf{k}.$$

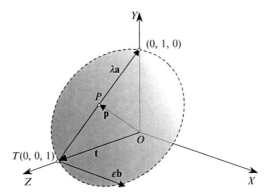

Fig. 10.33 The vectors **a** and **b** are parallel to the plane and the point $(0, 0, 1)$ is on the plane.

Substituting these components in (10.29) and (10.30) we have

$$\lambda = \frac{(0)(0) - (-1) \times 1}{2 \times 1 - (0)} = 0.5$$

$$\varepsilon = \frac{(0)(-1) - (0) \times 2}{2 \times 1 - (0)} = 0$$

therefore,

$$x_P = 0 + 0.5 \times 0 + 0 \times 1 = 0$$
$$y_P = 0 + 0.5 \times 1 + 0 \times 0 = 0.5$$
$$z_P = 1 + 0.5 \times (-1) + 0 \times 0 = 0.5.$$

The point $(0, 0.5, 0.5)$ has position vector **p**, where

$$|\mathbf{p}| = \sqrt{0^2 + 0.5^2 + 0.5^2} = \frac{\sqrt{2}}{2}$$

the plane equation is

$$0x + \frac{0.5}{\sqrt{2}/2}y + \frac{0.5}{\sqrt{2}/2}z - \sqrt{2}/2 = 0$$

which simplifies to

$$y + z - 1 = 0.$$

10.8.5 Plane Equation from Three Points

Very often in computer graphics problems we need to find the plane equation from three known points. To begin with, the three points must be distinct and not lie on a line. Figure 10.34 shows three points R, S and T, from which we create two

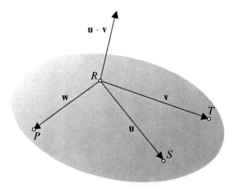

Fig. 10.34 The vectors used to determine a plane equation from three points R, S and T.

vectors $\mathbf{u} = \overrightarrow{RS}$ and $\mathbf{v} = \overrightarrow{RT}$. The vector product $\mathbf{u} \times \mathbf{v}$ then provides a vector normal to the plane containing the original points. We now take another point $P(x, y, z)$ and form a vector $\mathbf{w} = \overrightarrow{RP}$. The scalar product $\mathbf{w} \cdot (\mathbf{u} \times \mathbf{v}) = 0$ if P is in the plane containing the original points. This condition can be expressed as a determinant and converted into the general equation of a plane. The three points are assumed to be in an anticlockwise sequence viewed from the direction of the surface normal.

We begin with

$$\mathbf{u} \times \mathbf{v} = \begin{vmatrix} \mathbf{i} & \mathbf{j} & \mathbf{k} \\ x_u & y_u & z_u \\ x_v & y_v & z_v \end{vmatrix}.$$

As $\mathbf{w}$ is perpendicular to $\mathbf{u} \times \mathbf{v}$

$$\mathbf{w} \cdot (\mathbf{u} \times \mathbf{v}) = \begin{vmatrix} x_w & y_w & z_w \\ x_u & y_u & z_u \\ x_v & y_v & z_v \end{vmatrix} = 0.$$

Expanding the determinant we obtain

$$x_w \begin{vmatrix} y_u & z_u \\ y_v & z_v \end{vmatrix} + y_w \begin{vmatrix} z_u & x_u \\ z_v & x_v \end{vmatrix} + z_w \begin{vmatrix} x_u & y_u \\ x_v & y_v \end{vmatrix} = 0$$

which becomes

$$(x - x_R) \begin{vmatrix} y_S - y_R & z_S - z_R \\ y_T - y_R & z_T - z_R \end{vmatrix} + (y - y_R) \begin{vmatrix} z_S - z_R & x_S - x_R \\ z_T - z_R & x_T - x_R \end{vmatrix}$$

$$+ (z - z_R) \begin{vmatrix} x_S - x_R & y_S - y_R \\ x_T - x_R & y_T - y_R \end{vmatrix} = 0.$$

This can be arranged in the form $ax + by + cz + d = 0$ where

$$a = \begin{vmatrix} y_S - y_R & z_S - z_R \\ y_T - y_R & z_T - z_R \end{vmatrix} \qquad b = \begin{vmatrix} z_S - z_R & x_S - x_R \\ x_T - z_R & x_T - x_R \end{vmatrix}$$

$$c = \begin{vmatrix} x_S - x_R & y_S - y_R \\ x_T - x_R & y_T - y_R \end{vmatrix} \qquad d = -(ax_R + by_R + cz_R)$$

or

$$a = \begin{vmatrix} 1 & y_R & z_R \\ 1 & y_S & z_S \\ 1 & y_T & z_T \end{vmatrix} \qquad b = \begin{vmatrix} x_R & 1 & z_R \\ x_S & 1 & z_S \\ x_T & 1 & z_T \end{vmatrix} \qquad c = \begin{vmatrix} x_R & y_R & 1 \\ x_S & y_S & 1 \\ x_T & y_T & 1 \end{vmatrix}$$

$$d = -(ax_R + by_R + cz_R).$$

As an example, consider the three points $R(0, 0, 1)$, $S(1, 0, 0)$, $T(0, 1, 0)$. Therefore,

$$a = \begin{vmatrix} 1 & 0 & 1 \\ 1 & 0 & 0 \\ 1 & 1 & 0 \end{vmatrix} = 1, \quad b = \begin{vmatrix} 0 & 1 & 1 \\ 1 & 1 & 0 \\ 0 & 1 & 0 \end{vmatrix} = 1, \quad c = \begin{vmatrix} 0 & 0 & 1 \\ 1 & 0 & 1 \\ 0 & 1 & 1 \end{vmatrix} = 1,$$

$$d = -(1 \times 0 + 1 \times 0 + 1 \times 1) = -1$$

and the plane equation is

$$x + y + z - 1 = 0.$$

10.9 Intersecting Planes

When two non-parallel planes intersect they form a straight line at the intersection, which is parallel to both planes. This line can be represented as a vector, whose direction is revealed by the vector product of the planes' surface normals. However, we require a point on this line to establish a unique vector equation; a useful point is chosen as P_0, whose position vector $\mathbf{p_0}$ is perpendicular to the line.

Figure 10.35 shows two planes with normal vectors $\mathbf{n_1}$ and $\mathbf{n_2}$ intersecting to create a line represented by $\mathbf{n_3}$, whilst $P_0(x_0, y_0, z_0)$ is a particular point on $\mathbf{n_3}$ and $P(x, y, z)$ is any point on the line.

We start the analysis by defining the surface normals:

$$\mathbf{n_1} = a_1\mathbf{i} + b_1\mathbf{j} + c_1\mathbf{k}$$
$$\mathbf{n_2} = a_2\mathbf{i} + b_2\mathbf{j} + c_2\mathbf{k}$$

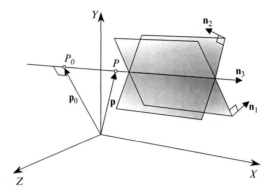

Fig. 10.35 Two intersecting planes create a line of intersection.

next we define $\mathbf{p}$ and $\mathbf{p}_0$:

$$\mathbf{p} = x\mathbf{i} + y\mathbf{j} + z\mathbf{k}$$
$$\mathbf{p}_0 = x_0\mathbf{i} + y_0\mathbf{j} + z_0\mathbf{k}.$$

Now we state the plane equations in vector form:

$$\mathbf{n}_1 \cdot \mathbf{p} + d_1 = 0$$
$$\mathbf{n}_2 \cdot \mathbf{p} + d_2 = 0.$$

The geometric significance of the scalars d_1 and d_2 has already been described above. Let's now define the line of intersection as

$$\mathbf{p} = \mathbf{p}_0 + \lambda \mathbf{n}_3$$

where λ is a scalar.

Because the line of intersection must be orthogonal to $\mathbf{n}_1$ and $\mathbf{n}_2$

$$\mathbf{n}_3 = a_3\mathbf{i} + b_3\mathbf{j} + c_3\mathbf{k} = \mathbf{n}_1 \times \mathbf{n}_2.$$

Now we introduce P_0 as this must satisfy both plane equations, therefore,

$$\mathbf{n}_1 \cdot \mathbf{p}_0 = -d_1 \tag{10.31}$$
$$\mathbf{n}_2 \cdot \mathbf{p}_0 = -d_2 \tag{10.32}$$

and as P_0 is such that $\mathbf{p}_0$ is orthogonal to $\mathbf{n}_3$

$$\mathbf{n}_3 \cdot \mathbf{p}_0 = 0. \tag{10.33}$$

Equations (10.31)–(10.33) form three simultaneous equations, which reveal the point P_0. These can be represented in matrix form as

$$\begin{bmatrix} -d_1 \\ -d_2 \\ 0 \end{bmatrix} = \begin{bmatrix} a_1 & b_1 & c_1 \\ a_2 & b_2 & c_2 \\ a_3 & b_3 & c_3 \end{bmatrix} \begin{bmatrix} x_0 \\ y_0 \\ z_0 \end{bmatrix}$$

or

$$\begin{bmatrix} d_1 \\ d_2 \\ 0 \end{bmatrix} = -\begin{bmatrix} a_1 & b_1 & c_1 \\ a_2 & b_2 & c_2 \\ a_3 & b_3 & c_3 \end{bmatrix} \begin{bmatrix} x_0 \\ y_0 \\ z_0 \end{bmatrix}$$

therefore,

$$\frac{x_0}{\begin{vmatrix} d_1 & b_1 & c_1 \\ d_2 & b_2 & c_2 \\ 0 & b_3 & c_3 \end{vmatrix}} = \frac{y_0}{\begin{vmatrix} a_1 & d_1 & c_1 \\ a_2 & d_2 & c_2 \\ a_3 & 0 & c_3 \end{vmatrix}} = \frac{z_0}{\begin{vmatrix} a_1 & b_1 & d_1 \\ a_2 & b_2 & d_2 \\ a_3 & b_3 & 0 \end{vmatrix}} = \frac{-1}{DET}$$

which enables us to state

$$x_0 = \frac{d_2 \begin{vmatrix} b_1 & c_1 \\ b_3 & c_3 \end{vmatrix} - d_1 \begin{vmatrix} b_2 & c_2 \\ b_3 & c_3 \end{vmatrix}}{DET}$$

$$y_0 = \frac{d_2 \begin{vmatrix} a_3 & c_3 \\ a_1 & c_1 \end{vmatrix} - d_1 \begin{vmatrix} a_3 & c_3 \\ a_2 & c_2 \end{vmatrix}}{DET}$$

$$z_0 = \frac{d_2 \begin{vmatrix} a_1 & b_1 \\ a_3 & b_3 \end{vmatrix} - d_1 \begin{vmatrix} a_2 & b_2 \\ a_3 & b_3 \end{vmatrix}}{DET}$$

where

$$DET = \begin{vmatrix} a_1 & b_1 & c_1 \\ a_2 & b_2 & c_2 \\ a_3 & b_3 & c_3 \end{vmatrix}.$$

The line of intersection is then given by

$$\mathbf{p} = \mathbf{p}_0 + \lambda \mathbf{n}_3.$$

If $DET = 0$ the line and plane are parallel.

To illustrate this, let the two intersecting planes be the xy-plane and the xz-plane, which means that the line of intersection will be the y-axis, as shown in Fig. 10.36.

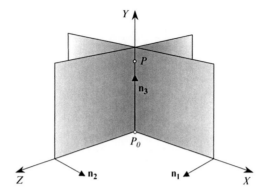

Fig. 10.36 Two intersecting planes creating a line of intersection coincident with the y-axis.

The plane equations are $z = 0$ and $x = 0$, therefore,

$$\mathbf{n}_1 = \mathbf{k}$$
$$\mathbf{n}_2 = \mathbf{i}$$

and $d_1 = d_2 = 0$.

We now compute $\mathbf{n}_3$, DET, x_0, y_0, z_0:

$$\mathbf{n}_3 = \begin{vmatrix} \mathbf{i} & \mathbf{j} & \mathbf{k} \\ 0 & 0 & 1 \\ 1 & 0 & 0 \end{vmatrix} = \mathbf{j}$$

$$DET = \begin{vmatrix} 0 & 0 & 1 \\ 1 & 0 & 0 \\ 0 & 1 & 0 \end{vmatrix} = 1$$

$$x_0 = \frac{0 \begin{vmatrix} 0 & 1 \\ 1 & 0 \end{vmatrix} - 0 \begin{vmatrix} 0 & 0 \\ 1 & 0 \end{vmatrix}}{1} = 0$$

$$y_0 = \frac{0 \begin{vmatrix} 0 & 0 \\ 0 & 1 \end{vmatrix} - 0 \begin{vmatrix} 0 & 0 \\ 1 & 0 \end{vmatrix}}{1} = 0$$

$$z_0 = \frac{0 \begin{vmatrix} 0 & 0 \\ 0 & 1 \end{vmatrix} - 0 \begin{vmatrix} 1 & 0 \\ 0 & 1 \end{vmatrix}}{1} = 0.$$

Therefore, the line equation is $\mathbf{p} = \lambda \mathbf{n}_3$, where $\mathbf{n}_3 = \mathbf{j}$, which is the y-axis.

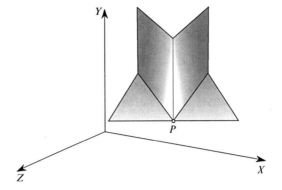

Fig. 10.37 Three mutually intersecting planes.

10.9.1 Intersection of Three Planes

Three mutually intersecting planes will intersect at a point as shown in Fig. 10.37, and we can find this point by using a similar strategy to the one used in two intersecting planes by creating three simultaneous plane equations using determinants.

Figure 10.37 shows three planes intersecting at the point $P(x, y, z)$. The three planes can be defined by the following equations:

$$a_1x + b_1y + c_1z + d_1 = 0$$
$$a_2x + b_1y + c_2z + d_2 = 0$$
$$a_3x + b_1y + c_3z + d_3 = 0$$

which means that they can be rewritten as

$$\begin{bmatrix} -d_1 \\ -d_2 \\ -d_3 \end{bmatrix} = \begin{bmatrix} a_1 & b_1 & c_1 \\ a_2 & b_2 & c_2 \\ a_3 & b_3 & c_3 \end{bmatrix} \begin{bmatrix} x \\ y \\ z \end{bmatrix}$$

or

$$\begin{bmatrix} d_1 \\ d_2 \\ d_3 \end{bmatrix} = - \begin{bmatrix} a_1 & b_1 & c_1 \\ a_2 & b_2 & c_2 \\ a_3 & b_3 & c_3 \end{bmatrix} \begin{bmatrix} x \\ y \\ z \end{bmatrix}$$

or in determinant form

$$\frac{x}{\begin{vmatrix} d_1 & b_1 & c_1 \\ d_2 & b_2 & c_2 \\ d_3 & b_3 & c_3 \end{vmatrix}} = \frac{y}{\begin{vmatrix} a_1 & d_1 & c_1 \\ a_2 & d_2 & c_2 \\ a_3 & d_3 & c_3 \end{vmatrix}} = \frac{z}{\begin{vmatrix} a_1 & b_1 & d_1 \\ a_2 & b_2 & d_2 \\ a_3 & b_3 & d_3 \end{vmatrix}} = \frac{-1}{DET}$$

where

$$DET = \begin{vmatrix} a_1 & b_1 & c_1 \\ a_2 & b_2 & c_2 \\ a_3 & b_3 & c_3 \end{vmatrix}.$$

Therefore, we can state that

$$x = -\frac{\begin{vmatrix} d_1 & b_1 & c_1 \\ d_2 & b_2 & c_2 \\ d_3 & b_3 & c_3 \end{vmatrix}}{DET}$$

$$y = -\frac{\begin{vmatrix} a_1 & d_1 & c_1 \\ a_2 & d_2 & c_2 \\ a_3 & d_3 & c_3 \end{vmatrix}}{DET}$$

$$z = -\frac{\begin{vmatrix} a_1 & b_1 & d_1 \\ a_2 & b_2 & d_2 \\ a_3 & b_3 & d_3 \end{vmatrix}}{DET}.$$

If $DET = 0$ two of the planes, at least, are parallel. Let's test these equations with a simple example.

The planes shown in Fig. 10.38 have the following equations:

$$x + y + z - 2 = 0$$
$$z = 0$$
$$y - 1 = 0$$

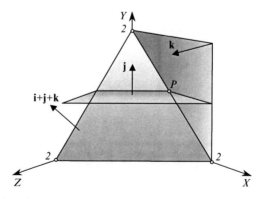

Fig. 10.38 Three planes intersecting at a point P.

therefore,

$$DET = \begin{vmatrix} 1 & 1 & 1 \\ 0 & 0 & 1 \\ 0 & 1 & 0 \end{vmatrix} = -1$$

$$x = -\frac{\begin{vmatrix} -2 & 1 & 1 \\ 0 & 0 & 1 \\ -1 & 1 & 0 \end{vmatrix}}{-1} = 1$$

$$y = -\frac{\begin{vmatrix} 1 & -2 & 1 \\ 0 & 0 & 1 \\ 0 & -1 & 0 \end{vmatrix}}{-1} = 1$$

$$z = -\frac{\begin{vmatrix} 1 & 1 & -2 \\ 0 & 0 & 0 \\ 0 & 1 & -1 \end{vmatrix}}{-1} = 0$$

which means that the intersection point is $(1, 1, 0)$, which is correct.

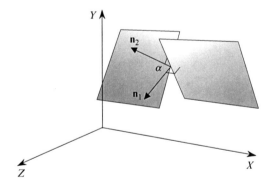

Fig. 10.39 The angle between two planes is the angle between their surface normals.

10.9.2 Angle Between Two Planes

Calculating the angle between two planes is relatively easy and can be found by taking the dot product of the planes' normals. Figure 10.39 shows two planes with α representing the angle between the two surface normals and $\mathbf{n}_1$ and $\mathbf{n}_2$.

Let the plane equations be

$$ax_1 + by_1 + cz_1 + d_1 = 0$$
$$ax_2 + by_2 + cz_2 + d_2 = 0$$

therefore, the surface normals are

$$\mathbf{n}_1 = a_1\mathbf{i} + b_1\mathbf{j} + c_1\mathbf{k}$$
$$\mathbf{n}_2 = a_2\mathbf{i} + b_2\mathbf{j} + c_2\mathbf{k}.$$

Taking the dot product of $\mathbf{n}_1$ and $\mathbf{n}_2$:

$$\mathbf{n}_1 \cdot \mathbf{n}_2 = |\mathbf{n}_1|\,|\mathbf{n}_2|\cos\alpha$$

and

$$\alpha = \cos^{-1}\left(\frac{\mathbf{n}_1 \cdot \mathbf{n}_2}{|\mathbf{n}_1|\,|\mathbf{n}_2|}\right).$$

Figure 10.40 shows two planes with normal vectors $\mathbf{n}_1$ and $\mathbf{n}_2$. The plane equations are

$$x + y + z - 1 = 0$$

and

$$z = 0$$

therefore,

$$\mathbf{n}_1 = \mathbf{i} + \mathbf{j} + \mathbf{k}$$

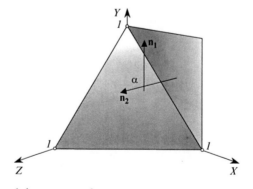

Fig. 10.40 α is the angle between two planes.

and

$$\mathbf{n}_2 = \mathbf{k}$$

therefore,

$$|\mathbf{n}_1| = \sqrt{3} \quad \text{and} \quad |\mathbf{n}_2| = 1$$

and

$$\alpha = \cos^{-1}\left(\frac{1}{\sqrt{3}}\right) \approx 54.74°.$$

10.9.3 Angle between a Line and a Plane

The angle between a line and a plane is calculated using a similar technique used for calculating the angle between two planes. If the line equation employs a direction vector, the angle is determined by taking the dot product of this vector and between the plane's normal. Figure 10.41 shows such a scenario where $\mathbf{n}$ is the plane's surface normal and $\mathbf{v}$ is the line's direction vector.

If the plane equation is

$$ax + by + cz + d = 0$$

then its surface normal is

$$\mathbf{n} = a\mathbf{i} + b\mathbf{j} + c\mathbf{k}.$$

If the line's direction vector is $\mathbf{v}$ and $T(x_T, y_T, z_T)$ is a point on the line, then any point on the line is given by the position vector $\mathbf{p}$:

$$\mathbf{p} = \mathbf{t} + \lambda \mathbf{v}$$

therefore, we can write

$$\mathbf{n} \cdot \mathbf{v} = |\mathbf{n}|\, |\mathbf{v}| \cos \alpha$$

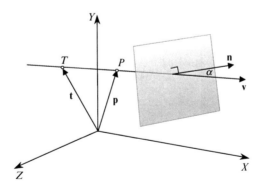

Fig. 10.41 α is the angle between the plane's surface normal and the line's direction vector.

and

$$\alpha = \cos^{-1}\left(\frac{\mathbf{n} \cdot \mathbf{v}}{|\mathbf{n}|\, |\mathbf{v}|}\right).$$

When the line is parallel to the plane $\mathbf{n} \cdot \mathbf{v} = 0$.

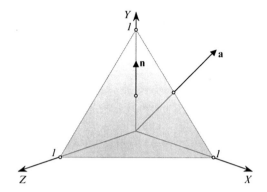

Fig. 10.42 The required angle is between **a** and **b**.

As an example, consider the scenario illustrated in Fig. 10.42 where the plane equation is

$$x + y + z - 1 = 0$$

therefore, the surface normal is given by **n**:

$$\mathbf{n} = \mathbf{i} + \mathbf{j} + \mathbf{k}$$

and the line's direction vector is **a**:

$$\mathbf{a} = \mathbf{i} + \mathbf{j}$$

therefore,

$$|\mathbf{n}| = \sqrt{3} \quad \text{and} \quad |\mathbf{a}| = \sqrt{2}$$

and

$$\alpha = \cos^{-1}\left(\frac{2}{\sqrt{6}}\right) \approx 35.26°.$$

10.9.4 Intersection of a Line with a Plane

Given a line and a plane, they will either intersect or are parallel. Either way, both conditions can be found using some simple vector analysis, as shown in Fig. 10.43. The objective is to identify a point P that is on the line and the plane. Let the plane equation be

$$ax + by + cz + d = 0$$

where

$$\mathbf{n} = a\mathbf{i} + b\mathbf{j} + c\mathbf{k}.$$

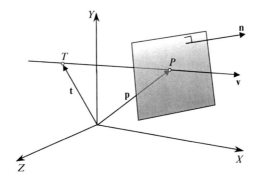

Fig. 10.43 The vectors required to determine whether a line and plane intersect.

P is a point on the plane with position vector

$$\mathbf{p} = x\mathbf{i} + y\mathbf{j} + z\mathbf{k}$$

therefore,

$$\mathbf{n} \cdot \mathbf{p} + d = 0.$$

Let the line equation be

$$\mathbf{p} = \mathbf{t} + \lambda\mathbf{v}$$

where

$$\mathbf{t} = x_T\mathbf{i} + y_T\mathbf{j} + z_T\mathbf{k}$$

and

$$\mathbf{v} = x_v\mathbf{i} + y_v\mathbf{j} + z_v\mathbf{k}$$

therefore, the line and plane will intersect for some λ such that

$$\mathbf{n} \cdot (\mathbf{t} + \lambda\mathbf{v}) + d = \mathbf{n} \cdot \mathbf{t} + \lambda\mathbf{n} \cdot \mathbf{v} + d = 0$$

therefore,

$$\lambda = \frac{-(\mathbf{n} \cdot \mathbf{t} + d)}{\mathbf{n} \cdot \mathbf{v}}$$

for the intersection point. The position vector for P is $\mathbf{p} = \mathbf{t} + \lambda\mathbf{v}$.

If $\mathbf{n} \cdot \mathbf{v} = 0$ the line and plane are parallel. Let's test this result with the scenario shown in Fig. 10.44.

Given the plane

$$x + y + z - 1 = 0$$
$$\mathbf{n} = \mathbf{i} + \mathbf{j} + \mathbf{k}$$

and the line

$$\mathbf{p} = \mathbf{t} + \lambda\mathbf{v}$$

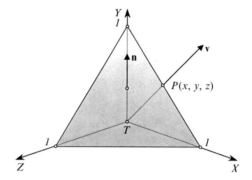

Fig. 10.44 *P* identifies the point where a line intersects a plane.

where

$$\mathbf{t} = 0$$

$$\mathbf{v} = \mathbf{i} + \mathbf{j}$$

then

$$\lambda = \frac{-(1 \times 0 + 1 \times 0 + 1 \times 0 - 1)}{1 \times 1 + 1 \times 1 + 1 \times 0} = 0.5$$

therefore, the point of intersection is $P(0.5, 0.5, 0)$.

10.10 Summary

Mixing vectors with geometry is a powerful analytical tool, and helps us to solve many problems associated with computer graphics, such as rendering, modelling, collision detection and physically-based animation. Unfortunately, there has not been space to investigate every topic, but hopefully, what has been covered, will enable you to solve other problems with greater confidence.

Chapter 11
Barycentric Coordinates

11.1 Introduction

Cartesian coordinates are a fundamental concept in mathematics and are central to computer graphics. Such rectangular coordinates are just offsets relative to some origin. Other coordinate systems also exist such as polar, spherical and cylindrical coordinates, and they, too, require an origin. Barycentric coordinates, on the other hand, locate points relative to existing points, rather than to an origin and are known as *local coordinates*. The German mathematician August Möbius (1790–1868) is credited with their discovery.

'*barus*' is the Greek entomological root for '*heavy*', and barycentric coordinates were originally used for identifying the centre of mass of shapes and objects. It is interesting to note that the prefixes '*bari*', '*bary*' and '*baro*' have also influenced other words such as baritone, baryon (heavy atomic particle) and barometer.

Although barycentric coordinates are used in geometry, computer graphics, relativity and global time systems, they do not appear to be a major topic in a typical math syllabus. Nevertheless, they are important and I would like to describe what they are and how they can be used in computer graphics.

The idea behind barycentric coordinates can be approached from different directions, and I have chosen mass points and linear interpolation. But before we begin this analysis, it will be useful to investigate a rather elegant theorem known as Ceva's Theorem, which we will invoke later in this chapter.

11.2 Ceva's Theorem

Giovanni Ceva (1647–1734) is credited with a theorem associated with the concurrency of lines in a triangle. It states that: In triangle $\triangle ABC$, the lines AA', BB' and CC', where A', B' and C' are points on the opposite sides facing vertices A, B and C respectively, are concurrent (intersect at a common point) if, and only if

J. Vince, *Mathematics for Computer Graphics*, Undergraduate Topics in Computer Science, DOI 10.1007/978-1-84996-023-6_11,
© Springer-Verlag London Limited 2010

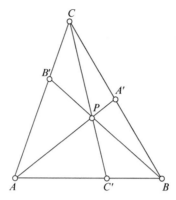

Fig. 11.1 The geometry associated with Ceva's Theorem.

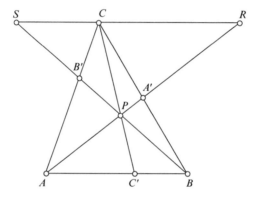

Fig. 11.2 The geometry for proving Ceva's Theorem.

$$\frac{AC'}{C'B} \cdot \frac{BA'}{A'C} \cdot \frac{CB'}{B'A} = 1.$$

Figure 11.1 shows such a scenario.

There are various ways of proving this theorem, (see *Advanced Euclidean Geometry* by Alfred Posamentier) and perhaps the simplest proof is as follows.

Figure 11.2 shows triangle $\triangle ABC$ with line AA' extended to R and BB' extended to S, where line SR is parallel to line AB. The resulting geometry creates a number of similar triangles:

$$\triangle ABA' \quad : \quad \triangle RCA' \quad \Rightarrow \quad \frac{A'C}{BA'} = \frac{CR}{AB} \tag{11.1}$$

$$\triangle ABB' \quad : \quad \triangle CSB' \quad \Rightarrow \quad \frac{B'A}{CB'} = \frac{AB}{SC} \tag{11.2}$$

$$\triangle BPC' \quad : \quad \triangle CSP \quad \Rightarrow \quad \frac{C'B}{SC} = \frac{C'P}{PC} \qquad (11.3)$$

$$\triangle AC'P \quad : \quad \triangle RCP \quad \Rightarrow \quad \frac{AC'}{CR} = \frac{C'P}{PC}. \qquad (11.4)$$

From (11.3) and (11.4) we get

$$\frac{C'B}{SC} = \frac{AC'}{CR}$$

which can be rewritten as

$$\frac{C'B}{AC'} = \frac{SC}{CR}. \qquad (11.5)$$

The product of (11.1), (11.2) and (11.5) is

$$\frac{A'C}{BA'} \cdot \frac{B'A}{CB'} \cdot \frac{C'B}{AC'} = \frac{CR}{AB} \cdot \frac{AB}{SC} \cdot \frac{SC}{CR} = 1. \qquad (11.6)$$

Rearranging the terms of (11.6) we get

$$\frac{AC'}{C'B} \cdot \frac{BA'}{A'C} \cdot \frac{CB'}{B'A} = 1$$

which is rather an elegant relationship.

11.3 Ratios and Proportion

Central to barycentric coordinates are ratios and proportion, so let's begin by revising some fundamental formulae used in calculating ratios.

Imagine the problem of dividing £100 between two people in the ratio $2 : 3$. The solution lies in the fact that the money is divided into five parts $(2 + 3)$, where two parts go to one person and three parts to the other person. In this case, one person receives £40 and the other £60. At a formal level, we can describe this as follows.

A scalar A can be divided into the ratio $r : s$ using the following expressions:

$$\frac{r}{r + s} A \quad \text{and} \quad \frac{s}{r + s} A.$$

Note that

$$\frac{r}{r + s} + \frac{s}{r + s} = 1$$

and

$$1 - \frac{r}{r + s} = \frac{s}{r + s}.$$

Furthermore, the above formulae can be extended to incorporate any number of ratio divisions. For example, A can be divided into the ratio $r : s : t$ by the following:

$$\frac{r}{r + s + t} A, \quad \frac{s}{r + s + t} A \quad \text{and} \quad \frac{t}{r + s + t} A$$

similarly,

$$\frac{r}{r+s+t} + \frac{s}{r+s+t} + \frac{t}{r+s+t} = 1.$$

These expressions are very important as they show the emergence of barycentric coordinates. For the moment, though, just remember their structure and we will investigate some ideas associated with balancing weights.

Fig. 11.3 Two masses fixed at the ends of a massless rod.

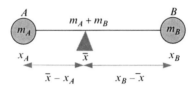

Fig. 11.4 The geometry used for equating turning moments.

11.4 Mass Points

We begin by calculating the centre of mass – the centroid – of two masses. Consider the scenario shown in Fig. 11.3 where two masses m_A and m_B are placed at the ends of a massless rod.

If $m_A = m_B$ a state of equilibrium is achieved by placing the fulcrum mid-way between the masses. If the fulcrum is moved towards m_A, mass m_B will have a turning advantage and the rod rotates clockwise.

To calculate a state of equilibrium for a general system of masses, consider the geometry illustrated in Fig. 11.4, where two masses m_A and m_B are positioned x_A and x_B at A and B respectively. When the system is in balance we can replace the two masses by a single mass $m_A + m_B$ at the centroid denoted by $\bar{x}$.

A balance condition arises when the LHS turning moment equals the RHS turning moment. The turning moment being the product of a mass by its offset from the fulcrum. Equating turning moments, equilibrium is reached when

$$m_B(x_B - \bar{x}) = m_A(\bar{x} - x_A)$$
$$m_B x_B - m_B \bar{x} = m_A \bar{x} - m_A x_A$$
$$(m_A + m_B)\bar{x} = m_A x_A + m_B x_B$$

$$\bar{x} = \frac{m_A x_A + m_B x_B}{m_A + m_B} = \frac{m_A}{m_A + m_B}x_A + \frac{m_B}{m_A + m_B}x_B. \qquad (11.7)$$

For example, if $m_A = 6$ and $m_B = 12$, and positioned at $x_A = 0$ and $x_B = 12$ respectively, the centroid is located at

$$\bar{x} = \frac{6}{18} \times 0 + \frac{12}{18} \times 12 = 8.$$

Thus we can replace the two masses by a single mass of 18 located at $\bar{x} = 8$.

Note that the terms in (11.7) $m_A/(m_A + m_B)$ and $m_B/(m_A + m_B)$ sum to 1 and are identical to those used above for calculating ratios. They are also called the *barycentric coordinates* of $\bar{x}$ relative to the points A and B.

Using the general form of (11.7) any number of masses can be analysed using

$$\bar{x} = \frac{\sum\limits_{i=1}^{n} m_i x_i}{\sum\limits_{i=1}^{n} m_i}$$

where m_i is a mass located at x_i. Furthermore, we can compute the y-component of the centroid $\bar{y}$ using

$$\bar{y} = \frac{\sum\limits_{i=1}^{n} m_i y_i}{\sum\limits_{i=1}^{n} m_i}$$

and in 3D the z-component of the centroid $\bar{z}$ is

$$\bar{z} = \frac{\sum\limits_{i=1}^{n} m_i z_i}{\sum\limits_{i=1}^{n} m_i}.$$

To recap, (11.7) states that

$$\bar{x} = \frac{m_A}{m_A + m_B} x_A + \frac{m_B}{m_A + m_B} x_B$$

therefore, we can write

$$\bar{y} = \frac{m_A}{m_A + m_B} y_A + \frac{m_B}{m_A + m_B} y_B$$

which allows us to state

$$\bar{\mathbf{P}} = \frac{m_A}{m_A + m_B} \mathbf{A} + \frac{m_B}{m_A + m_B} \mathbf{B}$$

where $\mathbf{A}$ and $\mathbf{B}$ are the position vectors for the mass locations A and B respectively, and $\bar{\mathbf{P}}$ is the position vector for the centroid $\bar{P}$.

If we extend the number of masses to three: m_A, m_B and m_C, which are organized as a triangle, then we can write

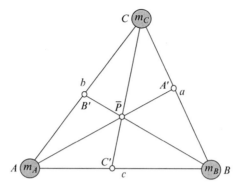

Fig. 11.5 The geometry used for equating turning moments.

$$\bar{\mathbf{P}} = \frac{m_A}{m_A + m_B + m_C}\mathbf{A} + \frac{m_B}{m_A + m_B + m_C}\mathbf{B} + \frac{m_C}{m_A + m_B + m_C}\mathbf{C}. \qquad (11.8)$$

The three multipliers of **A**, **B** and **C** are the barycentric coordinates of $\bar{P}$ relative to the points A, B and C. Note that the number of coordinates is not associated with the number of spatial dimensions, but the number of reference points. Now consider the scenario shown in Fig. 11.5. If $m_A = m_B = m_C$ then we can determine the location of A', B' and C' as follows:

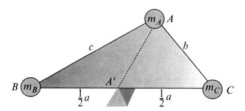

Fig. 11.6 Balancing the triangle along AA'.

1. We begin by placing a fulcrum under A mid-way along BC as shown in Fig. 11.6. The triangle will balance because $m_B = m_C$ and A' is $\frac{1}{2}a$ from C and $\frac{1}{2}a$ from B.
2. Now we place the fulcrum under B mid-way along CA as shown in Fig. 11.7. Once more the triangle will balance, because $m_C = m_A$ and B' is $\frac{1}{2}b$ from C and $\frac{1}{2}b$ from A.
3. Finally, we do the same for C and AB. Figure 11.8 shows the final scenario.

Ceva's Theorem confirms that the medians AA', BB' and CC' are concurrent at $\bar{P}$ because

$$\frac{AC'}{C'B} \cdot \frac{BA'}{A'C} \cdot \frac{CB'}{B'A} = \frac{\frac{1}{2}c}{\frac{1}{2}c} \cdot \frac{\frac{1}{2}a}{\frac{1}{2}a} \cdot \frac{\frac{1}{2}b}{\frac{1}{2}b} = 1.$$

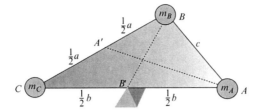

Fig. 11.7 Balancing the triangle along BB'.

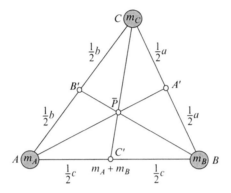

Fig. 11.8 $\bar{P}$ is the centroid of the triangle.

Arbitrarily, we select the median $C'C$. At C' we have an effective mass of $m_A + m_B$ and m_C at C. For a balance condition

$$(m_A + m_B) \times C'\bar{P} = m_C \times \bar{P}C$$

and as the masses are equal, $C'\bar{P}$ must be $\frac{1}{3}$ along the median $C'C$.

If we use (11.8) we obtain

$$\bar{P} = \frac{1}{3}A + \frac{1}{3}B + \frac{1}{3}C$$

which locates the coordinates of the centroid correctly.

Now let's consider another example where $m_A = 1$, $m_B = 2$ and $m_C = 3$, as shown in Fig. 11.9. For a balance condition A' must be $\frac{3}{5}a$ from B and $\frac{2}{5}a$ from C. Equally, B' must be $\frac{1}{4}b$ from C and $\frac{3}{4}b$ from A. Similarly, C' must be $\frac{2}{3}c$ from A and $\frac{1}{3}c$ from B.

Ceva's Theorem confirms that the lines AA', BB' and CC' are concurrent at $\bar{P}$ because

$$\frac{AC'}{C'B} \cdot \frac{BA'}{A'C} \cdot \frac{CB'}{B'A} = \frac{\frac{2}{3}c}{\frac{1}{3}c} \cdot \frac{\frac{3}{5}a}{\frac{2}{5}a} \cdot \frac{\frac{1}{4}b}{\frac{3}{4}b} = 1.$$

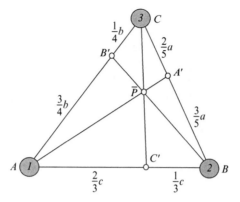

Fig. 11.9 How the masses determine the positions of A', B' and C'.

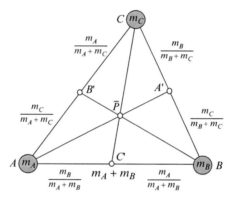

Fig. 11.10 How the masses determine the positions of A', B' and C'.

Arbitrarily select $C'C$. At C' we have an effective mass of 3 $(1+2)$ and 3 at C, which means that for a balance condition $\bar{P}$ is mid-way along $C'C$. Similarly, $\bar{P}$ is $\frac{1}{6}$ along $A'A$ and $\frac{1}{3}$ along $B'B$.

Once more, using (11.8) in this scenario we obtain

$$\bar{P} = \frac{1}{6}\mathbf{A} + \frac{1}{3}\mathbf{B} + \frac{1}{2}\mathbf{C}.$$

Note that the multipliers of $\mathbf{A}$, $\mathbf{B}$ and $\mathbf{C}$ are identical to the proportions of $\bar{P}$ along $A'A$, $B'B$ and $C'C$. Let's prove why this is so.

Figure 11.10 shows three masses with the triangle's sides divided into their various proportions to derive $\bar{P}$.

On the line $A'A$ we have m_A at A and effectively $m_B + m_C$ at A', which means that $\bar{P}$ divides $A'A$ in the ratio $m_A/(m_A + m_B + m_C) : (m_B + m_C)/(m_A + m_B + m_C)$.

On the line $B'B$ we have m_B at B and effectively $m_A + m_C$ at B', which means that $\bar{P}$ divides $B'B$ in the ratio $m_B/(m_A + m_B + m_C) : (m_A + m_C)/(m_A + m_B + m_C)$.

Similarly, on the line $C'C$ we have m_C at C and effectively $m_A + m_B$ at C', which means that $\bar{P}$ divides $C'C$ in the ratio $m_C/(m_A + m_B + m_C) : (m_A + m_B)/(m_A + m_B + m_C)$.

To summarize, given three masses m_A, m_B and m_C located at A, B and C respectively, the centroid $\bar{P}$ is given by

$$\bar{\mathbf{P}} = \frac{m_A}{m_A + m_B + m_C}\mathbf{A} + \frac{m_B}{m_A + m_B + m_C}\mathbf{B} + \frac{m_C}{m_A + m_B + m_C}\mathbf{C}. \qquad (11.9)$$

If we accept that m_A, m_B and m_C can have any value, including zero, then the barycentric coordinates of $\bar{P}$ will be affected by these values. For example, if $m_B = m_C = 0$ and $m_A = 1$, then $\bar{P}$ will be located at A with barycentric coordinates $(1,0,0)$. Similarly, if $m_A = m_C = 0$ and $m_B = 1$, then $\bar{P}$ will be located at B with barycentric coordinates $(0,1,0)$. And if $m_A = m_B = 0$ and $m_C = 1$, then $\bar{P}$ will be located at C with barycentric coordinates $(0,0,1)$.

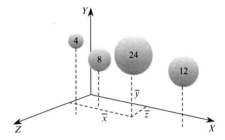

Fig. 11.11 Three masses can be represented by a single mass located at the centroid.

Now let's examine a 3D example as illustrated in Fig. 11.11. The figure shows three masses 4, 8 and 12 and their equivalent mass 24 located at $(\bar{x}, \bar{y}, \bar{z})$.

Table 11.1 The magnitude and coordinates of three masses

m_i	t_i	x_i	y_i	z_i	$t_i x_i$	$t_i y_i$	$t_i z_i$
12	$\frac{1}{2}$	8	6	2	4	3	1
8	$\frac{1}{3}$	2	3	3	$\frac{2}{3}$	1	1
4	$\frac{1}{6}$	2	6	6	$\frac{1}{3}$	1	1
					$\bar{x} = 5$	$\bar{y} = 5$	$\bar{z} = 3$

The magnitude and coordinates of three masses are shown in Table 11.1, together with the barycentric coordinate t_i. The column headed t_i expresses the masses as fractions of the total mass: i.e.,

$$t_i = \frac{m_i}{m_1 + m_2 + m_3}$$

and we see that the centroid is located at $(5, 5, 3)$.

Having discovered barycentric coordinates in weight balancing, let's see how they emerge in linear interpolation.

11.5 Linear Interpolation

Suppose that we wish to find a value mid-way between two scalars A and B. We could proceed as follows:

$$V = A + \frac{1}{2}(B - A)$$
$$= A + \frac{1}{2}B - \frac{1}{2}A$$
$$V = \frac{1}{2}A + \frac{1}{2}B$$

which seems rather obvious. Similarly, to find a value one-third between A and B, we can write

$$V = A + \frac{1}{3}(B - A)$$
$$= A + \frac{1}{3}B - \frac{1}{3}A$$
$$V = \frac{2}{3}A + \frac{1}{3}B.$$

Generalizing, to find some fraction t between A and B we can write

$$V = (1 - t)A + tB. \tag{11.10}$$

For example, to find a value $\frac{3}{4}$ between 10 and 18 we have

$$V = \left(1 - \frac{3}{4}\right) \times 10 + \frac{3}{4} \times 18 = 16.$$

Although this is a trivial formula, it is very useful when interpolating between two numerical values. Let us explore (11.10) in greater detail.

To begin with, it is worth noting that the multipliers of A and B sum to 1:

$$(1 - t) + t = 1.$$

Rather than using $(1 - t)$ as a multiplier, it is convenient to make a substitution such as $s = 1 - t$, and we have

$$V = sA + tB$$

where

$$s = 1 - t$$

and
$$s + t = 1.$$

Equation (11.10) is called a *linear interpolant* as it linearly interpolates between A and B using the parameter t. It is also known as a *lerp*. The terms s and t are the barycentric coordinates of V as they determine the value of V relative to A and B.

Now let's see what happens when we substitute coordinates for scalars. We start with 2D coordinates $A(x_A, y_A)$ and $B(x_B, y_B)$, and position vectors $\mathbf{A}$, $\mathbf{B}$ and $\mathbf{C}$ and the following linear interpolant

$$\mathbf{V} = s\mathbf{A} + t\mathbf{B}$$

where
$$s = 1 - t$$

and
$$s + t = 1$$

then

$$x_V = s x_A + t x_B$$
$$y_V = s y_A + t y_B.$$

Figure 11.12 illustrates what happens when t varies between 0 and 1.

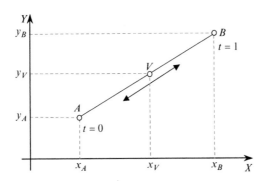

Fig. 11.12 The position of V slides between A and B as t varies between 0 and 1.

The point V slides along the line connecting A and B. When $t = 0$, V is coincident with A, and when $t = 1$, V is coincident with B. The reader should not be surprised that the same technique works in 3D.

Now let's extend the number of vertices to three in the form of a triangle as shown in Fig. 11.13. This time we will use r, s and t to control the interpolation. We would start as follows:

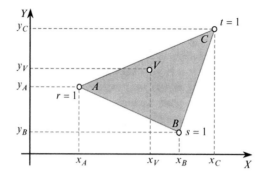

Fig. 11.13 The position of V moves between A, B and C depending on the value r, s and t.

$$\mathbf{V} = r\mathbf{A} + s\mathbf{B} + t\mathbf{C}$$

where $\mathbf{A}$, $\mathbf{B}$ and $\mathbf{C}$ are the position vectors for A, B and C respectively, and $\mathbf{V}$ is the position vector for the point V.

Let

$$r = 1 - s - t$$

and

$$r + s + t = 1.$$

Once more, we begin with 2D coordinates $A(x_A, y_A)$, $B(x_B, y_B)$ and $C(x_C, y_C)$ where

$$x_V = r x_A + s x_B + t x_C$$
$$y_V = r y_A + s y_B + t y_C.$$

When

$$r = 1, \quad V \text{ is coincident with } A;$$
$$s = 1, \quad V \text{ is coincident with } B;$$
$$t = 1, \quad V \text{ is coincident with } C.$$

Similarly, when

$$r = 0, \quad V \text{ is located on the edge } BC;$$
$$s = 0, \quad V \text{ is located on the edge } CA;$$
$$t = 0, \quad V \text{ is located on the edge } AB.$$

For all other values of r, s and t, where $r + s + t = 1$ and $0 \le r, s, t \le 1$, V is inside triangle $\triangle ABC$, otherwise it is outside the triangle.

The triple (r, s, t) are barycentric coordinates and locate points relative to A, B and C, rather than an origin. For example, the barycentric coordinates of A, B and C are $(1, 0, 0)$, $(0, 1, 0)$ and $(0, 0, 1)$ respectively.

All of the above formulae work equally well in three dimensions, so let's investigate how barycentric coordinates can locate points inside a 3D triangle. However, before we start, let's clarify what we mean by *inside* a triangle. Fortunately, barycentric coordinates can distinguish points within the triangle's three sides; points coincident with the sides; and points outside the triangle's boundary. The range and value of the barycentric coordinates provide the mechanism for detecting these three conditions.

Figure 11.14 illustrates a scenario with the points $P_1(x_1,y_1,z_1)$, $P_2(x_2,y_2,z_2)$ and $P_3(x_3,y_3,z_3)$. Using barycentric coordinates we can state that any point $P_0(x_0,y_0,z_0)$ inside or on the edge of triangle $\triangle P_1P_2P_3$ is defined by

$$x_0 = rx_1 + sx_2 + tx_3$$
$$y_0 = ry_1 + sy_2 + ty_3$$
$$z_0 = rz_1 + sz_2 + tz_3$$

where $r+s+t = 1$ and $0 \le r,s,t,\le 1$.

If the triangle's vertices are $P_1(0,2,0)$, $P_2(0,0,4)$ and $P_3(3,1,2)$ then we can choose different values of r, s and t to locate P_0 inside the triangle. However, I would also like to confirm that P_0 lies on the plane containing the three points. To do this we require the plane equation for the three points, which can be derived as follows.

Given $P_1(x_1,y_1,z_1)$, $P_2(x_2,y_2,z_2)$ and $P(x_3,y_3,z_3)$, and the target plane equation $ax + by + cz + d = 0$, then

$$a = \begin{vmatrix} 1 & y_1 & z_1 \\ 1 & y_2 & z_2 \\ 1 & y_3 & z_3 \end{vmatrix}$$

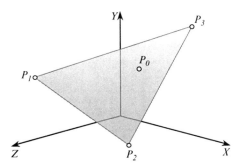

Fig. 11.14 A 3D triangle.

$$b = \begin{vmatrix} x_1 & 1 & z_1 \\ x_2 & 1 & z_2 \\ x_3 & 1 & z_3 \end{vmatrix}$$

$$c = \begin{vmatrix} x_1 & y_1 & 1 \\ x_2 & y_2 & 1 \\ x_3 & y_3 & 1 \end{vmatrix}$$

$$d = -(ax_1 + by_1 + cz_1)$$

thus

$$a = \begin{vmatrix} 1 & 2 & 0 \\ 1 & 0 & 4 \\ 1 & 1 & 2 \end{vmatrix} = 0$$

$$b = \begin{vmatrix} 0 & 1 & 0 \\ 0 & 1 & 4 \\ 3 & 1 & 2 \end{vmatrix} = 12$$

$$c = \begin{vmatrix} 0 & 2 & 1 \\ 0 & 0 & 1 \\ 3 & 1 & 1 \end{vmatrix} = 6$$

$$d = -24$$

therefore, the plane equation is

$$12y + 6z = 24. \tag{11.11}$$

If we substitute a point (x_0, y_0, z_0) in the LHS of (11.11) and obtain a value of 24, then the point is on the plane.

Table 11.2 shows various values of r, s and t, and the corresponding position of P_0. The table also confirms that is always on the plane containing the three points. Now we are in a position to test whether a point is inside, on the boundary or outside a 3D triangle.

Table 11.2 The barycentric coordinates of P_0

r	s	t	x_0	y_0	z_0	$12y_0 + 6z_0$
1	0	0	0	2	0	24
0	1	0	0	0	4	24
0	0	1	3	1	2	24
$\frac{1}{4}$	$\frac{1}{4}$	$\frac{1}{2}$	$1\frac{1}{2}$	1	2	24
0	$\frac{1}{2}$	$\frac{1}{2}$	$1\frac{1}{2}$	$\frac{1}{2}$	3	24
$\frac{1}{2}$	$\frac{1}{2}$	0	0	1	2	24
$\frac{1}{3}$	$\frac{1}{3}$	$\frac{1}{3}$	1	1	2	24

We begin by writing the three simultaneous equations defining P_0 in matrix form

$$\begin{bmatrix} x_0 \\ y_0 \\ z_0 \end{bmatrix} = \begin{bmatrix} x_1 & x_2 & x_3 \\ y_1 & y_2 & y_3 \\ z_1 & z_2 & z_3 \end{bmatrix} \cdot \begin{bmatrix} r \\ s \\ t \end{bmatrix}$$

therefore,

$$\frac{r}{\begin{vmatrix} x_0 & x_2 & x_3 \\ y_0 & y_2 & y_3 \\ z_0 & z_2 & z_3 \end{vmatrix}} = \frac{s}{\begin{vmatrix} x_1 & x_0 & x_3 \\ y_1 & y_0 & y_3 \\ z_1 & z_0 & z_3 \end{vmatrix}} = \frac{t}{\begin{vmatrix} x_1 & x_2 & x_0 \\ y_1 & y_2 & y_0 \\ z_1 & z_2 & z_0 \end{vmatrix}} = \frac{1}{\begin{vmatrix} x_1 & x_2 & x_3 \\ y_1 & y_2 & y_3 \\ z_1 & z_2 & z_3 \end{vmatrix}}$$

and

$$r = \frac{\begin{vmatrix} x_0 & x_2 & x_3 \\ y_0 & y_2 & y_3 \\ z_0 & z_2 & z_3 \end{vmatrix}}{DET}$$

$$s = \frac{\begin{vmatrix} x_1 & x_0 & x_3 \\ y_1 & y_0 & y_3 \\ z_1 & z_0 & z_3 \end{vmatrix}}{DET}$$

$$t = \frac{\begin{vmatrix} x_1 & x_2 & x_0 \\ y_1 & y_2 & y_0 \\ z_1 & z_2 & z_0 \end{vmatrix}}{DET}$$

$$DET = \begin{vmatrix} x_1 & x_2 & x_3 \\ y_1 & y_2 & y_3 \\ z_1 & z_2 & z_3 \end{vmatrix} .$$

Using the three points $P_1(0,2,0)$, $P_2(0,0,4)$, $P_3(3,1,2)$ and arbitrary positions of P_0, the values of r, s and t identify whether P_0 is inside or outside triangle $\triangle ABC$. For example, the point $P_0(0,2,0)$ is a vertex and is classified as being on the boundary. To confirm this we calculate r, s and t, and show that $r+s+t = 1$:

$$DET = \begin{vmatrix} 0 & 0 & 3 \\ 2 & 0 & 1 \\ 0 & 4 & 2 \end{vmatrix} = 24$$

$$r = \frac{\begin{vmatrix} 0 & 0 & 3 \\ 2 & 0 & 1 \\ 0 & 4 & 2 \end{vmatrix}}{24} = 1$$

$$s = \frac{\begin{vmatrix} 0 & 0 & 3 \\ 2 & 2 & 1 \\ 0 & 0 & 2 \end{vmatrix}}{24} = 0$$

$$t = \frac{\begin{vmatrix} 0 & 0 & 0 \\ 2 & 0 & 2 \\ 0 & 4 & 0 \end{vmatrix}}{24} = 0$$

therefore $r+s+t = 1$, but both s and t are zero which confirms that the point $(0,2,0)$ is on the boundary. In fact, as both coordinates are zero it confirms that the point is located on a vertex.

Now let's deliberately choose a point outside the triangle. For example, $P_0(4,0,3)$ is outside the triangle, which is confirmed by the corresponding values of r, s and t:

$$r = \frac{\begin{vmatrix} 4 & 0 & 3 \\ 0 & 0 & 1 \\ 3 & 4 & 2 \end{vmatrix}}{24} = -\frac{2}{3}$$

$$s = \frac{\begin{vmatrix} 0 & 4 & 3 \\ 2 & 0 & 1 \\ 0 & 3 & 2 \end{vmatrix}}{24} = \frac{3}{4}$$

$$t = \frac{\begin{vmatrix} 0 & 0 & 4 \\ 2 & 0 & 0 \\ 0 & 4 & 3 \end{vmatrix}}{24} = \frac{4}{3}$$

therefore,

$$r+s+t = -\frac{2}{3} + \frac{3}{4} + \frac{4}{3} = 1\frac{5}{12}$$

which confirms that the point $(4,0,3)$ is outside the triangle. Note that $r < 0$ and $t > 1$, which individually confirm that the point is outside the triangle's boundary.

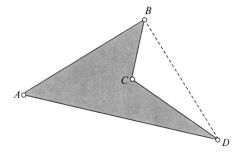

Fig. 11.15 A concave polygon.

11.6 Convex Hull Property

We have already shown that it is possible to determine whether a point is inside or outside a triangle. But remember that triangles are always convex. So can we test whether a point is inside or outside any polygon? Well the answer is no, unless the polygon is convex. The reason for this can be understood by considering the concave polygon shown in Fig. 11.15.

If we use barycentric coordinates to define a point P_0 as

$$\mathbf{P_0} = r\mathbf{A} + s\mathbf{B} + t\mathbf{C} + u\mathbf{D}$$

where $r + s + t + u = 1$. When $t = 0$, P_0 can exist anywhere inside triangle ΔABD. Thus, if any vertex creates a concavity, it will be ignored by barycentric coordinates.

11.7 Areas

Barycentric coordinates are also known as *areal coordinates* due to their area dividing properties. For example, in Fig. 11.16 the areas of the three internal triangles are in proportion to the barycentric coordinates of the point P.

To prove this, let P have barycentric coordinates

$$\mathbf{P} = r\mathbf{A} + s\mathbf{B} + t\mathbf{C}$$

where

$$r + s + t = 1$$

and

$$0 \leq (r, s, t) \leq 1.$$

If we use the notation *areaΔABC* to represent the area of the triangle formed from the vertices A, B and C then *areaΔABC* equals the sum of the areas of the smaller triangles:

$$area\Delta ABC = area\Delta ABP + area\Delta BCP + area\Delta CAP.$$

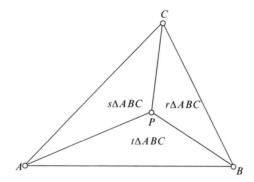

Fig. 11.16 The areas of the internal triangles are directly proportional to the barycentric coordinates of P.

But the area of any triangle $\Delta P_1 P_2 P_3$ equals

$$area\Delta P_1 P_2 P_3 = \frac{1}{2} \begin{vmatrix} x_1 & y_1 & 1 \\ x_2 & y_2 & 1 \\ x_3 & y_3 & 1 \end{vmatrix}$$

therefore,

$$area\Delta ABP = \frac{1}{2} \begin{vmatrix} x_A & y_A & 1 \\ x_B & y_B & 1 \\ x_P & y_P & 1 \end{vmatrix}$$

but

$$x_P = rx_A + sx_B + tx_C$$

and

$$y_P = ry_A + sy_B + ty_C$$

therefore,

$$area\Delta ABP = \frac{1}{2} \begin{vmatrix} x_A & y_A & 1 \\ x_B & y_B & 1 \\ rx_A + sx_B + tx_C & ry_A + sy_B + ty_C & 1 \end{vmatrix}$$

which expands to

$$area\Delta ABP = \frac{1}{2}\left[\begin{array}{l} x_A y_B + rx_B y_A + sx_B y_B + tx_B y_C + rx_A y_A + sx_B y_A + tx_C y_A - \\ rx_A y_A - sx_A y_B - tx_A y_C - x_B y_A - rx_A y_B - sx_B y_B - tx_C y_B \end{array} \right]$$

$$= \frac{1}{2}\left[\begin{array}{l} x_A y_B - x_B y_A + r(x_B y_A - x_A y_B) + s(x_B y_A - x_A y_B) + \\ t(x_B y_C - x_C y_B) + t(x_C y_A - x_A y_C) \end{array} \right]$$

$$= \frac{1}{2} \left[\begin{array}{c} x_A y_B - x_B y_A + (1-t)(x_B y_A - x_A y_B) + t(x_B y_C - x_C y_B) + \\ t(x_C y_A - x_A y_C) \end{array} \right]$$

$$= \frac{1}{2} [-t x_B y_A + t x_A y_B + t x_B y_C - t x_C y_B + t x_C y_A - t x_A y_C]$$

and simplifies to

$$area\Delta ABP = \frac{1}{2} t \begin{vmatrix} x_A & y_A & 1 \\ x_B & y_B & 1 \\ x_C & y_C & 1 \end{vmatrix} = t \times area\Delta ABC$$

therefore,

$$t = \frac{area\Delta ABP}{area\Delta ABC}$$

similarly,

$$area\Delta BCP = \frac{1}{2} r \begin{vmatrix} x_A & y_A & 1 \\ x_B & y_B & 1 \\ x_C & y_C & 1 \end{vmatrix} = r \times area\Delta ABC$$

$$r = \frac{area\Delta BCP}{area\Delta ABC}$$

and

$$area\Delta CAP = \frac{1}{2} s \begin{vmatrix} x_A & y_A & 1 \\ x_B & y_B & 1 \\ x_C & y_C & 1 \end{vmatrix} = s \times area\Delta ABC$$

$$s = \frac{area\Delta CAP}{area\Delta ABC}.$$

Thus, we see that the areas of the internal triangles are directly proportional to the barycentric coordinates of P.

This is quite a useful relationship and can be used to resolve various geometric problems. For example, let's use it to find the radius and centre of the inscribed circle for a triangle. We could approach this problem using classical Euclidean geometry, but barycentric coordinates provide a powerful analytical tool for resolving the problem very quickly. Consider triangle ΔABC with sides a, b and c as shown in Fig. 11.17. The point P is the centre of the inscribed circle with radius R. From our knowledge of barycentric coordinates we know that

$$\mathbf{P} = r\mathbf{A} + s\mathbf{B} + t\mathbf{C}$$

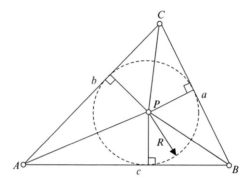

Fig. 11.17 The inscribed circle in triangle $\triangle ABC$.

where

$$r + s + t = 1. \tag{11.12}$$

We also know that the area properties of barycentric coordinates permit us to state

$$area\triangle BCP = r \times area\triangle ABC = \frac{1}{2}aR$$

$$area\triangle CAP = s \times area\triangle ABC = \frac{1}{2}bR$$

$$area\triangle ABP = t \times area\triangle ABC = \frac{1}{2}cR$$

therefore,

$$r = \frac{aR}{2 \times area\triangle ABC} \quad s = \frac{bR}{2 \times area\triangle ABC} \quad t = \frac{cR}{2 \times area\triangle ABC}$$

substituting r, s and t in (11.12) we get

$$\frac{R}{2 \times area\triangle ABC}(a + b + c) = 1$$

and

$$R = \frac{2 \times area\triangle ABC}{(a + b + c)}.$$

Substituting R in the definitions of r, s and t we obtain

$$r = \frac{a}{a + b + c} \quad s = \frac{b}{a + b + c} \quad t = \frac{c}{a + b + c}$$

and

$$x_P = rx_A + sx_B + tx_C$$
$$y_P = ry_A + sy_B + ty_C.$$

To test this solution, consider the right-angled triangle in Fig. 11.18, where $a = \sqrt{200}$, $b = 10$, $c = 10$ and $area \triangle ABC = 50$. Therefore

$$R = \frac{2 \times 50}{10 + 10 + \sqrt{200}} \approx 2.929$$

and

$$r = \frac{\sqrt{200}}{34.1421} \approx 0.4142 \quad s = \frac{10}{34.1421} \approx 0.2929 \quad t = \frac{10}{34.1421} \approx 0.2929$$

therefore,

$$x_P = 0.4142 \times 0 + 0.2929 \times 10 + 0.2929 \times 0 \approx 2.929$$
$$y_P = 0.4142 \times 0 + 0.2929 \times 0 + 0.2929 \times 0 \approx 2.929.$$

Therefore, the inscribed circle has a radius of 2.929 and a centre with coordinates (2.929, 2.929).

Let's explore another example where we determine the barycentric coordinates of a point using virtual mass points.

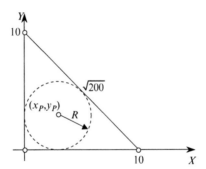

Fig. 11.18 The inscribed circle for a triangle.

Figure 11.19 shows triangle $\triangle ABC$ where A', B' and C' divide BC, CA and AB respectively, in the ratio 1 : 2. The objective is to find the barycentric coordinates of D, E and F, and the area of triangle $\triangle DEF$ as a proportion of triangle $\triangle ABC$.

We can approach the problem using mass points. For example, if we assume D is the centroid, all we have to do is determine the mass points that create this situation. Then the barycentric coordinates of D are given by (11.8). We proceed as follows.

The point D is on the intersection of lines CC' and AA'. Therefore, we begin by placing a mass of 1 at C. Then, for line BC to balance at A' a mass of 2 must be placed at B. Similarly, for line AB to balance at C' a mass of 4 must be placed at A. This configuration is shown in Fig. 11.20.

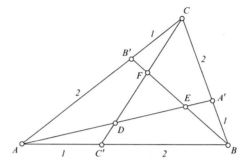

Fig. 11.19 Triangle $\triangle ABC$ with sides divided in the ratio $1 : 2$.

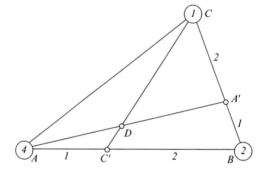

Fig. 11.20 The masses assigned to A, B and C to determine D.

The total mass is $7 = (1 + 2 + 4)$, therefore,

$$D = \frac{4}{7}A + \frac{2}{7}B + \frac{1}{7}C.$$

The point E is on the intersection of lines BB' and AA'. Therefore, we begin by placing a mass of 1 at A. Then, for line CA to balance at B' a mass of 2 must be placed at C. Similarly, for line BC to balance at A' a mass of 4 must be placed at B. This configuration is shown in Fig. 11.21. The total mass is still 7, therefore,

$$E = \frac{1}{7}A + \frac{4}{7}B + \frac{2}{7}C.$$

From the symmetry of the triangle we can state that

$$F = \frac{2}{7}A + \frac{1}{7}B + \frac{4}{7}C.$$

Thus we can locate the points and using the vector equations

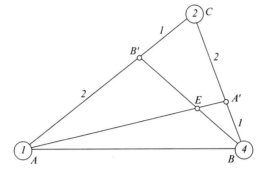

Fig. 11.21 The masses assigned to A, B and C to determine E.

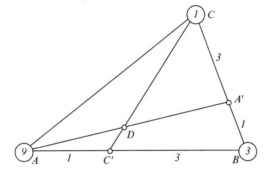

Fig. 11.22 The masses assigned to A, B and C to determine D.

$$\mathbf{D} = \frac{4}{7}\mathbf{A} + \frac{2}{7}\mathbf{B} + \frac{1}{7}\mathbf{C}$$

$$\mathbf{E} = \frac{1}{7}\mathbf{A} + \frac{4}{7}\mathbf{B} + \frac{2}{7}\mathbf{C}$$

$$\mathbf{F} = \frac{2}{7}\mathbf{A} + \frac{1}{7}\mathbf{B} + \frac{4}{7}\mathbf{C}.$$

The important feature of these equations is that the barycentric coordinates of D, E and F are independent of $\mathbf{A}$, $\mathbf{B}$ and $\mathbf{C}$ they arise from the ratio used to divide the triangle's sides.

Although it was not the original intention, we can quickly explore what the barycentric coordinates of D, E and F would be if the triangle's sides had been $1 : 3$ instead of $1 : 2$. Without repeating all of the above steps, we would proceed as follows.

The point D is on the intersection of lines CC' and AA'. Therefore, we begin by placing a mass of 1 at C. Then, for line BC to balance at A' a mass of 3 must be placed at B. Similarly, for line AB to balance at C' a mass of 9 must be placed at A. This configuration is shown in Fig. 11.22. The total mass is $13 = (1 + 3 + 9)$, therefore,

$$D = \frac{9}{13}\mathbf{A} + \frac{3}{13}\mathbf{B} + \frac{1}{13}\mathbf{C}$$

$$E = \frac{1}{13}\mathbf{A} + \frac{9}{13}\mathbf{B} + \frac{3}{13}\mathbf{C}$$

$$F = \frac{3}{13}\mathbf{A} + \frac{1}{13}\mathbf{B} + \frac{9}{13}\mathbf{C}.$$

We could even develop the general equations for a ratio $1 : n$. It is left to the reader to show that

$$D = \frac{n^2}{n^2+n+1}\mathbf{A} + \frac{n}{n^2+n+1}\mathbf{B} + \frac{1}{n^2+n+1}\mathbf{C}$$

$$E = \frac{1}{n^2+n+1}\mathbf{A} + \frac{n^2}{n^2+n+1}\mathbf{B} + \frac{n}{n^2+n+1}\mathbf{C}$$

$$F = \frac{n}{n^2+n+1}\mathbf{A} + \frac{1}{n^2+n+1}\mathbf{B} + \frac{n^2}{n^2+n+1}\mathbf{C}.$$

As a quick test for the above equations, let $n = 1$, which make D, E and F concurrent at the triangle's centroid:

$$D = \frac{1}{3}\mathbf{A} + \frac{1}{3}\mathbf{B} + \frac{1}{3}\mathbf{C}$$

$$E = \frac{1}{3}\mathbf{A} + \frac{1}{3}\mathbf{B} + \frac{1}{3}\mathbf{C}$$

$$F = \frac{1}{3}\mathbf{A} + \frac{1}{3}\mathbf{B} + \frac{1}{3}\mathbf{C}$$

which is rather reassuring!

Now let's return to the final part of the problem and determine the area of triangle ΔDEF in terms of ΔABC. The strategy is to split triangle ΔABC into four triangles: ΔBCF, ΔCAD, ΔABE and ΔDEF as shown in Fig. 11.23.

Therefore,

$$area \Delta ABC = area \Delta BCF + area \Delta CAD + area \Delta ABE + area \Delta DEF$$

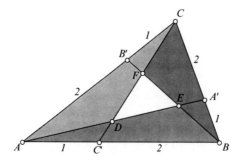

Fig. 11.23 Triangle ΔABC divides into four triangles ΔABE, ΔBCF, ΔCAD and ΔDEF.

and

$$1 = \frac{area\triangle BCF}{area\triangle ABC} + \frac{area\triangle CAD}{area\triangle ABC} + \frac{area\triangle ABE}{area\triangle ABC} + \frac{area\triangle DEF}{area\triangle ABC} \qquad (11.13)$$

But we have just discovered that the barycentric coordinates are intimately connected with the ratios of triangles. For example, if F has barycentric coordinates (r_F, s_F, t_F) relative to the points A, B and C respectively, then

$$r_F = \frac{area\triangle BCF}{area\triangle ABC}.$$

And if D has barycentric coordinates (r_D, s_D, t_D) relative to the points A, B and C respectively, then

$$s_D = \frac{area\triangle CAD}{area\triangle ABC}.$$

Similarly, if E has barycentric coordinates (r_E, s_E, t_E) relative to the points A, B and C respectively, then

$$t_E = \frac{area\triangle ABE}{area\triangle ABC}.$$

Substituting r_F, s_E and t_D in (11.7) we obtain

$$1 = r_F + s_D + t_E + \frac{area\triangle DEF}{area\triangle ABC}.$$

From (11.12) we see that

$$r_F = \frac{2}{7} \quad s_D = \frac{2}{7} \quad t_E = \frac{2}{7}$$

therefore,

$$1 = \frac{6}{7} + \frac{area\triangle DEF}{area\triangle ABC}$$

and

$$area\triangle DEF = \frac{1}{7} area\triangle ABC$$

which is rather neat!

But just before we leave this example, let's state a general expression for the $area\triangle DEF$ for a triangle whose sides are divided in the ratio $1 : n$ Once again, I'll leave it to the reader to prove that

$$area\triangle DEF = \frac{n^2 - 2n + 1}{n^2 + n + 1} \times area\triangle ABC.$$

Note that when $n = 1$, $area\triangle DEF = 0$, which is correct.

[Hint: The corresponding values of r_F, s_D and t_E are $n/(n^2 + n + 1)$.]

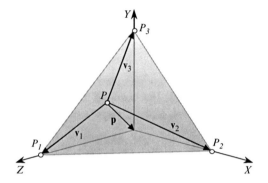

Fig. 11.24 A tetrahedron.

11.8 Volumes

We have now seen that barycentric coordinates can be used to locate a scalar within a 1D domain, a point within a 2D area, so it seems logical that the description should extend to 3D volumes, which is the case.

To demonstrate this, consider the tetrahedron shown in Fig. 11.24. The volume of a tetrahedron is give by

$$V = \frac{1}{6} \begin{vmatrix} x_1 & y_1 & z_1 \\ x_2 & y_2 & z_2 \\ x_3 & y_3 & z_3 \end{vmatrix}$$

where $[x_1\ y_1\ z_1]^T$, $[x_2\ y_2\ z_2]^T$ and $[x_3\ y_3\ z_3]^T$ are the three vectors extending from the fourth vertex to the other three vertices. However, if we locate the fourth vertex at the origin, (x_1, y_1, z_1), (x_2, y_2, z_2) and (x_3, y_3, z_3) become the coordinates of the three vertices.

Let's locate a point $P(x_P, y_P, z_P)$ inside the tetrahedron with the following barycentric definition

$$\mathbf{P} = r\mathbf{P}_1 + s\mathbf{P}_2 + t\mathbf{P}_3 + u\mathbf{P}_4 \tag{11.14}$$

where $\mathbf{P}$, $\mathbf{P}_1$, $\mathbf{P}_2$ and $\mathbf{P}_4$ are the position vectors for P, P_1, P_2, P_3 and P_4 respectively. The fourth barycentric term $u\mathbf{P}_4$ can be omitted as P_4 has coordinates $(0,0,0)$.

Therefore, we can state that the volume of the tetrahedron formed by the three vectors $\mathbf{P}$, $\mathbf{P}_2$ and $\mathbf{P}_3$ is given by

$$V = \frac{1}{6} \begin{vmatrix} x_P & y_P & z_P \\ x_2 & y_2 & z_2 \\ x_3 & y_3 & z_3 \end{vmatrix}. \tag{11.15}$$

Substituting (11.14) in (11.15) we obtain

$$V = \frac{1}{6} \begin{vmatrix} rx_1 + sx_2 + tx_3 & ry_1 + sy_2 + ty_3 & rz_1 + sz_2 + tz_3 \\ x_2 & y_2 & z_2 \\ x_3 & y_3 & z_3 \end{vmatrix} \quad (11.16)$$

which expands to

$$V = \frac{1}{6} \begin{vmatrix} y_2z_3(rx_1 + sx_2 + tx_3) + x_2y_3(rz_1 + sz_2 + tz_3) + x_3z_2(ry_1 + sy_2 + ty_3) \\ -y_3z_2(rx_1 + sx_2 + tx_3) - x_3y_2(rz_1 + sz_2 + tz_3) - x_2z_3(ry_1 + sy_2 + ty_3) \end{vmatrix}$$

$$= \frac{1}{6} \begin{vmatrix} r(x_1y_2z_3 + x_2y_3z_1 + x_3y_1z_2 - x_1y_3z_2 - x_3y_2z_1 - x_2y_1z_3) \\ +s(x_2y_2z_3 + x_2y_3z_2 + x_3y_1z_2 - x_2y_3z_2 - x_3y_1z_2 - x_2y_2z_3) \\ +t(x_3y_2z_3 + x_2y_3z_3 + x_3y_3z_2 - x_3y_3z_2 - x_3y_2z_3 - x_2y_3z_3) \end{vmatrix}$$

and simplifies to

$$V = \frac{1}{6} r \begin{vmatrix} x_1 & y_1 & z_1 \\ x_2 & y_2 & z_2 \\ x_3 & y_3 & z_3 \end{vmatrix}.$$

This states that the volume of the smaller tetrahedron is r times the volume of the larger tetrahedron V_T, where r is the barycentric coordinate modifying the vertex not included in the volume. By a similar process we can develop volumes for the other tetrahedra:

$$V(P, P_2P_4, P_3) = rV_T$$
$$V(P, P_1P_3, P_4) = sV_T$$
$$V(P, P_1P_2, P_4) = tV_T$$
$$V(P, P_1P_2, P_3) = uV_T$$

where $r + s + t + u = 1$.

Similarly, the barycentric coordinates of a point inside the volume sum to unity.

Let's test the above statements with an example. Figure 11.25 shows a tetrahedron and a point $P(\frac{1}{3}, \frac{1}{3}, \frac{1}{3})$ located within its interior.

The volume of the tetrahedron V_T is

$$V_T = \frac{1}{6} \begin{vmatrix} 0 & 0 & 1 \\ 1 & 0 & 0 \\ 0 & 1 & 0 \end{vmatrix} = \frac{1}{6}$$

$$r = \frac{V(P,P_2,P_4,P_3)}{V_T} = \frac{6}{6} \begin{vmatrix} \frac{2}{3} & -\frac{1}{3} & -\frac{1}{3} \\ -\frac{1}{3} & -\frac{1}{3} & -\frac{1}{3} \\ -\frac{1}{3} & \frac{2}{3} & -\frac{1}{3} \end{vmatrix} = \frac{1}{3}$$

$$s = \frac{V(P,P_1,P_3,P_4)}{V_T} = \frac{6}{6} \begin{vmatrix} -\frac{1}{3} & -\frac{1}{3} & \frac{2}{3} \\ -\frac{1}{3} & \frac{2}{3} & -\frac{1}{3} \\ -\frac{1}{3} & -\frac{1}{3} & -\frac{1}{3} \end{vmatrix} = \frac{1}{3}$$

$$t = \frac{V(P,P_1,P_2,P_4)}{V_T} = \frac{6}{6} \begin{vmatrix} -\frac{1}{3} & -\frac{1}{3} & \frac{2}{3} \\ \frac{2}{3} & -\frac{1}{3} & -\frac{1}{3} \\ -\frac{1}{3} & -\frac{1}{3} & -\frac{1}{3} \end{vmatrix} = \frac{1}{3}$$

$$u = \frac{V(P,P_1,P_2,P_3)}{V_T} = \frac{6}{6} \begin{vmatrix} -\frac{1}{3} & -\frac{1}{3} & \frac{2}{3} \\ \frac{2}{3} & -\frac{1}{3} & -\frac{1}{3} \\ -\frac{1}{3} & \frac{2}{3} & -\frac{1}{3} \end{vmatrix} = 0.$$

The barycentric coordinates (r,s,t,u) confirm that the point is located at the centre of triangle $\Delta P_1 P_2 P_3$. Note that the above determinants will create a negative volume if the vector sequences are reversed.

11.9 Bézier Curves and Patches

In Chapter 9 we examined Bézier curves and surface patches which are based on Bernstein polynomials:

$$\mathbf{B}_i^n(t) = \binom{n}{i} t^i (1-t)^{n-i}.$$

We discovered that these polynomials create the quadratic terms

$$(1-t)^2 \quad 2t(1-t) \quad t^2$$

and the cubic terms

$$(1-t)^3 \quad 3t(1-t)^2 \quad 3t^2(1-t) \quad t^3$$

which are used as scalars to multiply sequences of control points to create a parametric curve. Furthermore, these terms sum to unity, therefore they are also another form of barycentric coordinates. The only difference between these terms and the others described above is that they are controlled by a common parameter t. Another property of Bézier curves and patches is that they are constrained within the convex hull formed by the control points, which is also a property of barycentric coordinates.

11.10 Summary

To summarize, barycentric coordinates are regularly used to determine:

1. How a value is divided into various ratios. For example, a scalar A is divided into the ratios $r : s : t$ using

$$\frac{r}{r+s+t}A, \quad \frac{s}{r+s+t}A, \quad \frac{t}{r+s+t}A.$$

2. The mid-point between two points A and B:

$$P = \frac{1}{2}A + \frac{1}{2}B.$$

3. The centroid of triangle $\triangle ABC$:

$$\bar{P} = \frac{1}{3}A + \frac{1}{3}B + \frac{1}{3}C.$$

4. A point on a line through two points A and B:

$$P = (1-t)A + tB.$$

5. Whether a point is inside or outside triangle $\triangle ABC$:

$$P = rA + sB + tC.$$

P is inside or on the boundary of triangle $\triangle ABC$ when $0 \le (r,s,t) \le 1$, otherwise it is outside.

6. Whether a point is inside a tetrahedron (P_1, P_2, P_3, P_4):

$$P = rP_1 + sP_2 + tP_3 + uP_4.$$

P is inside the tetrahedron when $0 \le r,s,t,u \le 1$, otherwise it is outside.

7. Centres of gravity:

$$\bar{x} = \frac{\sum_{i=1}^{n} m_i x_i}{\sum_{i=1}^{n} m_i} \quad \bar{y} = \frac{\sum_{i=1}^{n} m_i y_i}{\sum_{i=1}^{n} m_i} \quad \bar{z} = \frac{\sum_{i=1}^{n} m_i z_i}{\sum_{i=1}^{n} m_i}$$

where m_i is a mass located at P_i.

Chapter 12
Geometric Algebra

12.1 Introduction

This can only be a brief introduction to geometric algebra as the subject really demands an entire book. Those readers who wish to pursue the subject further should consult the author's books: *Geometric Algebra for Computer Graphics* or *Geometric Algebra: An Algebraic System for Computer Games and Animation.*

Although geometric algebra introduces some new ideas, the subject should not be regarded as difficult. If you have read and understood the previous chapters, you should be familiar with vectors, vector products, transforms, and the idea that the product of two transforms is sensitive to the transform sequence. For example, in general, scaling an object after it has been translated, is not the same as translating an object after it has been scaled. Similarly, given two vectors **r** and **s** their vector product **r** × **s** creates a third vector **t**, using the right-hand rule, perpendicular to the plane containing **r** and **s**. However, just by reversing the vectors to **s** × **r**, creates a similar vector but in the opposite direction −**t**.

We regard vectors as *directed* lines or *oriented* lines, but if they exist, why shouldn't oriented planes and oriented volumes exist? Well the answer to this question is that they do, which is what geometric algebra is about. Unfortunately, when vectors were invented, geometric algebra was overlooked, and it has taken a further century for it to emerge through the work of William Kingdon Clifford (1845–1879) and David Hestenes. So let's continue and discover an exciting new algebra that will, in time, be embraced by the computer graphics community.

12.2 Symmetric and Antisymmetric Functions

It is possible to classify functions into two categories: *symmetric* (*even*) and *antisymmetric* (*odd*) functions. For example, given two symmetric functions $f(x)$ and $f(x, y)$:

$$f(-x) = f(x)$$

J. Vince, *Mathematics for Computer Graphics*, Undergraduate Topics in Computer Science, DOI 10.1007/978-1-84996-023-6_12,

and

$$f(y, x) = f(x, y)$$

an example being $\cos x$ where $\cos(-x) = \cos x$. Figure 12.1 illustrates how the cosine function is reflected about the origin. However, if the functions are antisymmetric:

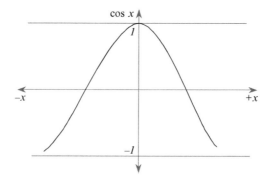

Fig. 12.1 The graph of the symmetric cosine function.

$$f(-x) = -f(x)$$

and

$$f(y, x) = -f(x, y)$$

an example being $\sin x$ where $\sin(-x) = -\sin x$. Figure 12.2 illustrates how the sine function is reflected about the origin.

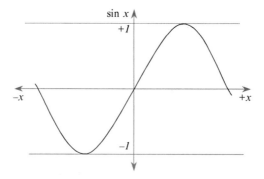

Fig. 12.2 The graph of the antisymmetric sine function.

The reason why we have examined symmetric and antisymmetric functions is that they play an important role in geometric algebra. Now let's continue with this introduction and explore some important trigonometric foundations.

12.3 Trigonometric Foundations

Figure 12.3 shows two line segments a and b with coordinates (a_1, a_2), (b_1, b_2) respectively. The lines are separated by an angle θ, and we will compute the expressions $ab \cos \theta$ and $ab \sin \theta$, as these play an important role in geometric algebra.

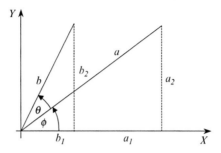

Fig. 12.3 Two line segments a and b separated by $+\theta$.

Using the trigonometric identities

$$\sin(\theta + \phi) = \sin \theta \cos \phi + \cos \theta \sin \phi \tag{12.1}$$

$$\cos(\theta + \phi) = \cos \theta \cos \phi - \sin \theta \sin \phi \tag{12.2}$$

and the following observations

$$\cos \phi = \frac{a_1}{a} \quad \sin \phi = \frac{a_2}{a} \quad \cos(\theta + \phi) = \frac{b_1}{b} \quad \sin(\theta + \phi) = \frac{b_2}{b}$$

we can rewrite (12.1) and (12.2) as

$$\frac{b_2}{b} = \frac{a_1}{a} \sin \theta + \frac{a_2}{a} \cos \theta \tag{12.3}$$

$$\frac{b_1}{b} = \frac{a_1}{a} \cos \theta - \frac{a_2}{a} \sin \theta. \tag{12.4}$$

To isolate $\cos \theta$ we multiply (12.3) by a_2 and (12.4) by a_1:

$$\frac{a_2 b_2}{b} = \frac{a_1 a_2}{a} \sin \theta + \frac{a_2^2}{a} \cos \theta \tag{12.5}$$

$$\frac{a_1 b_1}{b} = \frac{a_1^2}{a} \cos \theta - \frac{a_1 a_2}{a} \sin \theta. \tag{12.6}$$

Adding (12.5) and (12.6) we obtain

$$\frac{a_1 b_1 + a_2 b_2}{b} = \frac{a_1^2 + a_2^2}{a} \cos \theta = a \cos \theta$$

therefore,

$$ab \cos \theta = a_1 b_1 + a_2 b_2.$$

To isolate $\sin \theta$ we multiply (12.3) by a_1 and (12.4) by a_2

$$\frac{a_1 b_2}{b} = \frac{a_1^2}{a} \sin \theta + \frac{a_1 a_2}{a} \cos \theta \qquad (12.7)$$

$$\frac{a_2 b_1}{b} = \frac{a_1 a_2}{a} \cos \theta - \frac{a_2^2}{a} \sin \theta. \qquad (12.8)$$

Subtracting (12.8) from (12.7) we obtain

$$\frac{a_1 b_2 - a_2 b_1}{b} = \frac{a_1^2 + a_2^2}{a} \sin \theta = a \sin \theta$$

therefore,

$$ab \sin \theta = a_1 b_2 - a_2 b_1.$$

If we form the product of b's projection on a with a, we get $ab \cos \theta$ which we have shown equals $a_1 b_1 + a_2 b_2$. Similarly, if we form the product $ab \sin \theta$ we compute the area of the parallelogram formed by sweeping a along b, which equals $a_1 b_2 - a_2 b_1$. What is noteworthy, is that the product $ab \cos \theta$ is independent of the sign of the angle θ, whereas the product $ab \sin \theta$ is sensitive to the sign of θ. Consequently, if we construct the lines a and b such that b is rotated $-\theta$ relative to a as shown in Fig. 12.4, $ab \cos \theta = a_1 b_1 + a_2 b_2$, but $ab \sin \theta = -(a_1 b_2 - a_2 b_1)$. The antisymmetric nature of the sine function reverses the sign of the area.

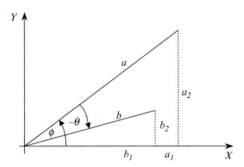

Fig. 12.4 Two line segments a and b separated by $-\theta$.

Having shown that area is a signed quantity just by using trigonometric identities, let's explore how vector algebra responds to this idea.

12.4 Vectorial Foundations

When we form the algebraic product of two 2D vectors **a** and **b**:

$$\mathbf{a} = a_1\mathbf{i} + a_2\mathbf{j}$$
$$\mathbf{b} = b_1\mathbf{i} + b_2\mathbf{j}$$

we obtain

$$\mathbf{ab} = a_1b_1\mathbf{i}^2 + a_2b_2\mathbf{j}^2 + a_1b_2\mathbf{ij} + a_2b_1\mathbf{ji} \qquad (12.9)$$

and it is obvious that $a_1b_1\mathbf{i}^2 + a_2b_2\mathbf{j}^2$ has something to do with $ab\cos\theta$, and $a_1b_2\mathbf{ij} + a_2b_1\mathbf{ji}$ has something to do with $ab\sin\theta$. The product **ab** creates the terms $\mathbf{i}^2$, $\mathbf{j}^2$, $\mathbf{ij}$ and $\mathbf{ji}$, which can be resolved as follows.

12.5 Inner and Outer Products

I like to believe that mathematics is a game – a game where we make the rules. Some rules might take us nowhere; others might take us so far in a particular direction and then restrict any further development; whilst other rules might open up a fantastic landscape that would have remained hidden had we not stumbled upon them. There are no 'wrong' or 'right' rules – there are just rules where some work better than others. Fortunately, the rules behind geometric algebra have been tested for over a 100 years, so we know they work. But these rules were not hiding somewhere waiting to be discovered, they arose due to the collective intellectual endeavour of many mathematicians over several decades.

Let's begin with the products **ij** and **ji** in (12.9) and assume that they anticommute: $\mathbf{ji} = -\mathbf{ij}$. Therefore,

$$\mathbf{ab} = a_1b_1\mathbf{i}^2 + a_2b_2\mathbf{j}^2 + (a_1b_2 - a_2b_1)\mathbf{ij} \qquad (12.10)$$

and if we reverse the product to **ba** we obtain

$$\mathbf{ba} = a_1b_1\mathbf{i}^2 + a_2b_2\mathbf{j}^2 - (a_1b_2 - a_2b_1)\mathbf{ij}. \qquad (12.11)$$

From (12.10) and (12.11) we see that the product of two vectors contains a symmetric component

$$a_1b_1\mathbf{i}^2 + a_2b_2\mathbf{j}^2$$

and an antisymmetric component

$$(a_1b_2 - a_2b_1)\mathbf{ij}.$$

It is interesting to observe that the symmetric component has $0°$ between its vector pairs ($\mathbf{i}^2$ or $\mathbf{j}^2$), whereas the antisymmetric component has $90°$ between its vector pairs (**i** and **j**). Therefore, the sine and cosine functions play a natural role in our rules. What we are looking for are two functions that, when given our vectors **a** and **b**, one function returns the symmetric component and the other returns the antisymmetric component. We call these the *inner* and *outer* functions respectively.

It should be clear that if the inner function includes the cosine of the angle between the two vectors it will reject the antisymmetric component and return the symmetric element. Similarly, if the outer function includes the sine of the angle between the vectors, the symmetric component is rejected, and returns the antisymmetric element.

If we declare the inner function as the *inner product*

$$\mathbf{a} \cdot \mathbf{b} = |\mathbf{a}||\mathbf{b}| \cos \theta \tag{12.12}$$

then

$$\begin{aligned} \mathbf{a} \cdot \mathbf{b} &= (a_1\mathbf{i} + a_2\mathbf{j}) \cdot (b_1\mathbf{i} + b_2\mathbf{j}) \\ &= a_1b_1\mathbf{i} \cdot \mathbf{i} + a_1b_2\mathbf{i} \cdot \mathbf{j} + a_2b_1\mathbf{j} \cdot \mathbf{i} + a_2b_2\mathbf{j} \cdot \mathbf{j} \\ &= a_1b_1 + a_2b_2 \end{aligned}$$

which is perfect!

Next, we declare the outer function as the *outer product* using the wedge "∧" symbol; which is why it is also called the *wedge product*:

$$\mathbf{a} \wedge \mathbf{b} = |\mathbf{a}||\mathbf{b}| \sin \theta \, \mathbf{i} \wedge \mathbf{j}. \tag{12.13}$$

Note that product includes a strange $\mathbf{i} \wedge \mathbf{j}$ term. This is included as we just can't ignore the **ij** term in the antisymmetric component:

$$\begin{aligned} \mathbf{a} \wedge \mathbf{b} &= (a_1\mathbf{i} + a_2\mathbf{j}) \wedge (b_1\mathbf{i} + b_2\mathbf{j}) \\ &= a_1b_1\mathbf{i} \wedge \mathbf{i} + a_1b_2\mathbf{i} \wedge \mathbf{j} + a_2b_1\mathbf{j} \wedge \mathbf{i} + a_2b_2\mathbf{j} \wedge \mathbf{j} \\ &= (a_1b_2 - a_2b_1)\mathbf{i} \wedge \mathbf{j} \end{aligned}$$

which enables us to write

$$\mathbf{ab} = \mathbf{a} \cdot \mathbf{b} + \mathbf{a} \wedge \mathbf{b} \tag{12.14}$$

$$\mathbf{ab} = |\mathbf{a}||\mathbf{b}| \cos \theta + |\mathbf{a}||\mathbf{b}| \sin \theta \, \mathbf{i} \wedge \mathbf{j}. \tag{12.15}$$

12.6 The Geometric Product in 2D

Clifford named the sum of the two products the *geometric product*, which means that (12.14) reads: The geometric product **ab** is the sum of the inner product "**a** dot **b**" and the outer product "**a** wedge **b**". Remember that all this assumes that $\mathbf{ji} = -\mathbf{ij}$ which seems a reasonable assumption.

Given the definition of the geometric product, let's evaluate $\mathbf{i}^2$

$$\mathbf{ii} = \mathbf{i} \cdot \mathbf{i} + \mathbf{i} \wedge \mathbf{i}.$$

Using the definition for the inner product (12.12) we have

$$\mathbf{i} \cdot \mathbf{i} = 1 \times 1 \times \cos 0° = 1$$

whereas using the definition of the outer product (12.13) we have

$$\mathbf{i} \wedge \mathbf{i} = 1 \times 1 \times \sin 0° \ \mathbf{i} \wedge \mathbf{i} = 0.$$

Thus $\mathbf{i}^2 = 1$ and $\mathbf{j}^2 = 1$, and $\mathbf{aa} = |\mathbf{a}|^2$:

$$\mathbf{aa} = \mathbf{a} \cdot \mathbf{a} + \mathbf{a} \wedge \mathbf{a}$$
$$= |\mathbf{a}||\mathbf{a}| \cos 0° + |\mathbf{a}||\mathbf{a}| \sin 0° \mathbf{i} \wedge \mathbf{j}$$
$$\mathbf{aa} = |\mathbf{a}|^2.$$

Now let's evaluate $\mathbf{ij}$:

$$\mathbf{ij} = \mathbf{i} \cdot \mathbf{j} + \mathbf{i} \wedge \mathbf{j}.$$

Using the definition for the inner product (12.12) we have

$$\mathbf{i} \cdot \mathbf{j} = 1 \times 1 \times \cos 90° = 0$$

whereas using the definition of the outer product (12.13) we have

$$\mathbf{i} \wedge \mathbf{j} = 1 \times 1 \times \sin 90° \ \mathbf{i} \wedge \mathbf{j} = \mathbf{i} \wedge \mathbf{j}.$$

Thus $\mathbf{ij} = \mathbf{i} \wedge \mathbf{j}$. But what is $\mathbf{i} \wedge \mathbf{j}$? Well, it is a new object and is called a *bivector* and defines the orientation of the plane containing $\mathbf{i}$ and $\mathbf{j}$.

As the order of the vectors is from $\mathbf{i}$ to $\mathbf{j}$, the angle is $+90°$ and $\sin(+90)° = 1$. Whereas, if the order is from $\mathbf{j}$ to $\mathbf{i}$ the angle is $-90°$ and $\sin(-90°) = -1$. Consequently,

$$\mathbf{ji} = \mathbf{j} \cdot \mathbf{i} + \mathbf{j} \wedge \mathbf{i}$$
$$= 0 + 1 \times 1 \times \sin(-90°)\mathbf{i} \wedge \mathbf{j}$$
$$\mathbf{ji} = -\mathbf{i} \wedge \mathbf{j}.$$

A useful way of visualizing the bivector $\mathbf{i} \wedge \mathbf{j}$ is to imagine moving along the vector $\mathbf{i}$ and then along the vector $\mathbf{j}$, which creates an anticlockwise rotation. Conversely, for the bivector $\mathbf{j} \wedge \mathbf{i}$, imagine moving along the vector $\mathbf{j}$ followed by vector $\mathbf{i}$, which creates a clockwise rotation. Another useful picture is to sweep vector $\mathbf{j}$ along vector $\mathbf{i}$ to create an anticlockwise rotation, and vice versa for $\mathbf{j} \wedge \mathbf{i}$. These ideas are shown in Fig. 12.5.

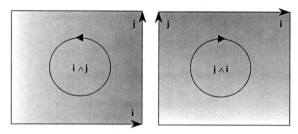

Fig. 12.5 An anticlockwise and clockwise bivector.

So far, so good. Our rules seem to be leading somewhere. The inner product (12.12) is our old friend the dot product, and does not need explaining. However, the outer product (12.13) does require some further explanation.

So the equation

$$\mathbf{ab} = 9 + 12\mathbf{i} \wedge \mathbf{j}$$

simply means that the geometric product of two vectors **a** and **b** creates a scalar, inner product of 9, and an outer product of 12 on the **i**–**j** plane. For example, if

$$\mathbf{a} = 3\mathbf{i}$$
$$\mathbf{b} = 3\mathbf{i} + 4\mathbf{j}$$

then

$$\mathbf{ab} = 3\mathbf{i} \cdot (3\mathbf{i} + 4\mathbf{j}) + 3\mathbf{i} \wedge (3\mathbf{i} + 4\mathbf{j})$$
$$= 9 + 9\mathbf{i} \wedge \mathbf{i} + 12\mathbf{i} \wedge \mathbf{j}$$
$$\mathbf{ab} = 9 + 12\mathbf{i} \wedge \mathbf{j}.$$

The 9 represents $|\mathbf{a}||\mathbf{b}| \cos \theta$, whereas the 12 represents an area $|\mathbf{a}||\mathbf{b}| \sin \theta$ on the **i**–**j** plane. The angle between the two vectors θ is given by

$$\theta = \cos^{-1}(3/5).$$

However, reversing the product, we obtain

$$\mathbf{ba} = (3\mathbf{i} + 4\mathbf{j}) \cdot 3\mathbf{i} + (3\mathbf{i} + 4\mathbf{j}) \wedge 3\mathbf{i}$$
$$= 9 + 9\mathbf{i} \wedge \mathbf{i} + 12\mathbf{j} \wedge \mathbf{i}$$
$$\mathbf{ab} = 9 - 12\mathbf{i} \wedge \mathbf{j}.$$

The sign of the outer (wedge) product has flipped to reflect the new orientation of the vectors relative to the accepted orientation of the basis bivectors.

So the geometric product combines the scalar and wedge products into a single product, where the scalar product is the symmetric component and the wedge product is the antisymmetric component. Now let's see how these products behave in 3D.

12.7 The Geometric Product in 3D

Before we consider the geometric product in 3D we need to introduce some new notation, which will simplify future algebraic expressions. Rather than use $\mathbf{i}$, $\mathbf{j}$ and $\mathbf{k}$ to represent the unit basis vectors let's employ $\mathbf{e}_1$, $\mathbf{e}_2$ and $\mathbf{e}_3$ respectively. This implies that (12.15) can be written

$$\mathbf{ab} = |\mathbf{a}||\mathbf{b}|\cos\theta + |\mathbf{a}||\mathbf{b}|\sin\theta\,\mathbf{e}_1 \wedge \mathbf{e}_2.$$

We begin with two 3D vectors:

$$\mathbf{a} = a_1\mathbf{e}_1 + a_2\mathbf{e}_2 + a_3\mathbf{e}_3$$
$$\mathbf{b} = b_1\mathbf{e}_1 + b_2\mathbf{e}_2 + b_3\mathbf{e}_3$$

therefore, their inner product is

$$\mathbf{a} \cdot \mathbf{b} = (a_1\mathbf{e}_1 + a_2\mathbf{e}_2 + a_3\mathbf{e}_3) \cdot (b_1\mathbf{e}_1 + b_2\mathbf{e}_2 + b_3\mathbf{e}_3)$$
$$= a_1b_1 + a_2b_2 + a_3b_3$$

and their outer product is

$$\mathbf{a} \wedge \mathbf{b} = (a_1\mathbf{e}_1 + a_2\mathbf{e}_2 + a_3\mathbf{e}_3) \wedge (b_1\mathbf{e}_1 + b_2\mathbf{e}_2 + b_3\mathbf{e}_3)$$
$$= a_1b_2\mathbf{e}_1 \wedge \mathbf{e}_2 + a_1b_3\mathbf{e}_1 \wedge \mathbf{e}_3 + a_2b_1\mathbf{e}_2 \wedge \mathbf{e}_1 + a_2b_3\mathbf{e}_2 \wedge \mathbf{e}_3$$
$$+ a_3b_1\mathbf{e}_3 \wedge \mathbf{e}_1 + a_3b_2\mathbf{e}_3 \wedge \mathbf{e}_2$$

$$\mathbf{a} \wedge \mathbf{b} = (a_1b_2 - a_2b_1)\mathbf{e}_1 \wedge \mathbf{e}_2 + (a_2b_3 - a_3b_2)\mathbf{e}_2 \wedge \mathbf{e}_3 + (a_3b_1 - a_1b_3)\mathbf{e}_3 \wedge \mathbf{e}_1. \quad (12.16)$$

This time we have three unit basis bivectors: $\mathbf{e}_1 \wedge \mathbf{e}_2$, $\mathbf{e}_2 \wedge \mathbf{e}_3$, $\mathbf{e}_3 \wedge \mathbf{e}_1$, and three associated scalar multipliers: $(a_1b_2 - a_2b_1)$, $(a_2b_3 - a_3b_2)$, $(a_3b_1 - a_1b_3)$ respectively.

Continuing with the idea described in the previous section, the three bivectors represent the three planes containing the respective vectors as shown in Fig. 12.6, and the scalar multipliers are projections of the area of the vector parallelogram onto the three bivectors as shown in Fig. 12.7.

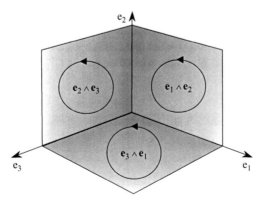

Fig. 12.6 The 3D bivectors.

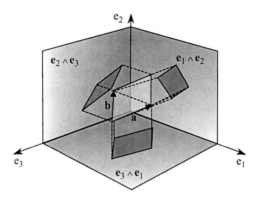

Fig. 12.7 The projections on the three bivectors.

The orientation of the vectors **a** and **b** determine whether the projected areas are positive or negative.

You may think that (12.16) looks familiar. In fact, it looks very similar to the cross product $\mathbf{a} \times \mathbf{b}$:

$$\mathbf{a} \times \mathbf{b} = (a_1 b_2 - a_2 b_1)\mathbf{e}_3 + (a_2 b_3 - a_3 b_2)\mathbf{e}_1 + (a_3 b_1 - a_1 b_3)\mathbf{e}_2. \qquad (12.17)$$

This similarity is no accident. For when Hamilton invented quaternions, he did not recognise the possibility of bivectors, and invented some rules, which eventually became the cross product! Later in this chapter we discover that quaternions are really bivectors in disguise.

We can see that a simple relationship exists between (12.16) and (12.17):

$$\mathbf{e}_1 \wedge \mathbf{e}_2 \text{ and } \mathbf{e}_3$$
$$\mathbf{e}_2 \wedge \mathbf{e}_3 \text{ and } \mathbf{e}_1$$
$$\mathbf{e}_3 \wedge \mathbf{e}_1 \text{ and } \mathbf{e}_2$$

the wedge product bivectors are perpendicular to the vector components of the cross product. So the wedge product is just another way of representing the cross product. However, the wedge product introduces a very important bonus: it works in space of any dimension, whereas, the cross product is only comfortable in 3D. Not only that, the wedge (outer product) is a product that creates volumes, hypervolumes, and can also be applied to vectors, bivectors, trivectors, etc.

12.8 The Outer Product of Three 3D Vectors

Having seen that the outer product of two 3D vectors is represented by areal projections onto the three basis bivectors, let's explore the outer product of three 3D vectors.

Given

$$\mathbf{a} = a_1\mathbf{e}_1 + a_2\mathbf{e}_2 + a_3\mathbf{e}_3$$
$$\mathbf{b} = b_1\mathbf{e}_1 + b_2\mathbf{e}_2 + b_3\mathbf{e}_3$$
$$\mathbf{c} = c_1\mathbf{e}_1 + c_2\mathbf{e}_2 + c_3\mathbf{e}_3$$

then

$$\mathbf{a} \wedge \mathbf{b} \wedge \mathbf{c} = (a_1\mathbf{e}_1 + a_2\mathbf{e}_2 + a_3\mathbf{e}_3) \wedge (b_1\mathbf{e}_1 + b_2\mathbf{e}_2 + b_3\mathbf{e}_3) \wedge (c_1\mathbf{e}_1 + c_2\mathbf{e}_2 + c_3\mathbf{e}_3)$$
$$= [(a_1b_2 - a_2b_1)\mathbf{e}_1 \wedge \mathbf{e}_2 + (a_2b_3 - a_3b_2)\mathbf{e}_2 \wedge \mathbf{e}_3 + (a_3b_1 - a_1b_3)\mathbf{e}_3 \wedge \mathbf{e}_1]$$
$$\wedge (c_1\mathbf{e}_1 + c_2\mathbf{e}_2 + c_3\mathbf{e}_3).$$

At this stage we introduce another axiom: the outer product is associative. This means that $\mathbf{a} \wedge (\mathbf{b} \wedge \mathbf{c}) = (\mathbf{a} \wedge \mathbf{b}) \wedge \mathbf{c}$. Therefore, knowing that $\mathbf{a} \wedge \mathbf{a} = 0$:

$$\mathbf{a} \wedge \mathbf{b} \wedge \mathbf{c} = c_3(a_1b_2 - a_2b_1)\mathbf{e}_1 \wedge \mathbf{e}_2 \wedge \mathbf{e}_3 + c_1(a_2b_3 - a_3b_2)\mathbf{e}_2 \wedge \mathbf{e}_3 \wedge \mathbf{e}_1$$
$$+ c_2(a_3b_1 - a_1b_3)\mathbf{e}_3 \wedge \mathbf{e}_1 \wedge \mathbf{e}_2.$$

But we are left with the products $\mathbf{e}_1 \wedge \mathbf{e}_2 \wedge \mathbf{e}_3$, $\mathbf{e}_2 \wedge \mathbf{e}_3 \wedge \mathbf{e}_1$ and $\mathbf{e}_3 \wedge \mathbf{e}_1 \wedge \mathbf{e}_2$. Not to worry, because we know that $\mathbf{a} \wedge \mathbf{b} = -\mathbf{b} \wedge \mathbf{a}$. Therefore,

$$\mathbf{e}_2 \wedge \mathbf{e}_3 \wedge \mathbf{e}_1 = -\mathbf{e}_2 \wedge \mathbf{e}_1 \wedge \mathbf{e}_3 = \mathbf{e}_1 \wedge \mathbf{e}_2 \wedge \mathbf{e}_3$$

and

$$\mathbf{e}_3 \wedge \mathbf{e}_1 \wedge \mathbf{e}_2 = -\mathbf{e}_1 \wedge \mathbf{e}_3 \wedge \mathbf{e}_2 = \mathbf{e}_1 \wedge \mathbf{e}_2 \wedge \mathbf{e}_3.$$

Therefore, we can write $\mathbf{a} \wedge \mathbf{b} \wedge \mathbf{c}$ as

$$\mathbf{a} \wedge \mathbf{b} \wedge \mathbf{c} = c_3(a_1b_2 - a_2b_1)\mathbf{e}_1 \wedge \mathbf{e}_2 \wedge \mathbf{e}_3 + c_1(a_2b_3 - a_3b_2)\mathbf{e}_1 \wedge \mathbf{e}_2 \wedge \mathbf{e}_3$$
$$+ c_2(a_3b_1 - a_1b_3)\mathbf{e}_1 \wedge \mathbf{e}_2 \wedge \mathbf{e}_3$$

or

$$\mathbf{a} \wedge \mathbf{b} \wedge \mathbf{c} = [c_3(a_1b_2 - a_2b_1) + c_1(a_2b_3 - a_3b_2) + c_2(a_3b_1 - a_1b_3)]\mathbf{e}_1 \wedge \mathbf{e}_2 \wedge \mathbf{e}_3$$

or using a determinant:

$$\mathbf{a} \wedge \mathbf{b} \wedge \mathbf{c} = \begin{vmatrix} a_1 & b_1 & c_1 \\ a_2 & b_2 & c_2 \\ a_3 & b_3 & c_3 \end{vmatrix} \mathbf{e}_1 \wedge \mathbf{e}_2 \wedge \mathbf{e}_3$$

which is the well-known expression for the volume of a parallelpiped formed by three vectors.

The term $\mathbf{e}_1 \wedge \mathbf{e}_2 \wedge \mathbf{e}_3$ is a *trivector* and confirms that the volume is oriented. If the sign of the determinant is positive, the original three vectors possess the same orientation of the three basis vectors. If the sign of the determinant is negative, the three vectors possess an orientation opposing that of the three basis vectors.

12.9 Axioms

One of the features of geometric algebra is that it behaves very similar to the every-day algebra of scalars:
Axiom 1: The associative rule

$$\mathbf{a}(\mathbf{bc}) = (\mathbf{ab})\mathbf{c}.$$

Axiom 2: The left and right distributive rules:

$$\mathbf{a}(\mathbf{b}+\mathbf{c}) = \mathbf{ab}+\mathbf{ac}$$
$$(\mathbf{b}+\mathbf{c})\mathbf{a} = \mathbf{ba}+\mathbf{ca}.$$

The next four axioms describe how vectors interact with a scalar (λ):
Axiom 3:
$$(\lambda\mathbf{a})\mathbf{b} = \lambda(\mathbf{ab}) = \lambda\mathbf{ab}.$$

Axiom 4:
$$\lambda(\phi\mathbf{a}) = (\lambda\phi)\mathbf{a}.$$

Axiom 5:
$$\lambda(\mathbf{a}+\mathbf{b}) = \lambda\mathbf{a}+\lambda\mathbf{b}.$$

Axiom 6:
$$(\lambda+\phi)\mathbf{a} = \lambda\mathbf{a}+\phi\mathbf{a}.$$

The next axiom that is adopted is
Axiom 7:
$$\mathbf{a}^2 = |\mathbf{a}|^2$$

which has already emerged as a consequence of the algebra. However, for non-Euclidean geometries, this can be set to $\mathbf{a}^2 = -|\mathbf{a}|^2$, which does not concern us here.

12.10 Notation

Having abandoned $\mathbf{i}, \mathbf{j}, \mathbf{k}$ for $\mathbf{e}_1, \mathbf{e}_2, \mathbf{e}_3$, it is convenient to convert geometric products $\mathbf{e}_1\mathbf{e}_2...\mathbf{e}_n$ to $\mathbf{e}_{12...n}$. For example, $\mathbf{e}_1\mathbf{e}_2\mathbf{e}_3 \equiv \mathbf{e}_{123}$. Furthermore, we must get used to the following substitutions:

$$\mathbf{e}_i\mathbf{e}_i\mathbf{e}_j = \mathbf{e}_j$$
$$\mathbf{e}_{21} = -\mathbf{e}_{12}$$
$$\mathbf{e}_{312} = \mathbf{e}_{123}$$
$$\mathbf{e}_{112} = \mathbf{e}_2$$
$$\mathbf{e}_{121} = -\mathbf{e}_2.$$

12.11 Grades, Pseudoscalars and Multivectors

As geometric algebra embraces such a wide range of objects, it is convenient to *grade* them as follows: scalars are grade 0, vectors are grade 1, bivectors are grade 2, and trivectors are grade 3, and so on for higher dimensions. In such a graded algebra it is traditional to call the highest grade element a *pseudoscalar*. Thus in 2D the pseudoscalar is e_{12} and in 3D the pseudoscalar is e_{123}.

One very powerful feature of geometric algebra is the idea of a *multivector*, which is a linear combination of a scalar, vector, bivector, trivector or any other higher dimensional object. For example the following are multivectors:

$$A = 3 + (2e_1 + 3e_2 + 4e_3) + (5e_{12} + 6e_{23} + 7e_{31}) + 8e_{123}$$
$$B = 2 + (2e_1 + 2e_2 + 3e_3) + (4e_{12} + 5e_{23} + 6e_{31}) + 7e_{123}$$

and we can form their sum:

$$A + B = 5 + (4e_1 + 5e_2 + 7e_3) + (9e_{12} + 11e_{23} + 13e_{31}) + 15e_{123}$$

or their difference:

$$A - B = 1 + (e_2 + e_3) + (e_{12} + e_{23} + e_{31}) + e_{123}.$$

We can even form their product AB, but at the moment we have not explored the products between all these elements.

We can isolate any grade of a multivector using the following notation:

$$\langle multivector \rangle_g$$

where g identifies a particular grade. For example, say we have the following multivector:

$$2 + 3e_1 + 2e_2 - 5e_{12} + 6e_{123}$$

we extract the scalar term using:

$$\langle 2 + 3e_1 + 2e_2 - 5e_{12} + 6e_{123} \rangle_0 = 2$$

the vector term using

$$\langle 2 + 3e_1 + 2e_2 - 5e_{12} + 6e_{123} \rangle_1 = 3e_1 + 2e_2$$

the bivector term using:

$$\langle 2 + 3e_1 + 2e_2 - 5e_{12} + 6e_{123} \rangle_2 = -5e_{12}$$

and the trivector term using:

$$\langle 2 + 3e_1 + 2e_2 - 5e_{12} + 6e_{123} \rangle_3 = 6e_{123}.$$

It is also worth pointing out that the inner vector product converts two grade 1 elements, i.e., vectors, into a grade 0 element, i.e., a scalar, whereas the outer vector product converts two grade 1 elements into a grade 2 element, i.e., a bivector. Thus the inner product is a grade lowering operation, while the outer product is a grade raising operation. These qualities of the inner and outer products are associated with higher grade elements in the algebra. This is why the scalar product is renamed as the inner product, because the scalar product is synonymous with transforming vectors into scalars. Whereas, the inner product transforms two elements of grade n into a grade $n - 1$ element.

12.12 Redefining the Inner and Outer Products

As the geometric product is defined in terms of the inner and outer products, it seems only natural to expect that similar functions exist relating the inner and outer products in terms of the geometric product. Such functions do exist and emerge when we combine the following two equations:

$$\mathbf{ab} = \mathbf{a} \cdot \mathbf{b} + \mathbf{a} \wedge \mathbf{b} \tag{12.18}$$

$$\mathbf{ba} = \mathbf{a} \cdot \mathbf{b} - \mathbf{a} \wedge \mathbf{b}. \tag{12.19}$$

Adding and subtracting (12.18) and (12.19) we have

$$\mathbf{a} \cdot \mathbf{b} = \frac{1}{2}(\mathbf{ab} + \mathbf{ba}) \tag{12.20}$$

$$\mathbf{a} \wedge \mathbf{b} = \frac{1}{2}(\mathbf{ab} - \mathbf{ba}). \tag{12.21}$$

Equations (12.20) and (12.21) and used frequently to define the products between different grade elements.

12.13 The Inverse of a Vector

In traditional vector analysis we accept that it is impossible to divide by a vector, but that is not so in geometric algebra. In fact, we don't actually divide a multivector by another vector but find a way of representing the inverse of a vector. For example, we know that a unit vector $\hat{\mathbf{a}}$ is defined as

$$\hat{\mathbf{a}} = \frac{\mathbf{a}}{|\mathbf{a}|}$$

and using the geometric product

$$\hat{\mathbf{a}}^2 = \frac{\mathbf{a}^2}{|\mathbf{a}|^2} = 1$$

therefore,

$$\mathbf{b} = \frac{\mathbf{a}^2\mathbf{b}}{|\mathbf{a}|^2}$$

and exploiting the associative nature of the geometric product we have

$$\mathbf{b} = \frac{\mathbf{a}(\mathbf{ab})}{|\mathbf{a}|^2}. \tag{12.22}$$

Equation (12.22) is effectively stating that, given the geometric product $\mathbf{ab}$ we can recover the vector $\mathbf{b}$ by pre-multiplying by $\mathbf{a}^{-1}$:

$$\frac{\mathbf{a}}{|\mathbf{a}|^2}.$$

Similarly, we can recover the vector $\mathbf{a}$ as follows by post-multiplying by $\mathbf{b}^{-1}$:

$$\mathbf{a} = \frac{(\mathbf{ab})\mathbf{b}}{|\mathbf{b}|^2}.$$

For example, given two vectors

$$\mathbf{a} = \mathbf{e}_1 + 2\mathbf{e}_2$$
$$\mathbf{b} = 3\mathbf{e}_1 + 2\mathbf{e}_2$$

their geometric product is

$$\mathbf{ab} = 7 - 4\mathbf{e}_{12}.$$

Therefore, given $\mathbf{ab}$ and $\mathbf{a}$, we can recover $\mathbf{b}$ as follows:

$$\mathbf{b} = \frac{\mathbf{e}_1 + 2\mathbf{e}_2}{5}(7 - 4\mathbf{e}_{12})$$
$$= \frac{1}{5}(7\mathbf{e}_1 - 4\mathbf{e}_{112} + 14\mathbf{e}_2 - 8\mathbf{e}_{212})$$
$$= \frac{1}{5}(7\mathbf{e}_1 - 4\mathbf{e}_2 + 14\mathbf{e}_2 + 8\mathbf{e}_1)$$
$$\mathbf{b} = 3\mathbf{e}_1 + 2\mathbf{e}_2.$$

Similarly, give $\mathbf{ab}$ and $\mathbf{b}$, $\mathbf{a}$ is recovered as follows:

$$\mathbf{a} = (7 - 4\mathbf{e}_{12})\frac{3\mathbf{e}_1 + 2\mathbf{e}_2}{13}$$
$$= \frac{1}{13}(21\mathbf{e}_1 + 14\mathbf{e}_2 - 12\mathbf{e}_{121} - 8\mathbf{e}_{122}$$
$$= \frac{1}{13}(21\mathbf{e}_1 + 14\mathbf{e}_2 + 12\mathbf{e}_2 - 8\mathbf{e}_1)$$
$$\mathbf{a} = \mathbf{e}_1 + 2\mathbf{e}_2.$$

Note that the inverse of a unit vector is the original vector:

$$\hat{\mathbf{a}}^{-1} = \frac{\hat{\mathbf{a}}}{|\hat{\mathbf{a}}|^2} = \hat{\mathbf{a}}.$$

12.14 The Imaginary Properties of the Outer Product

So far we know that the outer product of two vectors is represented by one or more unit basis vectors, such as

$$\mathbf{a} \wedge \mathbf{b} = \lambda_1 \mathbf{e}_{12} + \lambda_2 \mathbf{e}_{23} + \lambda_3 \mathbf{e}_{31}$$

where, in this case, the λ_i terms represent areas projected onto their respective unit basis bivectors. But what has not emerged is that the outer product is an imaginary quantity, which is revealed by expanding $\mathbf{e}_{12}^2$:

$$\mathbf{e}_{12}^2 = \mathbf{e}_{1212}$$

but as

$$\mathbf{e}_{21} = -\mathbf{e}_{12}$$

then

$$\mathbf{e}_{1(21)2} = -\mathbf{e}_{1(12)2}$$
$$= -\mathbf{e}_1^2 \mathbf{e}_2^2$$
$$\mathbf{e}_{12}^2 = -1.$$

Consequently, the geometric product effectively creates a complex number! Thus in a 2D scenario, given two vectors

$$\mathbf{a} = a_1 \mathbf{e}_1 + a_2 \mathbf{e}_2$$
$$\mathbf{b} = b_1 \mathbf{e}_1 + b_2 \mathbf{e}_2$$

their geometric product is

$$\mathbf{ab} = (a_1 b_1 + a_2 b_2) + (a_1 b_2 - a_2 b_1) \mathbf{e}_{12}$$

and knowing that $\mathbf{e}_{12} = i$, then we can write $\mathbf{ab}$ as

$$\mathbf{ab} = (a_1 b_1 + a_2 b_2) + (a_1 b_2 - a_2 b_1) i. \tag{12.23}$$

However, this notation is not generally adopted by the geometric community. The reason being that i is normally only associated with a scalar, with which it commutes. Whereas in 2D, $\mathbf{e}_{12}$ is associated with scalars and vectors, and although scalars present no problem, under some conditions, it anticommutes with vectors.

Consequently, an upper-case I is used so that there is no confusion between the two elements. Thus (12.23) is written as

$$\mathbf{ab} = (a_1 b_1 + a_2 b_2) + (a_1 b_2 - a_2 b_1)I$$

where

$$I^2 = -1.$$

It goes without saying that the 3D unit basis bivectors are also imaginary quantities, so, too, is $\mathbf{e}_{123}$.

Multiplying a complex number by i rotates it $90°$ on the complex plane. Therefore, it should be no surprise that multiplying a 2D vector by $\mathbf{e}_{12}$ rotates it by $90°$. However, because vectors are sensitive to their product partners, we must remember that pre-multiplying a vector by $\mathbf{e}_{12}$ rotates a vector clockwise and post-multiplying rotates a vector anti-clockwise.

Whilst on the subject of rotations, let's consider what happens in 3D. We begin with a 3D vector

$$\mathbf{a} = a_1 \mathbf{e}_1 + a_2 \mathbf{e}_2 + a_3 \mathbf{e}_3$$

and the unit basis bivector $\mathbf{e}_{12}$ as shown in Fig. 12.8. Next we construct their geometric product

$$\mathbf{e}_{12} \mathbf{a} = a_1 \mathbf{e}_{12} \mathbf{e}_1 + a_2 \mathbf{e}_{12} \mathbf{e}_2 + a_3 \mathbf{e}_{12} \mathbf{e}_3$$

which becomes

$$\mathbf{e}_{12} \mathbf{a} = a_1 \mathbf{e}_{121} + a_2 \mathbf{e}_{122} + a_3 \mathbf{e}_{123}$$
$$= -a_1 \mathbf{e}_2 + a_2 \mathbf{e}_1 + a_3 \mathbf{e}_{123}$$
$$\mathbf{e}_{12} \mathbf{a} = a_2 \mathbf{e}_1 - a_1 \mathbf{e}_2 + a_3 \mathbf{e}_{123}$$

and contains two parts: a vector $(a_2 \mathbf{e}_1 - a_1 \mathbf{e}_2)$ and a volume $a_3 \mathbf{e}_{123}$.

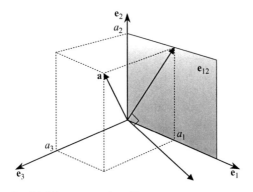

Fig. 12.8 The effect of multiplying a vector by a bivector.

Figure 12.8 shows how the projection of vector **a** is rotated anticlockwise on the bivector $\mathbf{e}_{12}$. A volume is also created perpendicular to the bivector. This enables us to predict that if the vector is coplanar with the bivector, the entire vector is rotated $90°$ and the volume component will be zero.

By post-multiplying **a** by $\mathbf{e}_{12}$ creates

$$\mathbf{a}\mathbf{e}_{12} = -a_2\mathbf{e}_1 + a_1\mathbf{e}_2 + a_3\mathbf{e}_{123}$$

which shows that while the volumetric element has remained the same, the projected vector is rotated anticlockwise.

You may wish to show that the same happens with the other two bivectors.

12.15 Duality

The ability to exchange pairs of geometric elements such as lines and planes involves a *dual* operation, which in geometric algebra is relatively easy to define. For example, given a multivector **A** its dual $\mathbf{A}^*$ is defined as

$$\mathbf{A}^* = I\mathbf{A}$$

where I is the local pseudoscalar. For 2D this is $\mathbf{e}_{12}$ and for 3D it is $\mathbf{e}_{123}$. Therefore, given a 2D vector

$$\mathbf{a} = a_1\mathbf{e}_1 + a_2\mathbf{e}_2$$

and its dual is

$$\mathbf{a}^* = \mathbf{e}_{12}(a_1\mathbf{e}_1 + a_2\mathbf{e}_2)$$
$$= a_1\mathbf{e}_{121} + a_2\mathbf{e}_{122}$$
$$\mathbf{a}^* = a_2\mathbf{e}_1 - a_1\mathbf{e}_2$$

which is another vector rotated $90°$ anticlockwise.

It is easy to show that $(\mathbf{a}^*)^* = -\mathbf{a}$, and two further dual operations return the vector back to **a**.

In 3D the dual of a vector $\mathbf{e}_1$ is

$$\mathbf{e}_{123}\mathbf{e}_1 = \mathbf{e}_{1231} = \mathbf{e}_{23}$$

which is the perpendicular bivector. Similarly, the dual of $\mathbf{e}_2$ is $\mathbf{e}_{31}$ and the dual of $\mathbf{e}_3$ is $\mathbf{e}_{12}$.

For a general vector $a_1\mathbf{e}_1 + a_2\mathbf{e}_2 + a_3\mathbf{e}_3$ its dual is

$$\mathbf{e}_{123}(a_1\mathbf{e}_1 + a_2\mathbf{e}_2 + a_3\mathbf{e}_3) = a_1\mathbf{e}_{1231} + a_2\mathbf{e}_{1232} + a_3\mathbf{e}_{1233}$$
$$= a_3\mathbf{e}_{12} + a_1\mathbf{e}_{23} + a_2\mathbf{e}_{31}.$$

The duals of the 3D basis bivectors are:

$$\mathbf{e}_{123}\mathbf{e}_{12} = \mathbf{e}_{12312} = -\mathbf{e}_3$$
$$\mathbf{e}_{123}\mathbf{e}_{23} = \mathbf{e}_{12323} = -\mathbf{e}_1$$
$$\mathbf{e}_{123}\mathbf{e}_{31} = \mathbf{e}_{12331} = -\mathbf{e}_2.$$

12.16 The Relationship Between the Vector Product and the Outer Product

We have already discovered that there is a very close relationship between the vector product and the outer product, and just to recap: Given two vectors

$$\mathbf{a} = a_1\mathbf{e}_1 + a_2\mathbf{e}_2 + a_3\mathbf{e}_3$$
$$\mathbf{b} = b_1\mathbf{e}_1 + b_2\mathbf{e}_2 + b_3\mathbf{e}_3$$

then

$$\mathbf{a} \times \mathbf{b} = (a_2b_3 - a_3b_2)\mathbf{e}_1 + (a_3b_1 - a_1b_3)\mathbf{e}_2 + (a_1b_2 - a_2b_1)\mathbf{e}_3 \qquad (12.24)$$

and

$$\mathbf{a} \wedge \mathbf{b} = (a_2b_3 - a_3b_2)\mathbf{e}_2 \wedge \mathbf{e}_3 + (a_3b_1 - a_1b_3)\mathbf{e}_3 \wedge \mathbf{e}_1 + (a_1b_2 - a_2b_1)\mathbf{e}_1 \wedge \mathbf{e}_2$$

or

$$\mathbf{a} \wedge \mathbf{b} = (a_2b_3 - a_3b_2)\mathbf{e}_{23} + (a_3b_1 - a_1b_3)\mathbf{e}_{31} + (a_1b_2 - a_2b_1)\mathbf{e}_{12}. \qquad (12.25)$$

If we multiply (12.25) by I_{123} we obtain

$$I_{123}(\mathbf{a} \wedge \mathbf{b}) = (a_2b_3 - a_3b_2)\mathbf{e}_{123}\mathbf{e}_{23} + (a_3b_1 - a_1b_3)\mathbf{e}_{123}\mathbf{e}_{31} + (a_1b_2 - a_2b_1)\mathbf{e}_{123}\mathbf{e}_{12}$$
$$= -(a_2b_3 - a_3b_2)\mathbf{e}_1 - (a_3b_1 - a_1b_3)\mathbf{e}_2 - (a_1b_2 - a_2b_1)\mathbf{e}_3$$

which is identical to the cross product (12.24) apart from its sign. Therefore, we can state:

$$\mathbf{a} \times \mathbf{b} = -I_{123}(\mathbf{a} \wedge \mathbf{b}).$$

12.17 The Relationship Between Quaternions and Bivectors

Hamilton's rules for the imaginaries i, j and k are shown in Table 12.1, whilst Table 12.2 shows the rules for 3D bivector products.

Table 12.1 Hamilton's quaternion product rules

	i	j	k
i	-1	k	$-j$
j	$-k$	-1	i
k	j	$-i$	-1

Table 12.2 3D bivector product rules

	$\mathbf{e}_{23}$	$\mathbf{e}_{31}$	$\mathbf{e}_{12}$
$\mathbf{e}_{23}$	-1	$-\mathbf{e}_{12}$	$\mathbf{e}_{31}$
$\mathbf{e}_{31}$	$\mathbf{e}_{12}$	-1	$-\mathbf{e}_{23}$
$\mathbf{e}_{12}$	$-\mathbf{e}_{31}$	$\mathbf{e}_{23}$	-1

Although there is some agreement between the table entries, there is a sign reversal in some of them. However, if we switch to a left-handed axial system the bivectors become $\mathbf{e}_{32}$, $\mathbf{e}_{13}$, $\mathbf{e}_{21}$ and their products are as shown in Table 12.3.

Table 12.3 Left-handed 3D bivector product rules

	$\mathbf{e}_{32}$	$\mathbf{e}_{13}$	$\mathbf{e}_{21}$
$\mathbf{e}_{32}$	-1	$\mathbf{e}_{21}$	$-\mathbf{e}_{13}$
$\mathbf{e}_{13}$	$-\mathbf{e}_{21}$	-1	$\mathbf{e}_{32}$
$\mathbf{e}_{21}$	$\mathbf{e}_{13}$	$-\mathbf{e}_{32}$	-1

If we now create a one-to-one correspondence (isomorphism) between the two systems:

$$i \leftrightarrow \mathbf{e}_{32} \quad j \leftrightarrow \mathbf{e}_{13} \quad k \leftrightarrow \mathbf{e}_{21}$$

there is a true correspondence between quaternions and a left-handed set of bivectors.

12.18 Reflections and Rotations

One of geometric algebra's strengths is the elegance it brings to calculating reflections and rotations. Unfortunately, there is insufficient space to examine the derivations of the formulae, but if you are interested, these can be found in the author's books. Let's start with 2D reflections.

12.18.1 2D Reflections

Given a line, whose perpendicular unit vector is $\hat{\mathbf{m}}$ and a vector $\mathbf{a}$ its reflection $\mathbf{a}'$ is given by

$$\mathbf{a}' = \hat{\mathbf{m}}\mathbf{a}\hat{\mathbf{m}}$$

which is rather elegant! For example, Fig. 12.9 shows a scenario where

$$\hat{\mathbf{m}} = \frac{1}{\sqrt{2}}(\mathbf{e}_1 + \mathbf{e}_2)$$

$$\mathbf{a} = \mathbf{e}_1$$

therefore,

$$\mathbf{a}' = \frac{1}{\sqrt{2}}(\mathbf{e}_1 + \mathbf{e}_2)(\mathbf{e}_1)\frac{1}{\sqrt{2}}(\mathbf{e}_1 + \mathbf{e}_2)$$

$$= \frac{1}{2}(1 - \mathbf{e}_{12})(\mathbf{e}_1 + \mathbf{e}_2)$$

$$= \frac{1}{2}(\mathbf{e}_1 + \mathbf{e}_2 + \mathbf{e}_2 - \mathbf{e}_1)$$

$$\mathbf{a}' = \mathbf{e}_2.$$

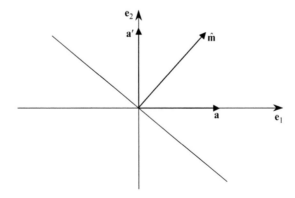

Fig. 12.9 The reflection of a 2D vector.

Note that in this scenario a reflection means a mirror image about the perpendicular vector.

12.18.2 3D Reflections

Let's explore the 3D scenario shown in Fig. 12.10 where

$$\mathbf{a} = \mathbf{e}_1 + \mathbf{e}_2 - \mathbf{e}_3$$

$$\hat{\mathbf{m}} = \mathbf{e}_2$$

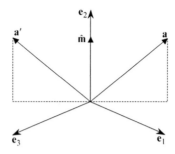

Fig. 12.10 The reflection of a 3D vector.

therefore,

$$\mathbf{a}' = \mathbf{e}_2(\mathbf{e}_1 + \mathbf{e}_2 - \mathbf{e}_3)\mathbf{e}_2$$
$$= \mathbf{e}_{212} + \mathbf{e}_{222} - \mathbf{e}_{232}$$
$$\mathbf{a}' = -\mathbf{e}_1 + \mathbf{e}_2 + \mathbf{e}_3.$$

As one might expect, it is also possible to reflect bivectors, trivectors and higher-dimensional objects, and for reasons of brevity, they are summarized as follows:

Reflecting about a line:

$$\begin{array}{rl} \textit{scalars} & \text{invariant} \\ \textit{vectors} & \mathbf{v}' = \hat{\mathbf{m}}\mathbf{v}\hat{\mathbf{m}} \\ \textit{bivectors} & \mathbf{B}' = \hat{\mathbf{m}}\mathbf{B}\hat{\mathbf{m}} \\ \textit{trivectors} & \mathbf{T}' = \hat{\mathbf{m}}\mathbf{T}\hat{\mathbf{m}}. \end{array}$$

Reflecting about a mirror:

$$\begin{array}{rl} \textit{scalars} & \text{invariant} \\ \textit{vectors} & \mathbf{v}' = -\hat{\mathbf{m}}\mathbf{v}\hat{\mathbf{m}} \\ \textit{bivectors} & \mathbf{B}' = \hat{\mathbf{m}}\mathbf{B}\hat{\mathbf{m}} \\ \textit{trivectors} & \mathbf{T}' = -\hat{\mathbf{m}}\mathbf{T}\hat{\mathbf{m}}. \end{array}$$

12.18.3 2D Rotations

Figure 12.11 shows a plan view of two mirrors M and N separated by an angle θ. The point P is in front of mirror M and subtends an angle α, and its reflection P_R exists in the virtual space behind M and also subtends an angle α with the mirror.

The angle between P_R and N must be $\theta - \alpha$, and its reflection P' must also lie $\theta - \alpha$ behind N. By inspection, the angle between P and the double reflection P' is 2θ.

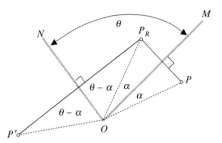

Fig. 12.11 Rotating a point by a double reflection.

If we apply this double reflection transform to a collection of points, they are effectively all rotated 2θ about the origin where the mirrors intersect. The only slight drawback with this technique is that the angle of rotation is twice the angle between the mirrors.

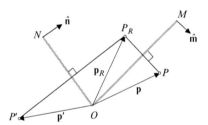

Fig. 12.12 Rotating a point by a double reflection.

Instead of using points, let's employ position vectors and substitute normal unit vectors for the mirrors' orientation. For example, Fig. 12.12 shows the same mirrors with unit normal vectors $\hat{\mathbf{m}}$ and $\hat{\mathbf{n}}$. After two successive reflections, P becomes P', and using the relationship:

$$\mathbf{v}' = -\hat{\mathbf{m}}\mathbf{v}\hat{\mathbf{m}}$$

we compute the reflections as follows:

$$\mathbf{p}_R = -\hat{\mathbf{m}}\mathbf{p}\hat{\mathbf{m}}$$
$$\mathbf{p}' = -\hat{\mathbf{n}}\mathbf{p}_R\hat{\mathbf{n}}$$
$$\mathbf{p}' = \hat{\mathbf{n}}\hat{\mathbf{m}}\mathbf{p}\hat{\mathbf{m}}\hat{\mathbf{n}}$$

which is also rather elegant and compact. However, we must remember that P is rotated twice the angle separating the mirrors, and the rotation is relative to the origin. Let's demonstrate this technique with an example.

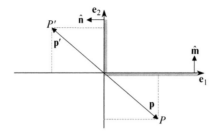

Fig. 12.13 Rotating a point by 180°.

Figure 12.13 shows two mirrors M and N with unit normal vectors $\hat{\mathbf{m}}$, $\hat{\mathbf{n}}$ and position vector $\mathbf{p}$:

$$\hat{\mathbf{m}} = \mathbf{e}_2$$
$$\hat{\mathbf{n}} = -\mathbf{e}_1$$
$$\mathbf{p} = \mathbf{e}_1 - \mathbf{e}_2.$$

As the mirrors are separated by 90° the point P is rotated 180°:

$$\mathbf{p}' = \hat{\mathbf{n}}\hat{\mathbf{m}}\mathbf{p}\hat{\mathbf{m}}\hat{\mathbf{n}}$$
$$= -\mathbf{e}_1\mathbf{e}_2(\mathbf{e}_1 - \mathbf{e}_2)\mathbf{e}_2(-\mathbf{e}_1)$$
$$= \mathbf{e}_{12121} - \mathbf{e}_{12221}$$
$$\mathbf{p}' = -\mathbf{e}_1 + \mathbf{e}_2.$$

12.19 Rotors

Quaternions are the natural choice for rotating vectors about an arbitrary axis, and although it my not be immediately obvious, we have already started to discover geometric algebra's equivalent.

We begin with

$$\mathbf{p}' = \hat{\mathbf{n}}\hat{\mathbf{m}}\mathbf{p}\hat{\mathbf{m}}\hat{\mathbf{n}}$$

and substitute $\mathbf{R}$ for $\hat{\mathbf{n}}\hat{\mathbf{m}}$ and $\tilde{\mathbf{R}}$ for $\hat{\mathbf{m}}\hat{\mathbf{n}}$, therefore,

$$\mathbf{p}' = \mathbf{R}\mathbf{p}\tilde{\mathbf{R}}$$

where $\mathbf{R}$ and $\tilde{\mathbf{R}}$ are called *rotors* which perform the same function as a quaternion.

Because geometric algebra is non-commutative, the sequence of elements, be they vectors, bivectors, trivectors, etc. is very important. Consequently, it is very useful to include a command that reverses a sequence of elements. The notation generally employed is the tilde ($\tilde{\ }$) symbol:

$$\mathbf{R} = \hat{\mathbf{n}}\hat{\mathbf{m}}$$

$$\tilde{\mathbf{R}} = \hat{\mathbf{m}}\hat{\mathbf{n}}.$$

Let's unpack a rotor in terms of its angle and bivector as follows:
The bivector defining the plane is $\hat{\mathbf{m}} \wedge \hat{\mathbf{n}}$ and θ is the angle between the vectors. Let

$$\mathbf{R} = \hat{\mathbf{n}}\hat{\mathbf{m}}$$

$$\tilde{\mathbf{R}} = \hat{\mathbf{m}}\hat{\mathbf{n}}$$

where

$$\hat{\mathbf{n}}\hat{\mathbf{m}} = \hat{\mathbf{n}} \cdot \hat{\mathbf{m}} - \hat{\mathbf{m}} \wedge \hat{\mathbf{n}}$$

$$\hat{\mathbf{m}}\hat{\mathbf{n}} = \hat{\mathbf{n}} \cdot \hat{\mathbf{m}} + \hat{\mathbf{m}} \wedge \hat{\mathbf{n}}$$

$$\hat{\mathbf{n}} \cdot \hat{\mathbf{m}} = \cos\theta$$

$$\hat{\mathbf{m}} \wedge \hat{\mathbf{n}} = \hat{\mathbf{B}}\sin\theta.$$

Therefore,

$$\mathbf{R} = \cos\theta - \hat{\mathbf{B}}\sin\theta$$

$$\tilde{\mathbf{R}} = \cos\theta + \hat{\mathbf{B}}\sin\theta.$$

We now have an equation that rotates a vector $\mathbf{p}$ through an angle 2θ about an axis defined by $\hat{\mathbf{B}}$:

$$\mathbf{p}' = \mathbf{R}\mathbf{p}\hat{\mathbf{R}}$$

or

$$\mathbf{p}' = (\cos\theta - \hat{\mathbf{B}}\sin\theta)\mathbf{p}(\cos\theta + \hat{\mathbf{B}}\sin\theta).$$

We can also express this such that it identifies the real angle of rotation α:

$$\mathbf{p}' = (\cos(\alpha/2) - \hat{\mathbf{B}}\sin(\alpha/2))\mathbf{p}(\cos(\alpha/2) + \hat{\mathbf{B}}\sin(\alpha/2)). \qquad (12.26)$$

Equation (12.26) references a bivector, which may make you feel uncomfortable! But remember, it simply identifies the axis perpendicular to its plane. Let's demonstrate how (12.26) works with two examples.

Example 1: Figure 12.14 shows a scenario where vector $\mathbf{p}$ is rotated $90°$ about $\mathbf{e}_2$ which is perpendicular to $\hat{\mathbf{B}}$, where

$$\alpha = 90°$$

$$\mathbf{a} = \mathbf{e}_2$$

$$\mathbf{p} = \mathbf{e}_1 + \mathbf{e}_2$$

$$\hat{\mathbf{B}} = \mathbf{e}_{31}.$$

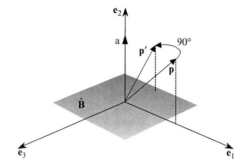

Fig. 12.14 Rotating a vector by 90°.

Therefore,

$$\mathbf{p}' = (\cos 45° - \mathbf{e}_{31} \sin 45°)(\mathbf{e}_1 + \mathbf{e}_2)(\cos 45° + \mathbf{e}_{31} \sin 45°)$$

$$= \left(\frac{\sqrt{2}}{2} - \frac{\sqrt{2}}{2}\mathbf{e}_{31} \right) (\mathbf{e}_1 + \mathbf{e}_2) \left(\frac{\sqrt{2}}{2} + \frac{\sqrt{2}}{2}\mathbf{e}_{31} \right)$$

$$= \left(\frac{\sqrt{2}}{2}\mathbf{e}_1 + \frac{\sqrt{2}}{2}\mathbf{e}_2 - \frac{\sqrt{2}}{2}\mathbf{e}_3 - \frac{\sqrt{2}}{2}\mathbf{e}_{312} \right) \left(\frac{\sqrt{2}}{2} + \frac{\sqrt{2}}{2}\mathbf{e}_{31} \right)$$

$$= \frac{1}{2}(\mathbf{e}_1 - \mathbf{e}_3 + \mathbf{e}_2 + \mathbf{e}_{231} - \mathbf{e}_3 - \mathbf{e}_1 - \mathbf{e}_{312} - \mathbf{e}_{31231})$$

$$\mathbf{p}' = \mathbf{e}_2 - \mathbf{e}_3.$$

Observe what happens when the bivector's sign is reversed to $-\mathbf{e}_{31}$:

$$\mathbf{p}' = (\cos 45° + \mathbf{e}_{31} \sin 45°)(\mathbf{e}_1 + \mathbf{e}_2)(\cos 45° - \mathbf{e}_{31} \sin 45°)$$

$$= \left(\frac{\sqrt{2}}{2} + \frac{\sqrt{2}}{2}\mathbf{e}_{31} \right) (\mathbf{e}_1 + \mathbf{e}_2) \left(\frac{\sqrt{2}}{2} - \frac{\sqrt{2}}{2}\mathbf{e}_{31} \right)$$

$$= \left(\frac{\sqrt{2}}{2}\mathbf{e}_1 + \frac{\sqrt{2}}{2}\mathbf{e}_2 + \frac{\sqrt{2}}{2}\mathbf{e}_3 + \frac{\sqrt{2}}{2}\mathbf{e}_{312} \right) \left(\frac{\sqrt{2}}{2} - \frac{\sqrt{2}}{2}\mathbf{e}_{31} \right)$$

$$= \frac{1}{2}(\mathbf{e}_1 + \mathbf{e}_3 + \mathbf{e}_2 + \mathbf{e}_{231} + \mathbf{e}_3 - \mathbf{e}_1 + \mathbf{e}_{312} - \mathbf{e}_{31231})$$

$$\mathbf{p}' = \mathbf{e}_2 + \mathbf{e}_3.$$

the rotation is clockwise about $\mathbf{e}_2$.

Example 2: Figure 12.15 shows a scenario where vector $\mathbf{p}$ is rotated 120° about the bivector $\mathbf{B}$, where

$$\mathbf{m} = \mathbf{e}_1 - \mathbf{e}_3$$
$$\mathbf{n} = \mathbf{e}_2 - \mathbf{e}_3$$

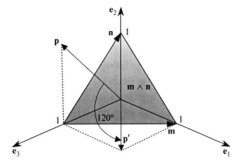

Fig. 12.15 Rotating a vector by 120°.

$$\alpha = 120°$$
$$\mathbf{p} = \mathbf{e}_2 + \mathbf{e}_3$$
$$\mathbf{B} = \mathbf{m} \wedge \mathbf{n}$$
$$= (\mathbf{e}_1 - \mathbf{e}_3) \wedge (\mathbf{e}_2 - \mathbf{e}_3)$$
$$\mathbf{B} = \mathbf{e}_{12} + \mathbf{e}_{31} + \mathbf{e}_{23}.$$

Next, we normalize $\mathbf{B}$ to $\hat{\mathbf{B}}$:

$$\hat{\mathbf{B}} = \frac{1}{\sqrt{3}}(\mathbf{e}_{12} + \mathbf{e}_{23} + \mathbf{e}_{31}$$

therefore,

$$\mathbf{p}' = (\cos 60° - \hat{\mathbf{B}} \sin 60°)\mathbf{p}(\cos 60° + \hat{\mathbf{B}} \sin 60°)$$
$$= \left(\frac{1}{2} - \frac{1}{\sqrt{3}}(\mathbf{e}_{12} + \mathbf{e}_{23} + \mathbf{e}_{31})\frac{\sqrt{3}}{2}\right)(\mathbf{e}_2 + \mathbf{e}_3)\left(\frac{1}{2} + \frac{1}{\sqrt{3}}(\mathbf{e}_{12} + \mathbf{e}_{23} + \mathbf{e}_{31})\frac{\sqrt{3}}{2}\right)$$
$$= \left(\frac{1}{2} - \frac{\mathbf{e}_{12}}{2} - \frac{\mathbf{e}_{23}}{2} - \frac{\mathbf{e}_{31}}{2}\right)(\mathbf{e}_2 + \mathbf{e}_3)\left(\frac{1}{2} + \frac{\mathbf{e}_{12}}{2} + \frac{\mathbf{e}_{23}}{2} + \frac{\mathbf{e}_{31}}{2}\right)$$
$$= \frac{1}{4}(\mathbf{e}_2 + \mathbf{e}_3 - \mathbf{e}_1 - \mathbf{e}_{123} + \mathbf{e}_3 - \mathbf{e}_2 - \mathbf{e}_{312} + \mathbf{e}_1)(1 + \mathbf{e}_{12} + \mathbf{e}_{23} + \mathbf{e}_{31})$$
$$= \frac{1}{2}(\mathbf{e}_3 - \mathbf{e}_{123})(1 + \mathbf{e}_{12} + \mathbf{e}_{23} + \mathbf{e}_{31})$$
$$= \frac{1}{2}(\mathbf{e}_3 + \mathbf{e}_{312} - \mathbf{e}_2 + \mathbf{e}_1 - \mathbf{e}_{123} - \mathbf{e}_{12312} - \mathbf{e}_{12323} - \mathbf{e}_{12331})$$
$$= \frac{1}{2}(\mathbf{e}_3 - \mathbf{e}_2 + \mathbf{e}_1 + \mathbf{e}_3 + \mathbf{e}_1 + \mathbf{e}_2)$$
$$\mathbf{p}' = \mathbf{e}_1 + \mathbf{e}_3.$$

These examples show that rotors behave just like quaternions. Rotors not only rotate vectors, but they can be used to rotate bivectors, and even trivectors, although, as one might expect, a rotated trivector remains unaltered in 3D.

12.20 Applied Geometric Algebra

This has been a very brief introduction to geometric algebra, and it has been impossible to cover all the algebra's features. However, if you have understood the above topics, you will have understood some of the fundamental ideas behind the algebra. Let's now consider some practical applications for geometric algebra.

12.20.1 Sine Rule

The sine rule states that for any triangle $\triangle ABC$ with angles α, β and χ, and respective opposite sides a, b and c, then

$$\frac{a}{\sin \alpha} = \frac{b}{\sin \beta} = \frac{c}{\sin \chi}.$$

This rule can be proved using the outer product of two vectors, which we know incorporates the sine of the angle between two vectors:

$$|\mathbf{a} \wedge \mathbf{b}| = |\mathbf{a}||\mathbf{b}| \sin \alpha.$$

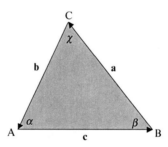

Fig. 12.16 The sine rule.

With reference to Fig. 12.16, we can state the triangle's area as

$$\text{area of } \triangle ABC = \frac{1}{2}|-\mathbf{c} \wedge \mathbf{a}| = \frac{1}{2}|\mathbf{c}||\mathbf{a}| \sin \beta$$

$$\text{area of } \triangle BCA = \frac{1}{2}|-\mathbf{a} \wedge \mathbf{b}| = \frac{1}{2}|\mathbf{a}||\mathbf{b}| \sin \chi$$

$$\text{area of } \triangle CAB = \frac{1}{2}|-\mathbf{b} \wedge \mathbf{c}| = \frac{1}{2}|\mathbf{b}||\mathbf{c}| \sin \alpha$$

which means that

$$|\mathbf{c}||\mathbf{a}|\sin\beta = |\mathbf{a}||\mathbf{b}|\sin\chi = |\mathbf{b}||\mathbf{c}|\sin\alpha$$

$$\frac{|\mathbf{a}|}{\sin\alpha} = \frac{|\mathbf{b}|}{\sin\beta} = \frac{|\mathbf{c}|}{\sin\chi}.$$

12.20.2 Cosine Rule

The cosine rule states that for any triangle $\triangle ABC$ with sides a, b and c, then

$$a^2 = b^2 + c^2 - 2bc\cos\alpha$$

where α is the angle between b and c.

Although this is an easy rule to prove using simple trigonometry, the geometric algebra solution is even easier.

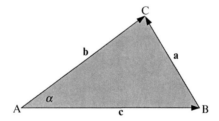

Fig. 12.17 The cosine rule.

Figure 12.17 shows a triangle $\triangle ABC$ constructed from vectors $\mathbf{a}$, $\mathbf{b}$ and $\mathbf{c}$. From Fig. 12.17

$$\mathbf{a} = \mathbf{b} - \mathbf{c}. \tag{12.27}$$

Squaring (12.27) we obtain

$$\mathbf{a}^2 = \mathbf{b}^2 + \mathbf{c}^2 - (\mathbf{b}\mathbf{c} + \mathbf{c}\mathbf{b}).$$

But

$$\mathbf{b}\mathbf{c} + \mathbf{c}\mathbf{b} = 2\mathbf{b}\cdot\mathbf{c} = 2|\mathbf{b}||\mathbf{c}|\cos\alpha$$

therefore,

$$|\mathbf{a}|^2 = |\mathbf{b}|^2 + |\mathbf{c}|^2 - 2|\mathbf{b}||\mathbf{c}|\cos\alpha.$$

12.20.3 A Point Perpendicular to a Point on a Line

Figure 12.18 shows a scenario where a line with direction vector $\hat{\mathbf{v}}$ passes through a point T. The objective is to locate another point P perpendicular to $\hat{\mathbf{v}}$ and a distance

δ from T. The solution is found by post-multiplying $\hat{\mathbf{v}}$ by the psuedoscalar $\mathbf{e}_{12}$, which rotates $\hat{\mathbf{v}}$ through an angle of $90°$.

As $\hat{\mathbf{v}}$ is a unit vector

$$\overrightarrow{TP} = \delta\hat{\mathbf{v}}\mathbf{e}_{12}$$

therefore,

$$\mathbf{p} = \mathbf{t} + \overrightarrow{TP}$$

and

$$\mathbf{p} = \mathbf{t} + \delta\hat{\mathbf{v}}\mathbf{e}_{12}. \qquad (12.28)$$

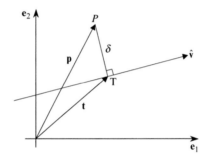

Fig. 12.18 A point P perpendicular to a point T on a line.

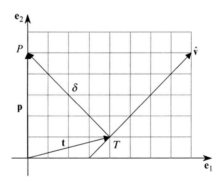

Fig. 12.19 A point P perpendicular to a point T on a line.

For example, Fig. 12.19 shows a 2D scenario where

$$\hat{\mathbf{v}} = \frac{1}{\sqrt{2}}(\mathbf{e}_1 + \mathbf{e}_2)$$
$$T = (4, 1)$$
$$\mathbf{t} = 4\mathbf{e}_1 + \mathbf{e}_2$$
$$\delta = \sqrt{32}.$$

Using (12.28)

$$\mathbf{p} = \mathbf{t} + \delta\hat{\mathbf{v}}\mathbf{e}_{12}$$
$$= 4\mathbf{e}_1 + \mathbf{e}_2 + \sqrt{32}\frac{1}{\sqrt{2}}(\mathbf{e}_1 + \mathbf{e}_2)\mathbf{e}_{12}$$
$$= 4\mathbf{e}_1 + \mathbf{e}_2 + 4\mathbf{e}_2 - 4\mathbf{e}_1$$
$$\mathbf{p} = 5\mathbf{e}_2$$

and

$$P = (0,5).$$

If $\mathbf{p}$ is required on the other side of the line, we pre-multiply $\hat{\mathbf{v}}$ by $\mathbf{e}_{12}$:

$$\mathbf{p} = \mathbf{t} + \delta\mathbf{e}_{12}\hat{\mathbf{v}}$$

which is the same as reversing the sign of δ.

12.20.4 Reflecting a Vector about a Vector

Reflecting a vector about another vector happens to be a rather easy problem for geometric algebra. Figure 12.20 shows the scenario where we see a vector $\mathbf{a}$ reflected about the normal to a line with direction vector $\hat{\mathbf{v}}$.

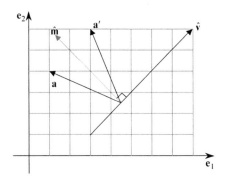

Fig. 12.20 Reflecting a vector about a vector.

We begin by calculating $\hat{\mathbf{m}}$:

$$\hat{\mathbf{m}} = \hat{\mathbf{v}}\mathbf{e}_{12} \tag{12.29}$$

then reflecting $\mathbf{a}$ about $\hat{\mathbf{m}}$:

$$\mathbf{a}' = \hat{\mathbf{m}}\mathbf{a}\hat{\mathbf{m}}$$

substituting $\hat{\mathbf{m}}$ we have

$$\mathbf{a}' = \hat{\mathbf{v}}\mathbf{e}_{12}\mathbf{a}\hat{\mathbf{v}}\mathbf{e}_{12}. \tag{12.30}$$

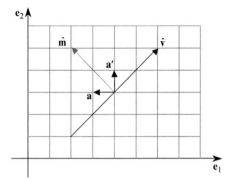

Fig. 12.21 Reflecting a vector about a vector.

As an illustration, consider the scenario shown in Fig. 12.21 where

$$\hat{\mathbf{v}} = \frac{1}{\sqrt{2}}(\mathbf{e}_1 + \mathbf{e}_2)$$

$$\mathbf{a} = -\mathbf{e}_1.$$

Therefore, using (12.29)

$$\hat{\mathbf{m}} = \frac{1}{\sqrt{2}}(\mathbf{e}_1 + \mathbf{e}_2)\mathbf{e}_{12}$$

$$\hat{\mathbf{m}} = \frac{1}{\sqrt{2}}(\mathbf{e}_2 - \mathbf{e}_1)$$

and using (12.30)

$$\mathbf{a}' = \frac{1}{\sqrt{2}}(\mathbf{e}_2 - \mathbf{e}_1)(-\mathbf{e}_1)\frac{1}{\sqrt{2}}(\mathbf{e}_2 - \mathbf{e}_1)$$

$$= \frac{1}{2}(\mathbf{e}_{12} + 1)(\mathbf{e}_2 - \mathbf{e}_1)$$

$$= \frac{1}{2}(\mathbf{e}_1 + \mathbf{e}_2 + \mathbf{e}_2 - \mathbf{e}_1)$$

$$\mathbf{a}' = \mathbf{e}_2.$$

12.20.5 Orientation of a Point with a Plane

In computer graphics we often need to test whether a point is above, below or on a planar surface. If we already have the plane equation for the surface it is just a question of substituting the test point in the equation and investigating its signed value. But here is another way. For example, if a bivector is used to represent the orientation of a plane, the outer product of the test point's position vector with the bivector computes an oriented volume. Figure 12.22 shows a bivector $\mathbf{a} \wedge \mathbf{b}$ and a test point P with position vector $\mathbf{p}$ relative to the bivector.

If

$\mathbf{a} \wedge \mathbf{b} \wedge \mathbf{p}$ is +ve, then P is 'above' the bivector.

$\mathbf{a} \wedge \mathbf{b} \wedge \mathbf{p}$ is −ve, then P is 'below' the bivector.

$\mathbf{a} \wedge \mathbf{b} \wedge \mathbf{p}$ is zero, then P is coplanar with the bivector.

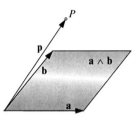

Fig. 12.22 Point relative to a bivector.

The terms 'above' and 'below' mean in the bivector's positive and negative half-space respectively. As an example, consider the scenario shown in Fig. 12.23 where the plane's orientation is represented by the bivector $\mathbf{a} \wedge \mathbf{b}$, and three test points P, Q and R.

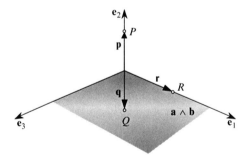

Fig. 12.23 Three points relative to a bivector.

If $P = (0,1,0)$ $Q = (0,-1,0)$ $R = (1,0,0)$

$$\mathbf{a} = \mathbf{e}_1 + \mathbf{e}_3$$
$$\mathbf{b} = \mathbf{e}_1$$

then

$$\mathbf{p} = \mathbf{e}_2$$
$$\mathbf{q} = -\mathbf{e}_2$$
$$\mathbf{r} = \mathbf{e}_1$$

and

$$\mathbf{a} \wedge \mathbf{b} \wedge \mathbf{p} = (\mathbf{e}_1 + \mathbf{e}_3) \wedge \mathbf{e}_1 \wedge \mathbf{e}_2$$
$$= \mathbf{e}_{123}$$
$$\mathbf{a} \wedge \mathbf{b} \wedge \mathbf{q} = (\mathbf{e}_1 + \mathbf{e}_3) \wedge \mathbf{e}_1 \wedge (-\mathbf{e}_2)$$
$$= -\mathbf{e}_{123}$$
$$\mathbf{a} \wedge \mathbf{b} \wedge \mathbf{r} = (\mathbf{e}_1 + \mathbf{e}_3) \wedge \mathbf{e}_1 \wedge \mathbf{e}_1$$
$$= 0.$$

We can see that the signs of the first two volumes show that P is in the positive half-space, Q is in the negative half-space, and R is on the plane.

12.21 Summary

Geometric algebra is a new and exciting subject and is destined to impact upon the way we solve problems in computer games and animation. Hopefully, you have found this chapter interesting, and if you are tempted to take the subject further, then look at the author's books.

Chapter 13
Worked Examples

13.1 Introduction

This chapter examines a variety of problems encountered in computer graphics and develops mathematical strategies for their solution. Such strategies may not be the most efficient, however, they will provide the reader with a starting point, which may be improved upon.

13.2 Area of Regular Polygon

Given a regular polygon with n sides, side length s, and radius r of the circumscribed circle, its area can be computed by dividing it into n isosceles triangles and summing their total area.

Figure 13.1 shows one of the isosceles triangles OAB formed by an edge s and the center O of the polygon. From Fig. 13.1 we observe that

$$\frac{s}{2h} = \tan\left(\frac{\pi}{n}\right)$$

therefore,

$$h = \frac{s}{2}\cot\left(\frac{\pi}{n}\right)$$

$$area\triangle OAB = \frac{sh}{2} = \frac{s^2}{4}\cot\left(\frac{\pi}{n}\right)$$

but there are n such triangles, therefore,

$$area = \frac{ns^2}{4}\cot\left(\frac{\pi}{n}\right).$$

J. Vince, *Mathematics for Computer Graphics*, Undergraduate Topics in Computer Science, DOI 10.1007/978-1-84996-023-6_13, © Springer-Verlag London Limited 2010

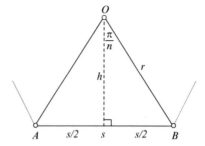

Fig. 13.1 One of the isosceles triangles forming a regular polygon.

If we let $s = 1$ the following table shows the area for the first six regular polygons.

n	$Area$
3	0.433
4	1
5	1.72
6	2.598
7	3.634
8	4.828

13.3 Area of any Polygon

Figure 13.2 shows a polygon with the following vertices in counter-clockwise sequence, and by inspection, the area is 9.5.

x	0	2	5	4	2
y	2	0	1	3	3

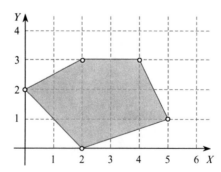

Fig. 13.2 A five-sided irregular polygon.

The area of a polygon is given by

$$area = \frac{1}{2}\sum_{i=0}^{n-1}\left(x_i y_{i+1(\bmod n)} - y_i x_{i+1(\bmod n)}\right)$$

$$= \frac{1}{2}(0 \times 0 + 2 \times 1 + 5 \times 3 + 4 \times 3 + 2 \times 2 - 2 \times 2 -$$

$$0 \times 5 - 1 \times 4 - 3 \times 2 - 3 \times 0)$$

$$area = \frac{1}{2}(33 - 14) = 9.5.$$

13.4 Dihedral Angle of a Dodecahedron

The dodecahedron is a member of the five Platonic solids, which are constructed from regular polygons. The dihedral angle is the internal angle between two touching faces. Figure 13.3 shows a dodecahedron with one of its pentagonal sides.

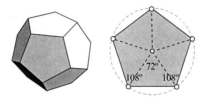

Fig. 13.3 A dodecahedron with one of its pentagonal sides.

Figure 13.4 illustrates the geometry required to fold two pentagonal sides through the dihedral angle γ.

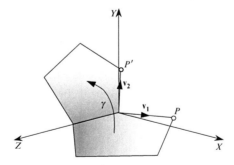

Fig. 13.4 The dihedral angle γ between two pentagonal sides.

The point P has coordinates

$$P(x,y,z) = (\sin 72°, 0, -\cos 72°)$$

and for simplicity, we will use a unit vector to represent an edge, therefore

$$|\mathbf{v}_1| = |\mathbf{v}_2| = 1.$$

The coordinates of the rotated point P' are given by the following transform:

$$\begin{bmatrix} x' \\ y' \\ z' \end{bmatrix} = \begin{bmatrix} \cos\gamma & -\sin\gamma & 0 \\ \sin\gamma & \cos\gamma & 0 \\ 0 & 0 & 1 \end{bmatrix} \begin{bmatrix} \sin 72° \\ 0 \\ -\cos 72° \end{bmatrix}$$

where

$$x' = \cos\gamma\sin 72°$$
$$y' = \sin\gamma\sin 72°$$
$$z' = -\cos 72°.$$

But

$$\mathbf{v}_1 \cdot \mathbf{v}_2 = |\mathbf{v}_1||\mathbf{v}_2|\cos\theta = xx' + yy' + zz'$$

therefore,

$$\cos\theta = \cos\gamma\sin^2 72° + \cos^2 72°$$

but $\theta = 108°$ (internal angle of a regular pentagon), therefore,

$$\cos\gamma = \frac{\cos 108° - \cos^2 72°}{\sin^2 72°} = \frac{\cos 72°}{\cos 72° - 1}.$$

The dihedral angle $\gamma \approx 116.56505°$.

A similar technique can be used to calculate the dihedral angles of the other Platonic objects.

13.5 Vector Normal to a Triangle

Very often in computer graphics we have to calculate a vector normal to a plane containing three points. The most effective tool to achieve this is the vector product. For example, given three points $P_1(5,0,0)$, $P_2(0,0,5)$ and $P_3(10,0,5)$, we can create two vectors $\mathbf{a}$ and $\mathbf{b}$ as follows:

$$\mathbf{a} = \begin{bmatrix} x_2 - x_1 \\ y_2 - y_1 \\ z_2 - z_1 \end{bmatrix} \qquad \mathbf{b} = \begin{bmatrix} x_3 - x_1 \\ y_3 - y_1 \\ z_3 - z_1 \end{bmatrix}$$

therefore,

$$\mathbf{a} = -5\mathbf{i} + 5\mathbf{k} \qquad \mathbf{b} = 5\mathbf{i} + 5\mathbf{k}.$$

The normal vector **n** is given by

$$\mathbf{n} = \mathbf{a} \times \mathbf{b} = \begin{vmatrix} \mathbf{i} & \mathbf{j} & \mathbf{k} \\ -5 & 0 & 5 \\ 5 & 0 & 5 \end{vmatrix} = 50\mathbf{j}.$$

13.6 Area of a Triangle Using Vectors

The vector product is also useful in calculating the area of a triangle using two of its sides as vectors. For example, using the same points and vectors in the previous example:

$$area = \frac{1}{2}|\mathbf{a} \times \mathbf{b}| = \frac{1}{2}\begin{vmatrix} \mathbf{i} & \mathbf{j} & \mathbf{k} \\ -5 & 0 & 5 \\ 5 & 0 & 5 \end{vmatrix} = \frac{1}{2}|50\mathbf{j}| = 25.$$

13.7 General Form of the Line Equation from Two Points

The general form of the line equation is given by

$$ax + by + c = 0$$

and it may be required to compute this equation from two known points. For example, Fig. 13.5 shows two points $P_1(x_1, y_1)$ and $P_2(x_2, y_2)$ from which it is possible to determine $P(x, y)$.

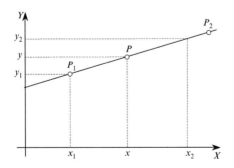

Fig. 13.5 A line formed from two points P_1 and P_2.

From Fig. 13.5

$$\frac{y_2 - y_1}{x_2 - x_1} = \frac{y - y_1}{x - x_1}$$
$$(y_2 - y_1)(x - x_1) = (x_2 - x_1)(y - y_1)$$
$$(y_2 - y_1)x - (y_2 - y_1)x_1 = (x_2 - x_1)y - (x_2 - x_1)y_1$$
$$(y_2 - y_1)x + (x_1 - x_2)y = x_1 y_2 - x_2 y_1$$

therefore,

$$a = y_2 - y_1 \quad b = x_1 - x_2 \quad c = -(x_1 y_2 - x_2 y_1).$$

If the two points are $P_1(1,0)$ and $P_2(3,4)$, then

$$(4 - 0)x + (1 - 3)y - (1 \times 4 - 3 \times 0) = 0$$

and

$$4x - 2y - 4 = 0$$

or

$$2x - y - 2 = 0.$$

13.8 Angle Between Two Straight Lines

Given two line equations it is possible to compute the angle between the lines using the scalar product. For example, if the line equations are

$$a_1 x + b_1 y + c_1 = 0$$
$$a_2 x + b_2 y + c_2 = 0$$

their normal vectors are $\mathbf{n} = a_1\mathbf{i} + b_1\mathbf{j}$ and $\mathbf{m} = a_2\mathbf{i} + b_2\mathbf{j}$ respectively, therefore,

$$\mathbf{n} \cdot \mathbf{m} = |\mathbf{n}||\mathbf{m}| \cos \alpha$$

and the angle between the lines α is given by

$$\alpha = \cos^{-1}\left(\frac{\mathbf{n} \cdot \mathbf{m}}{|\mathbf{n}||\mathbf{m}|}\right).$$

Figure 13.6 shows two lines with equations

$$2x + 2y - 4 = 0$$
$$2x + 4y - 4 = 0$$

therefore,

$$\alpha = \cos^{-1}\left(\frac{2 \times 2 + 2 \times 4}{\sqrt{2^2 + 2^2}\sqrt{2^2 + 4^2}}\right) \approx 18.435°.$$

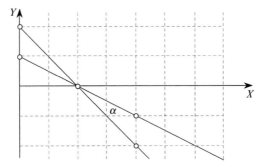

Fig. 13.6 Two lines intersecting at an angle α.

13.9 Test if Three Points Lie on a Straight Line

Figure 13.7 shows three points P_1, P_2 and P_3 which lie on a straight line. There are all sorts of ways to detect such a condition. For example, we could assume that the points are the vertices of a triangle, and if the triangle's area is zero, then the points lie on a line. Here is another approach.

Given $P_1(x_1, y_1)$, $P_2(x_2, y_2)$, $P_3(x_3, y_3)$ and $\mathbf{r} = \overrightarrow{P_1 P_2}$ and $\mathbf{s} = \overrightarrow{P_1 P_3}$, the three points lie on a straight line when $\mathbf{s} = \lambda \mathbf{r}$ where λ is a scalar.

If the points are

$$P_1(0, -2) \quad P_2(1, -1) \quad P_3(4, 2)$$

then

$$\mathbf{r} = \mathbf{i} + \mathbf{j} \quad \text{and} \quad \mathbf{s} = 4\mathbf{i} + 4\mathbf{j}$$

and

$$\mathbf{s} = 4\mathbf{r}$$

therefore, the points lie on a straight line as confirmed by the diagram.

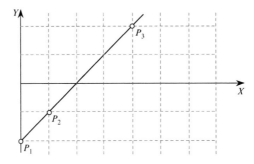

Fig. 13.7 Three points on a common line.

Another way is to compute

$$\begin{vmatrix} x_1 & y_1 & 1 \\ x_2 & y_2 & 1 \\ x_3 & y_3 & 1 \end{vmatrix}$$

which is twice the area of $\Delta P_1 P_2 P_3$. If this equals zero, the points must be co-linear.

13.10 Position and Distance of the Nearest Point on a Line to a Point

Suppose we have a line and some arbitrary point P, and we require to find the nearest point on the line to P. Vector analysis provides a very elegant way to solve such problems. Figure 13.8 shows a line and a point P and the nearest point Q on the line. The nature of the geometry is such that the line connecting P to Q is perpendicular to the reference line, which is exploited in the analysis. The objective is to determine the position vector $\mathbf{q}$.

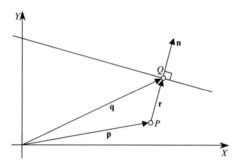

Fig. 13.8 Q is the nearest point on the line to P.

We start with the line equation

$$ax + by + c = 0$$

and declare $Q(x, y)$ as the nearest point on the line to P .
The normal to the line must be

$$\mathbf{n} = a\mathbf{i} + b\mathbf{j}$$

and the position vector for Q is

$$\mathbf{q} = x\mathbf{i} + y\mathbf{j}.$$

Therefore,

$$\mathbf{n} \cdot \mathbf{q} = -c. \tag{13.1}$$

$\mathbf{r}$ is parallel to $\mathbf{n}$, therefore,

$$\mathbf{r} = \lambda \mathbf{n} \tag{13.2}$$

where λ is some scalar.

Taking the scalar product of (13.2)

$$\mathbf{n} \cdot \mathbf{r} = \lambda \mathbf{n} \cdot \mathbf{n} \tag{13.3}$$

but as

$$\mathbf{r} = \mathbf{q} - \mathbf{p} \tag{13.4}$$
$$\mathbf{n} \cdot \mathbf{r} = \mathbf{n} \cdot \mathbf{q} - \mathbf{n} \cdot \mathbf{p}. \tag{13.5}$$

Substituting (13.1) and (13.3) in (13.5) we obtain

$$\lambda \mathbf{n} \cdot \mathbf{n} = -c - \mathbf{n} \cdot \mathbf{p}$$

therefore,

$$\lambda = \frac{-(\mathbf{n} \cdot \mathbf{p} + c)}{\mathbf{n} \cdot \mathbf{n}}.$$

From (13.4) we get

$$\mathbf{q} = \mathbf{p} + \mathbf{r}. \tag{13.6}$$

Substituting (13.2) in (13.6) we obtain the position vector for Q:

$$\mathbf{q} = \mathbf{p} + \lambda \mathbf{n}.$$

The distance PQ must be the magnitude of $\mathbf{r}$:

$$PQ = |\mathbf{r}| = \lambda |\mathbf{n}|.$$

Let's test this result with an example where the answer can be predicted.

Figure 13.9 shows a line whose equation is $x + y - 1 = 0$, and the associated point is $P(1, 1)$. By inspection, the nearest point is $Q(\frac{1}{2}, \frac{1}{2})$ and the distance $PQ \approx 0.7071$.

From the line equation

$$a = 1 \quad b = 1 \quad c = -1$$

therefore,

$$\lambda = -\frac{2 - 1}{2} = -\frac{1}{2}$$

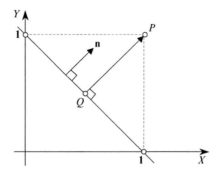

Fig. 13.9 Q is the nearest point on the line to P.

and

$$x_Q = x_P + \lambda x_n = 1 - \frac{1}{2} \times 1 = \frac{1}{2}$$
$$y_Q = y_P + \lambda y_n = 1 - \frac{1}{2} \times 1 = \frac{1}{2}.$$

The nearest point is $Q(\frac{1}{2}, \frac{1}{2})$ and the distance is

$$PQ = |\lambda \mathbf{n}| = \frac{1}{2}|\mathbf{i} + \mathbf{j}| \approx 0.7071.$$

13.11 Position of a Point Reflected in a Line

Suppose that instead of finding the nearest point on a line we require the reflection Q of P in the line. Once more, we set out to discover the position vector for Q. Figure 13.10 shows the vectors used in the analysis. We start with the line equation

$$ax + by + c = 0$$

and declare $T(x, y)$ as the nearest point on the line to O with $\mathbf{t} = x\mathbf{i} + y\mathbf{j}$ as its position vector.

From the line equation

$$\mathbf{n} = a\mathbf{i} + b\mathbf{j}$$

therefore,

$$\mathbf{n} \cdot \mathbf{t} = -c. \tag{13.7}$$

We note that $\mathbf{r} + \mathbf{r}'$ is orthogonal to $\mathbf{n}$, therefore,

$$\mathbf{n} \cdot (\mathbf{r} + \mathbf{r}') = 0$$

and

$$\mathbf{n} \cdot \mathbf{r} + \mathbf{n} \cdot \mathbf{r}' = 0. \tag{13.8}$$

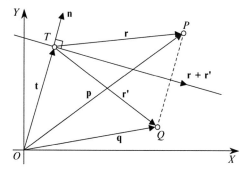

Fig. 13.10 The vectors required to find the reflection of P in the line.

We also note that $\mathbf{p} - \mathbf{q}$ is parallel to $\mathbf{n}$, therefore,

$$\mathbf{p} - \mathbf{q} = \mathbf{r} - \mathbf{r}' = \lambda\mathbf{n}$$

where λ is some scalar, therefore,

$$\lambda = \frac{\mathbf{r} - \mathbf{r}'}{\mathbf{n}}. \tag{13.9}$$

From the figure we note that

$$\mathbf{r} = \mathbf{p} - \mathbf{t}. \tag{13.10}$$

Substituting (13.7) in (13.10)

$$\mathbf{n} \cdot \mathbf{r} = \mathbf{n} \cdot \mathbf{p} - \mathbf{n} \cdot \mathbf{t} = \mathbf{n} \cdot \mathbf{p} + c. \tag{13.11}$$

Substituting (13.8) and (13.11) in (13.9)

$$\lambda = \frac{\mathbf{n} \cdot \mathbf{r} - \mathbf{n} \cdot \mathbf{r}'}{\mathbf{n} \cdot \mathbf{n}} = \frac{2\mathbf{n} \cdot \mathbf{r}}{\mathbf{n} \cdot \mathbf{n}}$$

$$\lambda = \frac{2(\mathbf{n} \cdot \mathbf{p} + c)}{\mathbf{n} \cdot \mathbf{n}}$$

and the position vector is

$$\mathbf{q} = \mathbf{p} - \lambda\mathbf{n}.$$

Let's again test this formula with a scenario that can be predicted in advance. Given the line equation

$$x + y - 1 = 0$$

and the point $P(1, 1)$, the reflection must be the origin, as shown in Fig. 13.11.
Now let's confirm this prediction.
From the line equation

$$a = 1 \quad b = 1 \quad c = -1$$

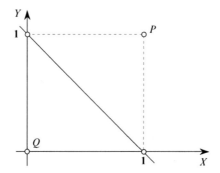

Fig. 13.11 Q is the reflection of P in the line.

and

$$x_P = 1$$
$$y_P = 1$$
$$\lambda = \frac{2 \times (2-1)}{2} = 1$$

therefore,

$$x_Q = x_P - \lambda x_n = 1 - 1 \times 1 = 0$$
$$y_Q = y_P - \lambda y_n = 1 - 1 \times 1 = 0$$

and the reflection point is $Q(0,0)$.

13.12 Intersection of a Line and a Sphere

In ray tracing and ray casting it is necessary to detect whether a ray (line) intersects objects within a scene. Such objects may be polygonal, constructed from patches, or defined by equations. In this example, we explore the intersection between a line and a sphere.

There are three possible scenarios: the line intersects, touches or misses the sphere. It just so happens, that the cosine rule proves very useful in setting up a geometric condition that identifies the above scenarios, which are readily solved using vector analysis.

Figure 13.12 shows a sphere with radius r located at C. The line is represented parametrically, which lends itself to this analysis. The objective is to discover whether there are points in space that satisfy both the line equation and the sphere equation. If there is a point, a position vector will locate it.

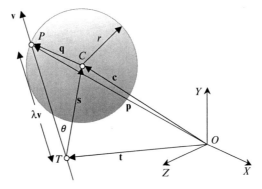

Fig. 13.12 The vectors required to locate a possible intersection.

The position vector for C is

$$\mathbf{c} = x_C\mathbf{i} + y_C\mathbf{j} + z_C\mathbf{k}$$

and the equation of the line is

$$\mathbf{p} = \mathbf{t} + \lambda\mathbf{v}$$

where λ is a scalar, and

$$|\mathbf{v}| = 1. \tag{13.12}$$

For an intersection at P

$$|\mathbf{q}| = r$$
$$|\mathbf{q}|^2 = r^2$$
$$|\mathbf{q}|^2 - r^2 = 0.$$

Using the cosine rule

$$|\mathbf{q}|^2 = |\lambda\mathbf{v}|^2 + |\mathbf{s}|^2 - 2|\lambda\mathbf{v}||\mathbf{s}|\cos\theta \tag{13.13}$$
$$|\mathbf{q}|^2 = \lambda^2|\mathbf{v}|^2 + |\mathbf{s}|^2 - 2|\mathbf{v}||\mathbf{s}|\lambda\cos\theta. \tag{13.14}$$

Substituting (13.12) in (13.14)

$$|\mathbf{q}|^2 = \lambda^2 + |\mathbf{s}|^2 - 2|\mathbf{s}|\lambda\cos\theta. \tag{13.15}$$

Now let's identify $\cos\theta$:

$$\mathbf{s} \cdot \mathbf{v} = |\mathbf{s}||\mathbf{v}|\cos\theta$$

therefore,

$$\cos\theta = \frac{\mathbf{s} \cdot \mathbf{v}}{|\mathbf{s}|}. \tag{13.16}$$

Substituting (13.16) in (13.15)

$$|\mathbf{q}|^2 = \lambda^2 - 2\mathbf{s}\cdot\mathbf{v}\lambda + |\mathbf{s}|^2$$

therefore,

$$|\mathbf{q}|^2 - r^2 = \lambda^2 - 2\mathbf{s}\cdot\mathbf{v}\lambda + |\mathbf{s}|^2 - r^2 = 0. \qquad (13.17)$$

Equation (13.17) is a quadratic in λ where

$$\lambda = \mathbf{s}\cdot\mathbf{v} \pm \sqrt{(\mathbf{s}\cdot\mathbf{v})^2 - |\mathbf{s}|^2 + r^2} \qquad (13.18)$$

and

$$\mathbf{s} = \mathbf{c} - \mathbf{t}.$$

The discriminant of (13.18) determines whether the line intersects, touches or misses the sphere.

   The position vector for P is given by

$$\mathbf{p} = \mathbf{t} + \lambda\mathbf{v}$$

where

$$\lambda = \mathbf{s}\cdot\mathbf{v} \pm \sqrt{(\mathbf{s}\cdot\mathbf{v})^2 - |\mathbf{s}|^2 + r^2}$$

and

$$\mathbf{s} = \mathbf{c} - \mathbf{t}.$$

For a miss condition

$$(\mathbf{s}\cdot\mathbf{v})^2 - |\mathbf{s}|^2 + r^2 < 0.$$

For a touch condition

$$(\mathbf{s}\cdot\mathbf{v})^2 - |\mathbf{s}|^2 + r^2 = 0.$$

For an intersect condition

$$(\mathbf{s}\cdot\mathbf{v})^2 - |\mathbf{s}|^2 + r^2 > 0.$$

To test these formulae we will create all three scenarios and show that the equations are well behaved.

   Figure 13.13 shows a sphere with three lines represented by their direction vectors $\lambda\mathbf{v}_1$, $\lambda\mathbf{v}_2$ and $\lambda\mathbf{v}_3$. The sphere has radius $r = 1$ and is centered at C with position vector

$$\mathbf{c} = \mathbf{i} + \mathbf{j}$$

whilst the three lines L_1, L_2 and L_3 miss, touch and intersect the sphere respectively.

   The lines are of the form

$$\mathbf{p} = \mathbf{t} + \lambda\mathbf{v}$$

therefore,

$$\mathbf{p}_1 = \mathbf{t}_1 + \lambda\mathbf{v}_1$$

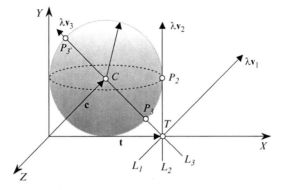

Fig. 13.13 Three lines that miss, touch and intersect the sphere.

$$\mathbf{p}_2 = \mathbf{t}_2 + \lambda\mathbf{v}_2$$
$$\mathbf{p}_3 = \mathbf{t}_3 + \lambda\mathbf{v}_3$$

where

$$\mathbf{t}_1 = 2\mathbf{i} \quad \mathbf{v}_1 = \frac{1}{\sqrt{2}}\mathbf{i} + \frac{1}{\sqrt{2}}\mathbf{j}$$
$$\mathbf{t}_2 = 2\mathbf{i} \quad \mathbf{v}_2 = \mathbf{j}$$
$$\mathbf{t}_3 = 2\mathbf{i} \quad \mathbf{v}_3 = -\frac{1}{\sqrt{2}}\mathbf{i} + \frac{1}{\sqrt{2}}\mathbf{j}$$

and

$$\mathbf{c} = \mathbf{i} + \mathbf{j}.$$

Let's substitute the lines in the original equations:

L_1: $\mathbf{s} = -\mathbf{i} + \mathbf{j}$

$$(\mathbf{s}\cdot\mathbf{v})^2 - |\mathbf{s}|^2 + r^2 = 0 - 2 + 1 = -1$$

the negative discriminant confirms a miss condition.

L_2: $\mathbf{s} = -\mathbf{i} + \mathbf{j}$

$$(\mathbf{s}\cdot\mathbf{v})^2 - |\mathbf{s}|^2 + r^2 = 1 - 2 + 1 = 0$$

the zero discriminant confirms a touch condition, therefore $\lambda = 1$ and the touch point is $P_2(2,1,0)$ which is correct.

L_3: $\mathbf{s} = -\mathbf{i} + \mathbf{j}$

$$(\mathbf{s}\cdot\mathbf{v})^2 - |\mathbf{s}|^2 + r^2 = 2 - 2 + 1 = 1$$

the positive discriminant confirms an intersect condition, therefore,

$$\lambda = \frac{2}{\sqrt{2}} \pm 1 = 1 + \sqrt{2} \quad \text{or} \quad \sqrt{2} - 1.$$

The intersection points are given by the two values of λ:
when $\lambda = 1 + \sqrt{2}$

$$x_P = 2 + \left(1 + \sqrt{2}\right)\left(-\frac{1}{\sqrt{2}}\right) = 1 - \frac{1}{\sqrt{2}}$$

$$y_P = 0 + \left(1 + \sqrt{2}\right)\frac{1}{\sqrt{2}} = 1 + \frac{1}{\sqrt{2}}$$

$$z_P = 0.$$

when $\lambda = \sqrt{2} - 1$

$$x_P = 1 + \left(\sqrt{2} - 1\right)\left(-\frac{1}{\sqrt{2}}\right) = 1 + \frac{1}{\sqrt{2}}$$

$$y_P = 0 + \left(\sqrt{2} - 1\right)\frac{1}{\sqrt{2}} = 1 - \frac{1}{\sqrt{2}}$$

$$z_P = 0.$$

The intersection points are

$$P_{3'}\left(1 - \frac{1}{\sqrt{2}}, 1 + \frac{1}{\sqrt{2}}, 0\right)$$

$$P_3\left(1 + \frac{1}{\sqrt{2}}, 1 - \frac{1}{\sqrt{2}}, 0\right)$$

which are correct.

13.13 Sphere Touching a Plane

A sphere will touch a plane if the perpendicular distance from its center to the plane equals its radius. The geometry describing this condition is identical to finding the position and distance of the nearest point on a plane to a point.

Figure 13.14 shows a sphere located at P with position vector $\mathbf{p}$. A potential touch condition occurs at Q, and the objective of the analysis is to discover its position vector $\mathbf{q}$. Given the following plane equation

$$ax + by + cz + d = 0$$

its surface normal is

$$\mathbf{n} = a\mathbf{i} + b\mathbf{j} + c\mathbf{k}.$$

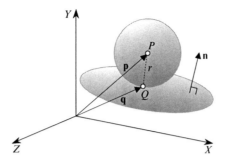

Fig. 13.14 The vectors used to detect when a sphere touches a plane.

The nearest point Q on the plane to a point P is given by the position vector

$$\mathbf{q} = \mathbf{p} + \lambda \mathbf{n} \qquad (13.19)$$

where

$$\lambda = -\frac{\mathbf{n} \cdot \mathbf{p} + d}{\mathbf{n}} \cdot \mathbf{n}$$

the distance

$$PQ = |\lambda \mathbf{n}|.$$

If P is the center of the sphere with radius r, and position vector $\mathbf{p}$ the touch point is also given by (13.19) when

$$PQ = |\lambda \mathbf{n}| = r.$$

Let's test the above equations with a simple example, as shown in Fig. 13.15, which shows a sphere with radius $r = 1$ and centered at $P(1, 1, 1)$.

The plane equation is

$$y - 2 = 0$$

therefore,

$$\mathbf{n} = \mathbf{j}$$

and

$$\mathbf{p} = \mathbf{i} + \mathbf{j} + \mathbf{k}$$

therefore,

$$\lambda = -(1 - 2) = 1$$

which equals the sphere's radius and therefore the sphere and plane touch. The touch point is

$$x_Q = 1 + 1 \times 0 = 1$$
$$y_Q = 1 + 1 \times 1 = 2$$
$$z_Q = 1 + 1 \times 0 = 1$$

$P(1, 2, 1)$ which is correct.

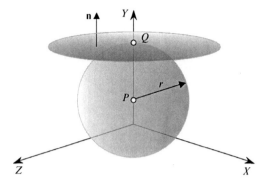

Fig. 13.15 A sphere touching a plane.

13.14 Summary

Unfortunately, problem solving is not always obvious, and it is possible to waste hours of analysis simply because the objective of the solution has not been well formulated. Hopefully, though, the reader has discovered some of the strategies used in solving the above geometric problems, and will be able to implement them in other scenarios. At the end of the day, practice makes perfect!

Chapter 14
Conclusion

In the previous 13 chapters I have attempted to introduce you to some of the important elements of mathematics employed in computer graphics. I knew from the start that this would be a challenge for two reasons: one was knowing where to start, and the other was where to stop. I assumed that most readers would already be interested in computer animation, games or virtual reality, and so on, and knew something about mathematics. So perhaps the chapters on numbers, algebra and trigonometry provided a common starting point.

The chapters on Cartesian coordinates, vectors, transforms, interpolation, barycentric coordinates, curves and patches are the real core of the book, but whilst revealing these subjects I was always wondering when to stop. On the one hand, I could have frustrated readers by stopping short of describing a subject completely, and on the other hand lost readers by pursuing a subject to a level beyond the book's objective. Hopefully, I have managed to keep the right balance.

I do hope that the chapter on geometric algebra will tempt you to explore this subject further. It's not often that something completely new comes along and challenges the way we solve geometric problems.

For many readers, what I have covered will be sufficient to enable them to design programs and solve a wide range of problems. For others, the book will provide a useful stepping stone to more advanced texts on mathematics. But what I really hope that I have managed to show is that mathematics is not that difficult, especially when it can be applied to an exciting subject such as computer graphics.

J. Vince, *Mathematics for Computer Graphics*, Undergraduate Topics
in Computer Science, DOI 10.1007/978-1-84996-023-6_14,
© Springer-Verlag London Limited 2010

Index

Breinigsville, PA USA
25 October 2010
248057BV00003B/20/P